MAROONS AND THE MAROONED

CARIBBEAN
STUDIES
SERIES

ANTON L. ALLAHAR AND NATASHA BARNES
Series Editors

MAROONS AND THE MAROONED

Runaways and Castaways
in the Americas

Edited by
Richard Bodek and Joseph Kelly

University Press of Mississippi / Jackson

The University Press of Mississippi is the scholarly publishing agency of the Mississippi Institutions of Higher Learning: Alcorn State University, Delta State University, Jackson State University, Mississippi State University, Mississippi University for Women, Mississippi Valley State University, University of Mississippi, and University of Southern Mississippi.

www.upress.state.ms.us

The University Press of Mississippi is a member of the Association of University Presses.

Copyright © 2020 by University Press of Mississippi
All rights reserved

First printing 2020

∞

Library of Congress Cataloging-in-Publication Data

Names: Bodek, Richard, 1961- editor. | Kelly, Joseph, 1962- editor.
Title: Maroons and the marooned: runaways and castaways in the Americas / edited by Richard Bodek and Joseph Kelly.
Description: Jackson: University Press of Mississippi, 2020. | Series: Caribbean studies series | Includes bibliographical references and index.
Identifiers: LCCN 2019058813 (print) | LCCN 2019058814 (ebook) | ISBN 9781496827203 (hardback) | ISBN 9781496827197 (trade paperback) | ISBN 9781496827210 (epub) | ISBN 9781496827227 (epub) | ISBN 9781496827234 (pdf) | ISBN 9781496827241 (pdf)
Subjects: LCSH: Maroons. | Maroons in literature. | AmericaHistory. | BISAC: HISTORY / Americas (North, Central, South, West Indies)
Classification: LCC E450 .M385 2020 (print) | LCC E450 (ebook) | DDC 305.5/122097dc23
LC record available at https://lccn.loc.gov/2019058813
LC ebook record available at https://lccn.loc.gov/2019058814

British Library Cataloging-in-Publication Data available

We would like to dedicate this book to all the students whom we taught in our College of Charleston Honors Course, "Marooned!" These students were always an inspiration, always pushed us to look at the phenomenon in a new light, and motivated us to mount the conference that inspired the book in your hands.

Spring 2008	**Spring 2012**	**Spring 2016**
Laurel Black	John Brooker	Alexandra Astor
Robyn Burrows	Cara Bujanowski	Peter Bruno
Anna Chard	Mary Crowe	Erik Cardwell
Jody Christian	Zachary Huey	Laura Cox
Jarryd de Boer	Mollianna Judd	Shana Devlin
Tan-ni Fan	Kristen McLinko	Joseph Dibrigida
Ashlee Fields	Andrew Nelson	Sarah Ford
Natasha Hoover	Franklin Peters	Wilson Ford
Valerie Kneece	Mary Rumble	Abigael Malcolm
Sophia Lee	Brandi Schumacher	Travis McGowin
Sharon McMullen	Jacqueline Tully	Sophie Naughton
Alex Modley	Margaret Turner	Julie Reams
Lucas Nelson	Alice Van Arsdale	Baylee Sims
Cindy Oliva	Samantha Wilds	Catherine Stiers
Kellie Osborne	Emily Wise	
Erica Sheftic		
Courtney Skibbe		
Kirsten Shumy		
Shanaya Suchak		
Mary Foster Williams		

Contents

ix   Acknowledgments

xi   Introduction

3   **Chapter One**
"Mingled Fear and Ferocity": A Glimpse into the Maroon Communities of the Great Dismal Swamp
J. Brent Morris

30   **Chapter Two**
Belonging and Alienation: Gullah Jack and Some Maroon Dimensions of the "Denmark Vesey Conspiracy"
James O'Neil Spady

55   **Chapter Three**
"We Will Never Surrender!": Quilombos, Their Descendants, and the Struggle for Land and Rights in Brazil's Ribeira
Edward Shore

82   **Chapter Four**
The Bermuda Assemblage: Toward a Posthuman Globalization
Steven Mentz

97   **Chapter Five**
Bookends of History: Maroonage in *The Female American* and *Die Wand*
Peter Sands

117 Chapter Six
Castaways, Re-Captive Slaves, and Resistance: Testing the Boundaries of Freedom in the Work of Yvette Christiansë
Simon Lewis

133 Chapter Seven
The Opacity of Home—Being Marooned at the End of the World
Claire Curtis

149 Chapter Eight
"Lest Darkness Fall": Castaways in Time and Space in Popular Turn-of-the-Century Fiction
Richard Bodek

165 Chapter Nine
Maroons and the American Epic
Joseph Kelly

189 List of Contributors

193 Index

Acknowledgments

We would like to acknowledge everybody who made this book possible. The College of Charleston's Program in the Carolina Lowcountry and Atlantic World, under its phenomenal director, Simon Lewis, provided the intellectual and institutional space for the conference that inspired this collection. The College's Anthropology, English, and History Departments provided both financial and intellectual support. Vijay Shah, our original editor at the University Press of Mississippi, always showed great enthusiasm for, and interest in, the work and its potential place in the field of cultural studies. Finally, perhaps our chief intellectual debt belongs to Sally and Richard Price, whose high standards forced both the original conference and this book to be as theoretically acute and precise as possible. They never allowed either us or any of our contributors to take the easy way out. For this we will always be grateful.

Introduction

"Marooned" is what happens to castaways. At least in common use, it is a transitive verb: the hand of God (usually through the agency of a sea storm) or one's ship captain (as a punishment) *maroons* the unfortunate voyager in a deserted wilderness. Zeus marooned Odysseus on Ogygia with a thunderbolt. A hurricane marooned the *Sea Venture* on the uninhabited Bermuda archipelago. The writer Daniel Defoe marooned Robinson Crusoe on a Caribbean island and in so doing helped define a cultural genre, with its concomitant themes, motifs, and conventions. In modern culture, the scene of action sometimes shifts to outer space or landscapes of the zombie apocalypse, strange new worlds in which survivors struggle to remake civilization. But the fundamentals remain. The *robinsonade* endures as one of our more ubiquitous narrative templates. It is the argument of this book that American culture uses such tales to redefine national identity and reaffirm democracy.

Most historians and anthropologists know that *maroon* has an older usage. Originally, it referred to cattle that escaped colonial farms on Hispaniola and fled into the backcountry, where they shucked off their domestication and regained their wildness. The Spanish called them *cimmarón*. Most scholars today accept that this usage was current in the Spanish language by 1535. Just five years later, the term was used (first metaphorically and later literally) to describe human chattel who did the same thing: bound to Spanish plantations or mines, Africans slipped their shackles and escaped into the wilderness, where, according to the Spanish point of view, they reverted to their own wildness. The English became familiar with the term through Francis Drake's pirate raids on Panama in the 1570s, when he teamed up with escaped slaves, or *Symerons*, living in the hinterland. The word *maroon* first appeared in English print in 1666, when John Davies, translating a history of Barbados, wrote that some of the enslaved people, like Panama's *Symerons*, would "run away and get into the Mountains and Forests, where they live like so many Beasts." These self-liberated people, he continued, were then "call'd Marons, that is to say Savages."[1]

Though they were often helped by and came to resemble the native peoples that Europeans called "savages," maroons found the mountains and swamps and jungles just as hostile and frightening as did Europeans. They only embraced these dangers through necessity, doing what they could to humanize the wilderness. Why take such risks? As Sylviane Diouf puts it in her 2014 *Slavery's Exiles: The Story of the American Maroons*, "autonomy was at the heart" of the maroons' "project." Exile, hiding "in the wilds," was their means of accomplishing such self-determination.[2] Scholars classify this phenomenon as *marronage*: the condition of people who escaped the site of bondage to construct new lives and sometimes new civil societies beyond the boundary of colonial law.[3]

Maroon did not refer to white castaways until 1699, more than a hundred years after Drake introduced England to the black *Symerons* of Panama. Upon losing his way while wandering from a hunting expedition, William Dampier, a white logger on the Campeche coast of Mexico, "began to see ... that I was (as we call it, I suppose from the Spaniards), Marooned, or Lost, and quite out of the Hearing of my Comrades Guns." For several days, he lived on "Wild-Pines" and suffered clouds of mosquitos before he was rescued.[4] As Dampier's usage indicates, marooned-as-lost began as a metaphoric comparison to fugitive societies living in the wildernesses abutting Spanish colonies. Because being marooned came to be associated almost exclusively with white European castaways, the etymology invites comparison between true maroons (escaped slaves establishing new lives in the wilderness) and people who were marooned (through punishment or maritime disaster). Like true maroons, castaways must construct new lives in the wilderness. If their numbers are sufficiently large, they must remake civil society. Nevertheless, there is no term equivalent to the escaped slaves' *marronage*. Thus, for the volume at hand, we have coined the term *maroonage*, meant both to signal the similarity and difference between castaways and true maroons.

Intrigued by this apparent similarity, the editors of this volume somewhat naively invited scholars to begin discussions that might bridge the gap between the historical, anthropological, and political study of maroons and the cultural study of castaways' narratives. In February 2016, under the sponsorship of the Carolina Lowcountry and Atlantic World Program at the College of Charleston, a diverse group of anthropologists, historians, and literary critics met to explore *marronage* and *maroonage* from the perspectives of their disciplines. Most of the essays in this volume were first drafted for presentation at that conference. It might be fair to say that Diouf was in most people's minds. She is the first historian since Herbert Aptheker (in the 1930s and '40s) to acknowledge not only the existence but also the importance of maroons to our understanding of slavery within the borders of the United States. In fact, as Diouf demonstrates, the previous generation's titanic figures (for example, scholars such as Eugene Genovese) did not think *marronage* had much of a place in the American experience. Consequently, discussions of maroons within the boundaries of the present-day United States often begin with the same rhetorical gesture, illustrated here by Ted Maris-Wolf: "Despite Herbert Aptheker's insistence long ago that dozens of maroon communities once existed within the present limits of the USA, little is known about the nature, composition or even the location of most of these communities." That is changing. Archaeologists (Daniel O. Sayers, Rosalyn Howard, Terrence Weik, and Uzi Baram, among others) have been uncovering new evidence, especially about maroons in Florida and the Great Dismal Swamp. Even so, Sayers asserted in 2012 that "historical archaeologists can—and in fact need to—dramatically expand the influence of their research and voices in discourses on *marronage*." In his view, "hundreds of thousands" of "captive people ... *did* maroon in the U. S." between 1550 and 1860, and archaeology can inform other disciplines of their importance.[5]

Some scholars in those disciplines have been doing such work. Anthropologicial studies and histories include Kenneth Bilby's *True Born Maroons*, Hugo Prosper Leaming's *Hidden Americans: Maroons of Virginia and the Carolinas*, Matthew Clavin's *Aiming for Pensacola: Fugitive Slaves on the Atlantic and Southern Frontiers*, Loren Sweninger and John Hope Franklin's *Runaway Slaves: Rebels on the Plantation*, Marcus Rediker and Peter Linebaugh's *The Many-Headed Hydra: Sailors, Slaves, Commoners and the Hidden History of Revolutionary Atlantic*, Steven Hahn's *The Political Worlds of Slavery and Freedom*, Timothy James Lockley's *Maroon Communities in South Carolina: A Documentary Record*, Ted Maris-Wolf's "Hidden in Plain Sight: Maroon Life and Labor in Virginia's Dismal Swamp," Kevin Mulroy's *Freedom on the Border: The Seminole Maroons in Florida, the Indian Territory, Coahuila, and Texas*, and Katherine Wilson's "The Performance of Freedom: Maroons and the Colonial Order in Eighteenth-Century Jamaica and the Atlantic Sound."[6] Diouf's *Slavery's Exiles* does not culminate but certainly concentrates a trend in recent historiography. This is by no means an exhaustive listing, but it indicates how such scholarship—from Sayers's revisionist interpretation of the Underground Railroad to Hahn's reconceptualization of black communities in antebellum Northern states—is redefining *marronage* and asserting its centrality to American history. The historically focused half of this volume contributes to this work, helping to develop our understanding of American *marronage*.

Historians have long acknowledged that the Great Dismal Swamp was a site of *marronage*; few historians have appreciated the scale and the persistent significance of this refuge. In the nineteenth century, the swamp carried heavy symbolic freight in the works of writers like Harriet Beecher Stowe, Henry Wadsworth Longfellow, Thomas Wentworth Higgenson, and Martin Delany. More significant is the role it played in the largely non-literary African American culture in the heart of the Confederacy. Sylviane Diouf devotes a chapter of her work to the Great Dismal Swamp. In chapter one of the present volume, J. Brent Morris augments Diouf's work with a tour de force summary of the historical record and with new archaeological evidence discovered by the Great Dismal Swamp Landscape Study.

The social historian Steven Hahn teaches us that scholars of American slavery have too long ignored the importance of *marronage* not only as an influence on cultural practice among slaves in the United States who were not fugitive, but as a framing concept by which to understand a wider range of American experience. For example, he suggests that it would be profitable "for us to consider the [antebellum] enclaves of African Americans in New England, the Middle Atlantic, and the Midwest not so much as 'free black communities,' but as entities that resembled 'maroons.'"[7] The psychological experience of free blacks living (for instance) in Boston or New York had something in common with true maroons. In chapter two, James Spady follows Hahn's lead, turning our attention to the streets of Charleston in 1822, when the so-called Denmark Vesey Rebellion convulsed South Carolina's slavocracy. According to court records, thousands of slaves (both urban and rural) attempted *marronage*: they meant to kill whites, burn Charleston, seize the ships in its harbor, and flee to Haiti. The archival record of the uprising has been more or less stable for years, but interpretations of that data have been highly controversial. Writing in the tradition of Michel Foucault, Spady's own method is fascinating and instructive, and his conclusions are startling. His research suggests that the keen historical focus on Vesey, a free man of color, is misplaced, and that the slave Gullah Jack was more central to the affair than is typically recognized. By mapping the relations between those who testified to the court, "who was related to whom, who was a close intimate of whom, who owned whom, and who lived or worked near whom," Spady concludes that even coerced evidence tends to be credible. Furthermore, testimony indicates that *marronage* was not merely a goal.

Spady explains that the "minds and social relations of the black community in 1822" were already experiencing a type of what he calls "psychic marronage" in certain spaces in the urban and rural landscapes.

Freedom, of course, is the *raison d'etre* of maroons. *Choosing freedom* is the pillar of maroon identity. Maroons escaped slavery; they braved the snakes, alligators, and cats of the jungle, swamp, and mountains, and had the courage to risk the retributive torture of pursuing slave catchers, all for freedom. Maroon identity, Richard Price tells us, "is predicated on a single opposition: freedom versus slavery." No other mode of society identifies so strongly with the unalienable human right of self-determination.[8] The philosopher Neil Roberts goes so far as to suggest that *marronage* exemplifies the "supreme ideal of freedom," and that to understand freedom correctly we must understand the psychological experience of flight from bondage and the subsequent reconstruction of civil society. For Roberts, *marronage* is the lens through which we must view freedom. As an existential human condition, freedom is not static but "perpetual, unfinished, and rooted in acts of flight."[9] People escaping bound labor take ownership of their fate, moving from victimhood toward sovereignty in an act not dissimilar to the existential "courage to be" described by the theologian Paul Tillich. Martin Luther King Jr. was thinking of Tillich when he led the marchers in Birmingham, which was undoubtedly a willful deed of courage, the existential assertion of people claiming their freedom.

The legacy clings to such people even into the twenty-first century. As Edward Shore argues in chapter three, Brazil's *Remanescentes de quilombo* carry the symbolic significance of historical freedom-seekers into our contemporary consciousness. They do so in the most quotidian, material sense possible: their claim to, and possession of, land first occupied by maroons. Many scholars make the claim that today's *quilombos* have no real connection to true maroons. Using the oral histories that he collected, Shore disputes that opinion. Tracing one maroon family through generations, he demonstrates how families in the rainforests of the Ribeira Valley still maintain a "deep historical consciousness" of their maroon ancestors.

The second half of this volume turns its attention away from literal maroons to consider how this consciousness is retained by non-maroon cultures when they tell tales of castaways. Though the scholars in this section come from various backgrounds—political science, utopian studies, history, and literary criticism—they all deal with more contemporary works of imaginative literature. Thus, we move from history to cultural criticism. When we first convened our interdisciplinary *Maroonage/Marronage* conference, neither of the editors fully appreciated how presumptuously we had planted ourselves in the territory of this "deep historical consciousness." Handled incautiously, the enthusiastic discovery of connections between people who escaped slavery and white castaways can too easily disrespect the legacy of people who suffered the worst kind of bound labor. The differences must not be forgotten. Maroons *chose* to fly towards the uncertainties of the wilderness. The castaway, at least initially, was hurled out of self-sovereignty into victimhood. Cultural critics, then, must avoid the facile path that suggests victims of *maroonage* like Robinson Crusoe or Shakespeare's Prospero are equivalent to the Quilombo of Brazil, the black Seminoles, or Charleston's Gullah Jack. After all, the marooned Crusoe and Prospero eagerly subjugate "this thing of darkness" they consider an inferior race. Presiding over the *Maroonage/Marronage* conference in Charleston in 2016, the anthropologists Richard and Sally Price consistently voiced this caution. Similarly, Diouf defines *maroons* very narrowly, as if to use the term loosely or figuratively diminishes its power.[10]

Two weeks after our group concluded its meeting in Charleston, another group of (mostly) young scholars, many of them associated with Leiden University or the International Institute of Social History at the University of Amsterdam, published a collection of essays about the Dutch empire. They grouped escaped slaves with other populations of "mass deserters," including indentured servants, convicts, and workers escaping naval and merchant ships. For example, circa 1600, about a quarter of a million people, mostly Europeans, labored under harsh discipline aboard Atlantic ships. The conditions of such bound labor were often intolerable; they fled in astoundingly high numbers. Flight from bound labor, these scholars concluded, was "widespread . . . throughout the early modern world." Despite the obvious differences between, say, fugitive slaves and fugitive sailors, the Leiden group insisted that the "dynamics" of desertion "can (and must) be studied in a comparative way."[11]

Emboldened by the usefulness of such comparative methods, we feel that it would be irresponsible to deny the similarities between *maroonage* and *marronage*. We must not erase the traces of slavery's exiles that are written beneath the surface of castaway narratives. This imperative is doubly important because *maroonage* tales are so vital to the formation of our national identity. The work they perform in our culture makes them the most important narratives we produce. And we produce them continually. Modern culture, the literary critic Steven Mentz points out, obsesses about shipwrecks. "We fear repeating" such tales, Mentz claims, "but cannot resist retelling" them. Readers of *Robinson Crusoe* "latched onto" that novel "for the same reason teenagers flocked to James Cameron's *Titanic* in the summer of 1997." Shipwrecks lure and terrify because they capture the essence of modern experience. They dramatize the tension between "our hopes for an ordered universe" and the "disorienting" effects of "the most powerful nonhuman actor in world history": the "inhospitable sea." The transoceanic voyages of Europe's Age of Discovery, as we all know, set in motion "catastrophic clashes of cultures, peoples, viruses, and ecosystems." These encounters so disrupted long-settled systems of life and thought that disruption itself became the defining characteristic of modernity. Shipwrecks are about rupture. As the solid-timbered ship founders and begins to disappear under the water or, stuck on a reef, is pried apart by the waves, cultural values and (perhaps more importantly) established authority disperse in the deep water, where, lifted free of gravity, they lose their purchase. The survivors watch them float away.

In his 2015 book, *Shipwreck Modernity*, Mentz uncovered the deep structure underlying shipwreck tales. They follow a three-part psychological pattern. As a ship breaks apart, as the deck disappears underfoot, cold seawater shocks the voyagers. Saltwater slaps them in the face, as if waking them from a dream. Then immersion in the sea "puts all forms of order in suspension." Voyagers float free of all connections. They become solitary, detached from each other and untethered from the forces that build ships and organize the old world. Even gravity is disengaged. Eventually, the sea coughs the voyagers out of the surf, gravity reorganizes itself, feet find sand, and the castaways begin the work of drying out, of salvage, of reordering the wreckage of the old world according to the new demands of a wild landscape.

Shock. Immersion. Salvage.

The first two stages hurl survivors into terrifying freedom; the third stage, which consumes most of the space in these stories, is what the castaways do with their liberty. The "microgenre" of shipwreck, Mentz argues, gives culture the narrative tools not only to work out its beliefs but to cope with the condition of uncertainty set loose by the age of exploration. Shipwreck emblemizes modern life, and our culture tells tales of shipwreck to "think through changing views of humanity and the natural world."[12] Mentz does not connect this genre to the freedom experienced by escaped slaves. But it is our conviction that the connection is there, latent, hidden in the deep structure of castaway tales. Just as *maroons* are the etymological root of *being marooned*, so too must *maroonage* be anchored to *marronage*. Literary scholars are just beginning to measure the value of *marronage* to American culture. Scholars such as William Tynes Cowan, David Kazanjian, Sean Gerrity, Nubia Kai, and Martha Schoolman have applied methodologies of cultural criticism to the texts associated with *marronage*, charting what we might call a discourse of *marronage*.[13] This volume enters into new stage of criticism that plots imaginative literature about castaways on this map. Failing to acknowledge this link would write off a national debt to an important cultural heritage. It would also settle for an incomplete understanding of *maroonage* narratives. Insisting on anchoring tales of castaways to this underappreciated discourse endorses the new claims—from archaeologists, historians, and anthropologists—that *marronage* is central to American identity.

In chapter four, Mentz provides the hinge swinging this volume from historical studies of *marronage* to cultural studies of *maroonage*. He begins in the same territory as his book. "The progressive encounter of European cultures with the world ocean and its islands," he writes, is "the central collective narrative of premodern history." One might say that European culture had "an obsessive love of islands." Beginning in the early Middle Ages, Europeans "turn[ed] to islands as sites of cultural fantasy." They were especially useful for "powerful utopian fictions," and the Atlantic exchange accelerated the phenomenon. Bermuda, the site of the most spectacular shipwreck in early modern English history, provides the model. Ever since Shakespeare's *Tempest*, Bermuda has served the narrative of British empire, and Mentz's "post-human" approach to the island aims to disturb that legacy. His nonlinear argument is inconclusive by design: Mentz wants to "reframe the ideological debates that such stories raise."

Daniel Defoe's *Robinson Crusoe* frames many of the tropes we associate with *maroonage*—the European castaway's isolation on a desert isle; the transformation through his encounter with wilderness; the simultaneous domination of nature; the racial and religious conflicts with natives—and the genre Defoe's novel spawned, the *robinsonade*, helped the English interpret and justify their colonial enterprise. Frequently welded to Defoe's tropes is the distinctly American utopian myth of the marriage of savage to civilization. That myth was first figured by the Pocahontas/Smith/Rolfe stories coming out of Jamestown. The native female acquiesces to the superiority of Christianity and modernity, embodied in the European male; the European absorbs the simplicity and innocence that is supposed to be the best part of the primitive, embodied by the native woman. One early American novel seems to invoke those tropes only to undermine them. Critics have long thought that *The Female American*, first published in 1767, dissented from the masculine, Eurocentric identity reproduced by the robinsonade. In chapter five, Peter Sands disputes this claim. Using the 1963 novel *Die Wand* (*The Wall*), by Austrian Marlen Haushofer, Sands draws the contours of a truly ecofeminist utopian robinsonade. These lines exclude *The Female American*, which, Sands concludes, turns out to be surprisingly conventional.

Yvette Christiansë sets her collection of poems, *Castaway*, on St. Helena, a "misty" island in the Caribbean, to borrow Simon Lewis's term. In chapter six, Lewis links Christiansë's work to several of the historical chapters in this book's first section. Christiansë troubles "the binary of slave and free, maroon (deliberate) and castaway (accidental)." Even more, she "exposes the 'mistiness' of race categorization." Many of her poems give voice to a population neglected and silenced by history: captives supposedly liberated by British naval vessels patrolling the Atlantic to suppress the slave trade. Just as Shore traces the resilience of maroon identities through generations, Lewis shows how Christiansë examines the construction of identity among these "re-captives" and their descendants. She elaborates a "liminal and transitional social space *between* slavery and freedom." According to Lewis, Christiansë's characters embody several of the features theorized by Neil Roberts' *Freedom as Marronage* even as she takes up important connections between naming and identity.

The next two essays expand the genre of *maroonage*. "[T]o be marooned," Claire Curtis asserts, "is to be human," at least in the contemporary cultural imagination. Curtis, a political scientist, reminds us that "utopias are often constructed in relation to the experience of being marooned." They might not always manifest as "classic maroonage tales," but "utopian accounts do use the maroonage experience to create or encounter new and better societies," and she suggests that the "the language of maroonage" gives us a lens through which we ought to read such utopias. In fact, her studies of utopian literature have convinced her that many post-apocalyptic narratives are, at their heart, *maroonage* tales. "What is an account of the end of the world," she asks, but the story of "survivors marooned from all that they once knew into a world of zombies, rising seas or plague wastelands?" It is the third stage of Mentz's three-part experience: salvage. Curtis examines how two post-apocalyptic utopian narratives, Margaret Atwood's MaddAddam trilogy and the novel *2312* by the felicitously named Kim Stanley Robinson, rewrite "the heroic" story at the heart of so many European *maroonage* tales: "conquering ... a wild space." In doing so, Curtis's analyses demonstrate what the *maroonage* premise contributes to the genre of "critical" utopias.

Richard Bodek examines yet another manifestation of the castaway story. He begins with the original time-castaway tale, Mark Twain's *A Connecticut Yankee in King Arthur's Court*, which hurls its modern-day protagonist, Hank Morgan, back in time to Camelot. For ages critics have treated this novel as Twain's detailed rumination on Romantic versus Enlightenment modes of thought, on the benefits and dangers of technology, etc. Bodek augments these interpretations using Claire Curtis's method, reading the genre through a *maroonage* lens. After all, Morgan is cast out of the modern world, encounters a comparatively primitive society, and attempts to remake the world using the salvage he has brought with him. Similar treatments of L. Sprague de Camp's *Lest Darkness Fall* and, most interestingly, Octavia Butler's *Kindred* demonstrate how much cultural work is accomplished by this popular version of the *maroonage* tale. Even as *Lest Darkness Fall* reconstructs American identity on the eve of World War II, when liberal democracy was menaced by the tenets of fascism, *Kindred* fundamentally reconstructs American identity by reminding readers how much of what they take as fundamentally American ideas are really late twentieth-century constructs.

Finally, Joseph Kelly's chapter serves as a sort of conclusion and peroration for the collection. The previous four essays, from Sands's chapter on *The Female American* through Bodek's study of time-castaways, demonstrate how ubiquitous *maroonage* is in American culture. They make a convincing case for the sizeable cultural work accomplished by such narratives. Considering how *useful* the creators of American culture have found the *maroonage* template, how each generation reproduces and reconfigures its deep structure, Kelly argues that *maroonage* is the origin of our national literature. Ultimately, this is an argument against the literary history we have been spinning for ourselves ever since the first invention of an American canon: that the Puritans who settled New England are the foundation of American culture. The essential fact of the *Mayflower* story and its sequel on the *Arabella* is the avoidance of shipwreck. Their story of Exodus—chosen people clinging to their old faith no matter their trials in the New World—has proven to be unhelpful in the construction of new narratives. Consequently, artists only infrequently dip into the Pilgrims' purse, and when on those rare occasions they do, they usually come back penniless. Revisiting Steven Mentz and those Jamestown settlers marooned on Bermuda, Kelly argues that our literary anthologies ought to discard William Bradford's *Of Plimoth Plantation* and install William Strachey's *True Reportory of the Wracke and Redemption of Sir Thomas Gates* as the starting point of American literature. This is not in any way an attempt to do justice by William Strachey, who subscribed to the triumphalist template of "conquering . . . a wild space." Strachey was a company man, literally, an executive of the Virginia Company. Consequently, the villains of his narrative are the fugitives of bound labor who tried to maroon themselves on Bermuda. Fugitives do not often get to write the narratives, and the *True Reportory* is no exception, but skimming below the surface of Strachey's tale we can amplify the voices of the fugitives. The tale that ought to open anthologies of American literature is the story of ordinary people bound to labor trying to flee into the wilderness.

Early as they were, these white castaways were not England's first maroons in America. The silenced and forgotten progenitors of America were true maroons, hundreds of Africans fleeing Spanish slavery, who found refuge among the natives of a brave new world. Ignored by most histories, overshadowed by the mystery of whites abandoned on Albemarle Sound, is a deeper mystery: the lost maroons of Roanoke. *Maroonage/Marronage* means to do justice by them and all other fugitives and castaways who dared to claim sovereignty over themselves. We continue to use their stories—with or without acknowledgment—in the twenty-first century.

Notes

1. Drake's exploits on this expedition were not widely published until the first printing of *Sir Francis Drake Revisited* in 1626. Nevertheless, Symerons were widely discussed as early as the 1580s, when they played a large role in England's plans for Sir Walter Raleigh's Roanoke colony. Such documents as Richard Hakluyt's 1584 *Discourse on Western Planting* indicate the extent to which England's elites were familiar with the term. Richard Price provides a succinct historiography of the term in *Maroon Societies*, p. 1 n1. John Davies, translator of Charles de Rochefort, *The History of the Barbados, St. Christophers . . . and the Rest of the Caribby-Islands* (London: 1666), p. 202; noted in the entry on "Maroon," *Oxford English Dictionary*, 3rd edition, December 2000, accessed February 17, 2016.

2. Sylviane Diouf, *Slavery's Exiles: The Story of American Maroons* (New York: New York University Press, 2014), 2.

3. Scholars tend to divide such experiences into two types, *petit marronage* (temporary escape) and *grand marronage* (permanent escape). Strictly speaking, we should speak of constructing new lives and civil society in relation to *grand marronage*.

4. See *OED*, "marooned, v."; William Dampier, *Voyages and Descriptions*, vol. II, part II, 3rd edition (London: James Knapton, 1705), 84. "Eighteenth Century Collections On-line," University of Michigan Library, September 2008, accessed July 18, 2016.

5. See Uzi Baram, "Cosmopolitan Meanings of Old Spanish Fields: Historical Archaeology of a Maroon Community in Southwest Florida," *Historical Archaeology* 46, no. 1 (2012): 108–122; Rosalyn Howard, "'Looking For Angola': An Archaeological and Ethnohistorical Search for a Nineteenth Century Florida Maroon Community and Its Caribbean Connections," *Florida Historical Quarterly* 92, no. 1 (2013): 32–68; Terrence Weik, "Allies, Adversaries, and Kin in the African Seminole Communities of Florida: Archaeology at Pilaklikaha," in *Archaeology of the Atlantic Africa and the African Diaspora*, eds. A. Ogundiran and T. Falola (Bloomington: Indiana University Press, 2007): 311–31; and Daniel O. Sayers, "Marronage Perspective for Historical Archaeology in the United States," *Historical Archaeology* 46, no. 4 (2012): 135–61. Quotation from Sayers, 135, 153.

6. Kenneth Bilby, *True-Born Maroons* (Gainesville: University Press of Florida, 2005); Hugo Prosper Leaming, *Hidden Americans: Maroons of Virginia and the Carolinas* (New York: Garland Publishing, 1995); Matthew J. Clavin, *Aiming for Pensacola: Fugitive Slaves on the Atlantic and Southern Frontiers* (Cambridge: Harvard University Press, 2015); John Hope Franklin and Loren Schweninger, *Runaway Slaves: Rebels on the Plantation* (Oxford:

Oxford University Press, 2000); Steven Hahn, *The Political Worlds of Slavery and Freedom* (Cambridge: Harvard University Press, 2009); Timothy James Lockley, ed., *Maroon Communities in South Carolina: A Documentary Record* (Columbia: University of South Carolina Press, 2009); Ted Maris-Wolf, "Hidden in Plain Sight: Maroon Life and Labor in Virginia's Dismal Swamp," *Slavery & Abolition* 34, no. 3 (2013): 446–64; Kevin Mulroy, *Freedom on the Border: The Seminole Maroons in Florida, the Indian Territory, Coahuila, and Texas* (Lubbock: Texas Tech University Press, 2003); Kathleen Wilson, "The Performance of Freedom: Maroons and the Colonial Order in Eighteenth-Century Jamaica and the Atlantic Sound," *William and Mary Quarterly*, third series, 66, no. 1 (2009): 45–86.

7. Steven Hahn, *The Political Worlds of Slavery and Freedom* (Cambridge, MA: Harvard University Press, 2009), 24. Diouf took issue with this very passage (p. 2).

8. Price, *First Time*, 11–12.

9. Neil Roberts, *Freedom as Marronage* (Chicago: University of Chicago Press, 2015). ProQuest ebrary, accessed February 7, 2016.

10. Diouf, *Slavery's Exiles*, 2.

11. Matthias van Rossum and Jeannette Kamp, eds. *Desertion in the Early Modern World: A Comparative History* (London: Bloomsbury, 2016), 6.

12. Steven Mentz, *Shipwreck Modernity: Ecologies of Globalization, 1550–1719* (Minneapolis, University of Minnesota Press, 2015), xxv–xxvi, 2.

13. William Tynes Cowan, *The Slave in the Swamp: Disrupting the Plantation Narrative* (New York: Routledge, 2006); David Kazanjian, *The Brink of Freedom: Improvising Life in the Nineteenth-Century Atlantic World* (Durham: Duke University Press, 2016); Sean Gerrity, "Freedom on the Move: Marronage in Martin Delany's *Blake; or, the Huts of America*," *MELUS: Multi-Ethnic Literature of the U.S.* 43, no. 3 (2018): 1–18; Nubia Kai, "Black Seminoles: The Maroons of Florida," *African and Black Diaspora: An International Journal* 8, no. 2 (2015): 146–57; Martha Schoolman, *Abolitionist Geographies* (Minneapolis: University of Minnesota Press, 2014).

Secondary Source Bibliography

Baram, Uzi. "Cosmopolitan Meanings of Old Spanish Fields: Historical Archaeology of a Maroon Community in Southwest Florida." *Historical Archaeology* 46, no. 1 (2012): 108–122.

Bilby, Kenneth. *True-Born Maroons*. Gainesville: University Press of Florida, 2005.

Clavin, Matthew J. *Aiming for Pensacola: Fugitive Slaves on the Atlantic and Southern Frontiers*. Cambridge, MA: Harvard University Press, 2015.

Cowan, William Tynes. *The Slave in the Swamp: Disrupting the Plantation Narrative*. New York: Routledge, 2006.

Desertion in the Early Modern World: A Comparative History. Edited by Matthias van Rossum and Jeannette Kamp. London: Bloomsbury, 2016.

Diouf, Sylviane. *Slavery's Exiles: The Story of American Maroons*. New York: New York University Press, 2014.

Franklin, John Hope, and Loren Schweninger. *Runaway Slaves: Rebels on the Plantation*. New York: Oxford University Press, 2000.

Gerrity, Sean. "Freedom on the Move: Marronage in Martin Delany's *Blake; or, the Huts of America*." *MELUS: Multi-Ethnic Literature of the U.S.* 43, no. 3 (2018): 1–18.

Hahn, Steven. *The Political Worlds of Slavery and Freedom*. Cambridge, MA: Harvard University Press, 2009.
Howard, Rosalyn. "'Looking For Angola': An Archaeological and Ethnohistorical Search for a Nineteenth Century Florida Maroon Community and Its Caribbean Connections." *Florida Historical Quarterly* 92, no. 1 (2013): 32–68.
Kai, Nubia. "Black Seminoles: The Maroons of Florida." *African and Black Diaspora: An International Journal* 8, no. 2 (2015): 146–57.
Kazanjian, David. *The Brink of Freedom: Improvising Life in the Nineteenth-Century Atlantic World*. Durham: Duke University Press, 2016.
Leaming, Hugo Prosper. *Hidden Americans: Maroons of Virginia and the Carolinas*. New York: Garland Publishing, 1995.
Maris-Wolf, Ted. "Hidden in Plain Sight: Maroon Life and Labor in Virginia's Dismal Swamp." *Slavery & Abolition* 34, no. 3 (2013): 446–64.
Maroon Communities in South Carolina: A Documentary Record. Edited by Timothy James Lockley. Columbia: University of South Carolina Press, 2009.
Mentz, Steven. *Shipwreck Modernity: Ecologies of Globalization, 1550–1719*. Minneapolis: University of Minnesota Press, 2015.
Mulroy, Kevin. *Freedom on the Border: The Seminole Maroons in Florida, the Indian Territory, Coahuila, and Texas*. Lubbock: Texas Tech University Press, 2003.
Roberts, Neil. *Freedom as Marronage*. Chicago: University of Chicago Press, 2015. ProQuest ebrary. Accessed February 7, 2016.
Sayers, Daniel O. "Marronage Perspective for Historical Archaeology in the United States." *Historical Archaeology* 46, no. 4 (2012): 135–61.
Schoolman, Martha. *Abolitionist Geographies*. Minneapolis: University of Minnesota Press, 2014.
Weik, Terrence. "Allies, Adversaries, and Kin in the African Seminole Communities of Florida: Archaeology at Pilaklikaha." In *Archaeology of the Atlantic Africa and the African Diaspora*. Edited by A. Ogundiran and T. Falola, 311–31. Bloomington: Indiana University Press, 2007.
Wilson, Kathleen. "The Performance of Freedom: Maroons and the Colonial Order in Eighteenth-Century Jamaica and the Atlantic Sound." *William and Mary Quarterly*, third series, 66, no. 1 (2009): 45–86.

MAROONS AND THE MAROONED

Chapter One

"Mingled Fear and Ferocity": A Glimpse into the Maroon Communities of the Great Dismal Swamp

J. Brent Morris

Writing for *The Liberty Bell* in 1852, abolitionist Edmund Jackson recounted the circumstances of the maroons of the Great Dismal Swamp, a "large colony of negroes, who originally obtained their freedom through the grace of God, and their own determined energy." "How long this colony has existed," he admitted, "what is its amount of population, what portion of the colonists are now Fugitives, and what the descendants of Fugitives, are questions not easily determined."[1] Many of these had lived their entire lives without setting their gaze upon the people or places outside of the swamp's depths. David Hunter Strother went on assignment to the Great Dismal for *Harper's Monthly* in 1856 with the specific purpose of catching a glimpse of one of these mythical "fugitives." When he did stumble upon the fierce-looking Osman, a leader of the Deep Swamp maroons, Strother's desires were quickly replaced by the terror of being himself discovered by the well-armed chief. Seconds seemed like an eternity, and the journalist could only shake off his paralysis once the "sable outlaw" had disappeared back into the swamp. In the 150 or so years since Strother's account of his journey rolled off the presses of *Harper's*, the maroons of the Great Dismal Swamp have been just as elusive to historians.

Maroons were highly successful in concealing themselves, but their flight into an impenetrable swamp, far beyond the gaze or reach of outsiders, has been more successful in hiding them than they ever would have imagined. Maroons usually only appear in the documentary record when their presence in the swamp was accidentally discovered or when their activities at the swamp's edge became intolerable or too dangerous to the safety or ideological comfort of white society that officials felt their destruction was necessary.[2] With no masters to chronicle their activities, no abolitionists to dictate letters describing swamp life, and no known internal record-keeping, the legacy of the maroons depends on a handful of brief travel accounts, a contemporary observation here and there, a few newspaper features, and the rare personal testimony of a former resident of the swamp. These sources have not merited the concerted attention of historians—it is a story that from first glance seems unknowable, or more likely, owing to the apparently thin documentary record, a very short story without much to tell.

This is an impediment that obscures the histories of all North American maroon communities. There is a rich literature devoted to the maroon communities of South and Central America and the Caribbean.[3] The maroons of Jamaica fought several wars with colonial authorities and won a treaty of independence. The maroon *quilombo* of Palmares in Brazil numbered in the tens of thousands, persisted for nearly a century, and also defeated colonial armies sent to destroy them. These communities among others thus left significant records (both maroon and colonial), a boon for historians who study these groups. South and Central American and Caribbean marronage on a grand scale presented military, economic, and ideological threats that often forced Europeans to action, and in the process, created a rich paper trail.

However, most North American maroon colonies were much smaller and did not often interact with the white governing authorities (compared to their counterparts to the south), resulting in a dearth of source material. Thus, only a few historians (usually in the context of Florida and the Seminoles) have focused to any extent on marronage in the British North American colonies or the United States.[4] When the topic of marronage is not completely ignored, historians of the past generation have taken great pains to dismiss North American marronage altogether. Michael Mullin, in his 1992 book *Africa in America: Slave Acculturation and Resistance in the American South and the British Caribbean, 1736–1831*, proclaims an "absence of a maroon dimension in the South."[5] Eugene Genovese's 1979 *From Rebellion to Revolution: Afro-American Slave Revolts in the Making of the Modern World* condescendingly describes maroons (in particular, those of the Great Dismal Swamp) as nothing more than a "nuisance," fugitives "huddled in small units" who should be called maroons "only as a courtesy." In his estimation, North American maroons were nothing more than loose bands of disorganized "desperadoes."⁶ John Hope Franklin and Loren Schweninger characterize North American marronage as an "ephemeral" phenomenon, and analyze the subject in just a single page in their 1999 book *Runaway Slaves: Rebels on the Plantation*.⁷ Another important work on colonial slavery, Philip D. Morgan's *Slave Counterpoint: Black Culture in the Eighteenth-Century Chesapeake & Lowcountry*, relegates discussion of marronage to six short paragraphs and concludes that when such fugitive communities did form, they were all "short-lived," especially in the Chesapeake, a region "not particularly conducive to maroon settlements."⁸ Alvin O. Thompson's *Flight to Freedom: African Runaways and Maroons in the Americas* gives relatively little attention to marronage north of the Caribbean, and then, only as synthesis of an admittedly sparse historiography and not based on original research.⁹ The only thorough study of marronage in North America is Sylviane Diouf's recent book *Slavery's Exiles: The Story of the American Maroons*. This largely synthetic work is a welcome addition to a near-nonexistent historiography, yet it does not devote more than a single chapter to any one maroon group.¹⁰

Historians have only recently started acknowledging the existence, numbers, and importance of the Great Dismal Swamp maroons, yet still not approaching the extent the story deserves.¹¹ Between the early seventeenth century and 1865, thousands of maroons and enslaved swamp-company timber workers settled in the swamp and formed permanent communities that varied significantly over time and swamp location. Altogether, these communities were central to a historically significant social and economic world deep within the swamp that endured for more than two centuries yet, at the same time, went under-recorded in the documentary record. However, despite the impression one might get from the historiography, these are not unknowable stories.

Today the Great Dismal Swamp extends north and south fifty miles inland and straddles the Virginia-North Carolina border. Before industrialists began large-scale drainage projects in the eighteenth century, the swamp's area was nearly the size of Delaware at 2,000 square miles, from the Atlantic shore in the east to the Suffolk Scarp, the ancient Pleistocene shoreline, to the west.¹² However, there were very few reasons for whites of the plantation country to approach the Dismal Swamp. One of the earliest descriptions of the swamp was by the man who would eventually be hired to survey it, William Byrd II. He imagined that "towards the heart of this humble desart [sic], no beast or bird approaches, not so much as an insect or reptile . . . Nor indeed do any birds care to fly over it . . . for fear of the noisome exhalations that rise from this vast body of dirt and nastiness."¹³ This, of course, was not remotely true, as the actual presence of Dismal Swamp wildlife (black bears, alligators, several varieties of poisonous snakes, feral cattle and hogs, and swarms of bloodthirsty mosquitoes and yellow flies) may well have been more terrifying than its absence in Byrd's narrative. Despite Byrd's proposals that the swamp might be drained, lumbered, and generally "redeemed" for immense profits, no one would attempt it in his lifetime. In the elite Georgian tradition that prized an ordered and subdued landscape, the untamable Dismal Swamp stood out as an anomalous curse on the landscape to be avoided and, if possible, ignored.

Yet each obstacle that kept whites comfortably outside the swamp and frustrated their attempts to subdue it served to protect those who sought their freedom in the swamp's depths. The Great Dismal was a natural defense to those who slaved on the outside and sought to escape. Moreover, once maroons had established themselves in the swamp, the nearby plantation country was a convenient target for plunder, resistance, and liberation of brothers and sisters still in bonds. The swamp's dark waters were believed by many to have medicinal qualities, and its acidity made it naturally antibiotic. There are "islands" of slightly higher elevation scattered throughout the swamp where homes could be built, crops grown, and even livestock raised, and the place teemed with game for hunting.[14]

The first inhabitants of the Dismal Swamp were Indigenous refugees from European aggression or fugitives from slavery. As an alternative to abandoning their homeland, these men and women of Tidewater tribes chose to move into the nearby swamp, a landscape that had very little value or significance to the colonists but was revered by Indigenous settlers for its shelter, protection, and natural gifts.[15] Prior to the first decades of the eighteenth century, there is also evidence that escaped indentured servants had entered the Dismal Swamp.[16] Judging from the presence of Africans in Virginia from 1619 and in and around Norfolk from the 1630s, there were probably self-emancipating Africans in the swamp early on as well, but not many. The black population of the region was still relatively small and would remain so until the next century.[17]

Although the numbers and organization of the earliest maroons were limited, some of them immediately began a campaign of raids against the outside society that had enslaved them, though more for survival than revenge. The first generations of Dismal Swamp maroons were a diverse assortment of men and women who sought to negate the dehumanization and criminalization imposed upon them in the dominant world by removing themselves from it. They transcended whatever differences might have obtained among them in the outside world in favor of a united enmity against a shared antagonist and dedication to self-determination. A 1709 uprising involving Native

Americans, slaves, and maroons led by an African American named Peter is but the best documented example of the concerted action of early maroons.[18]

After generations of steady maroon growth in the swamp, self-emancipating men and women could expect to find empathetic guides, teachers in the arts of survival, and communities and kin groups to which they might attach themselves. Guerrilla activity in the area increased through the 1720s, as refugees from the Tuscarora War entered the swamp from the South, and Africans, who were steadily increasing in number in Virginia tobacco fields, fled there from the north. When Byrd surveyed the swamp in 1728, he encountered people he characterized as maroons, and, fully aware of the Jamaican maroon wars that were then raging, compared the Dismal Swamp maroons to Romulus and Remus, the legendary founders of Rome, who had issued a call to the exiles, dispossessed, and self-emancipating slaves of Italy to join them in the building of a city of refuge in the wilderness. From such similar beginnings had grown one of the most powerful empires in history, and Byrd warned that if the growing maroon population of the Dismal Swamp were not soon checked, a dangerous power base hostile to the surrounding country might emerge.[19]

The early Dismal Swamp maroons appreciated their relatively small numbers, and like other hemispheric maroons, they sought all possible alliances. This is evident in the earliest days of Great Dismal Swamp maroons aligning with slaves and Native Americans. There are also indications later that the maroon community sent men to fight in Lord Dunmore's black regiment during the Revolutionary War.[20] Into the first years of the nineteenth century, maroon raids originating from the Dismal Swamp very likely coordinated with larger insurrection attempts, including the Easter Rebellion, or Sancho's Rebellion, of 1801–1802.[21] Maroons continued their raids from the swamp through the 1820s, and whites feared that the swamp was becoming a point of assembly for nearby slaves, a base and goal for concerted slave insurrection in the upper South. The Vesey scare in South Carolina in 1822 did little to ease their minds. An urban uprising in Charleston was one thing; whites in the Tidewater were terrified of what a similar rebellion might accomplish in their midst near a sanctuary as sprawling and impenetrable as the Dismal Swamp. Initial reports of Nat Turner's rebellion in 1831 suggested the fear had become a reality—the earliest accounts of the uprising assumed that it was the work of a band of Dismal Swamp maroons. Although this was not the case, fugitives from the defeated insurrection and its aftermath did flee to the Dismal Swamp, and some succeeded in their escape to the maroons.[22]

The alarm produced by the Turner rebellion and its proximity to the Great Dismal affected the number of fugitives' entering the swamp as well as the conduct of guerrilla activity during the next twenty years. Though the deeper portions of the swamp were never penetrated, there were regular raids into the more accessible interior areas by slave hunters and their bloodhounds. Contemporaries suggest that the maroon population of the Dismal Swamp had shrunk significantly by the 1840s.[23] However, structured communities continued to exist, and their growth and increased activity from the mid-1840s onward is reflected in local and national periodicals, as well as a burst of new legislation that sought to curb the incidence of marronage.[24] This expansion and the experience of guerilla raiding by a new generation of Dismal Swamp maroons would prove useful in their military alliance with the United States of America against the Confederacy during the Civil War of the 1860s.[25]

The primary objective of the Dismal Swamp maroons was to stay undetected below the radar. In this, they were extraordinarily successful. Nearly every aspect of their lives in some way reflected a desire to maintain their secrecy and concealment. Although abolitionists and romantics sympathetic to their circumstances often sentimentalized the story of the Dismal Swamp maroons, Southerners, loath to publicize the fact that they could often not even locate much less destroy the maroon threat, had no incentive to advertise their impotence. The combination of exaggeration and suppression has produced a record that contributes very little to our actual knowledge of maroon life in the swamp.[26] However, the recent discoveries of new primary source narratives included in this chapter and a larger work-in-progress, and the interdisciplinary work of the Great Dismal Swamp Landscape Study (GDSLS), an archaeology-focused research group (for which I have served as historian since 2009), have helped flesh out this history well beyond what any scholar has accomplished to date.[27]

Fundamentally, the Great Dismal Swamp did not shelter a single large maroon colony, despite what many contemporaries and commentators have since assumed. Instead, self-emancipators formed dozens of separate maroon communities across the swamp. Modern satellite imaging indicates that large mesic islands (greater than 20 acres) and large clusters of smaller islands (50 or more acres in aggregate) exist in the swamp that would have been conducive to larger-scale settlement. GDSLS excavations on some of these sites have produced conclusive evidence of continuous maroon occupation throughout the seventeenth through nineteenth centuries.[28] GDSLS cartographer Graham Callaway has suggested that there are potentially hundreds of such higher dry ground landforms located throughout the still largely undisturbed Great Dismal Swamp Wildlife Refuge (GDSWR, 175 square miles on the North Carolina side), and this does not include any such landforms located in developed former swamp land.[29] Islands surveyed by the GDSLS to date range from 1–39 acres, are often found in clusters with as little as 50 feet of swamp separating them, and are as high as 10 feet above swamp level in the most isolated, Deep Swamp islands.[30] Yet these islands spread over thousands of square acres, and though some are close enough to have been utilized by the same group of maroons, most are not. To be sure, there *were* large communities deep within the Great Dismal, but the basic topography of the swamp, social structure of the communities, and concerns for defense and safety preclude any possibility of their being more than loosely joined.

The overall maroon population of the Great Dismal Swamp likely fluctuated widely over two centuries, and it is impossible to state with any precision numbers for any given time. One Southerner estimated the swamp's population from the 1840s at an impossibly high 40,000.[31] The editor of the *Zions Herald* newspaper mentioned in 1848 the presence of "hundreds of fugitives" in "this damp and dreary region." During a lecture on December 8, 1850, Frederick Douglass, whose other writings suggest some knowledge of the Great Dismal Swamp maroons, told of "uncounted numbers of fugitives," a very accurate assessment.[32] Another frequent figure guessed for maroon population, 2,000, derives from the militia estimate at the time of the Turner revolt.[33] The GDSLS has uncovered evidence of "heavy" maroon use and dense populations deep in the swamp. Though considerably less than 1 percent of the GDSWR acreage has even been surveyed, every area of dry ground visited by the GDSLS was determined to be an archaeological site or an isolated find.[34] The most extensive excavation to date, called the "nameless" site, represents just 1/10 of 1 percent of the 20-acre mesic island upon which it was located.[35] At the island's highest elevation, in a 20-by-20 meter area, GDSLS has excavated ten significant structures and cultural landscape features, including six structural footprints, a defensive structure (fort/ammunition depot), and several other postholes and pits of unknown purpose.[36] With the general concurrence of the documentary sources that the swamp population was quite large, one could say with some confidence that dozens of maroons settled at any given time on this excavated spot, and as the GDSLS has only uncovered a tiny fraction of likely settlement locations, the aggregate population of the Great Dismal Swamp maroon communities at any given time likely numbered in at least the hundreds, perhaps thousands.

Three different types of marronage developed in the Great Dismal Swamp, groups I have termed "Fringe," "Liminal," and "Deep Swamp" maroons. Though there were cases where a maroon transitioned from one type of marronage to another, these were almost always in the direction of more structure and independence than less.[37] The Fringe maroons were semi-independent and included those who settled at the edge of the swamp, strategically situated for easy access to both the interior of the swamp and outside world. These were often the most transient maroons who were not necessarily seeking to remain in the swamp for extended periods of time. Before the significant encroachments of agriculture, lumbering, and canals in the late eighteenth century, these maroons sometimes formed small communities, but as the swamp's edge receded in the nineteenth century, Fringe maroons appeared only as very small groups or as individuals. As this transformation was occurring at the swamp's periphery, Liminal maroons developed as a distinct population alongside corporate and industrial enterprises in the swamp. These maroons often lived alongside enslaved swamp laborers, indeed, often really out in plain sight. They did not necessarily seek to limit contacts and connections with the outside world, and in fact were largely dependent on it for their survival. The Deep Swamp maroons were those who sought to separate themselves physically, socially, and economically from the exterior world as much as possible. These were the most permanently settled maroons of the swamp, often living for years (or decades) in their isolation.

The most ephemeral Dismal Swamp residents were the Fringe maroons. These men and women settled at the natural perimeter of the swamp and generally fell into one of three subcategories. The first were transient refugees from slavery who availed themselves of the swamp's secrecy and protection for a time before moving on to another location, often a step closer to a Free State or Canada. The North Star meant freedom to thousands of self-emancipating slaves over the years, and the Dismal Swamp was a bright spot lit in its path, earning it a reputation as a busy station of the "underground railroad."[38] More settled maroons around the perimeter were known to shelter self-emancipators, offering them temporary respite from the worst dangers of escape and advice for the next leg of their journey. Those already in the swamp knew of the routes to Canada and the Northern states, and even if they had not chosen to set out themselves, shared what they knew.[39]

Time spent at the edges of the swamp could also have been intentionally temporary and sometimes also included return to their enslavement after a period of "lying out." An amazingly efficient and vast communication network in the region helped these men and women maintain their fastness in the swamp yet remain in touch with loved ones still in bonds. Slave owners also appear to have been well-aware of the "grapevine telegraph," sometimes using it to contact their former slaves in the swamp. A postbellum source described the process by which a maroon named Pompey used the swamp's communication network to negotiate improved treatment and living conditions from his owner over the course of a three-month stay at the edges of the swamp. This episode demonstrates the fluidity and connections between the maroons of the swamp's edge and the external world.[40]

A third group of Fringe maroons (and there was likely some overlap with the other two) utilized the swamp's edge as a base of operations for guerilla raids on outside settlements. These maroons were often described by hostile outsiders as "too lazy" to work, filching from local granaries, or raiding nearby plantations or towns at night to help themselves to what they need "without leave asked or granted."[41] At times, these forays out of the swamp could turn violent. Travelers near to the swamp's edge were warned to exercise extreme caution against frequent maroon attacks.[42] The Great Dismal was one of the "strong swamps" from which maroons "commit many daring outrages."[43]

These "renegades" were well-prepared for battle. Their lives as hunters and butchers of raided stock already required it, as would their very survival in a tenuous and hostile world. Military reports of raids from the swamp frequently cite firearms, swords, knives, and pikes within the possession of maroons. The maroons also manufactured bows and arrows, useful to preserve powder and shot for emergencies.[44] One maroon raider, an outlawed fugitive slave from Suffolk, Virginia, with a $1,000 price on his head, was captured after leading several raids in the 1850s. Though shot several times, the captive was unhurt, thanks to his swamp-made body armor, a coat thickly wadded with turkey feathers that was impervious to small shot.[45]

All three groups of Fringe maroons, for their own reasons, strategically positioned themselves for quick access to worlds both inside and outside the swamp. In the seventeenth and eighteenth centuries, before significant tracts of swampland were drained and put to plow, this heavily wooded transitionary region from dry ground to swamp was several miles wide at places and offered maroons enough of the swamp's concealment without requiring the extreme level of commitment or exposure to as many dangers as the Deep Swamp interior. If necessary, they could retreat further into the swamp to avoid capture but would generally return to the perimeter once a threat had passed. By the late eighteenth century, however, much of the higher and drier land of the Suffolk Scarp, the western boundary of the Great Dismal Swamp, had been developed and the perimeter transition zone largely eliminated. This significantly reduced the degree to which Fringe maroons could hope to avoid detection and harassment from the outside world. With a transition zone around the perimeter that may have been a half-mile at most from a clearly demarcated outside world, marronage on the fringe gradually became limited to shorter stays, very small groups or (most often) individuals, and required an abundance of vigilance and caution.

At the other extreme were maroons who did everything they could to remain hidden and inaccessible to outsiders. These Deep Swamp maroons had made a conscious decision to not just escape from slavery, but to completely remove themselves from the world outside the swamp. They were also the most settled of all Dismal Swamp maroons, and nearly every aspect of their lives reflects a desire for permanence and independence.

Settled on and around mesic islands many miles into the swamp's interior, the life of Deep Swamp maroons reflected their isolation and unique living environments.[46] There, they were able to construct structures with the expectation of permanence. With a protective buffer of miles of nearly impenetrable swamp between themselves and the outside world, an expanse that might take an outsider unfamiliar with the terrain days to negotiate, Deep Swamp maroons could afford the investment in time and labor to craft structures they fully intended to last. Sections of architectural footprints excavated by the GDSLS bear this out. Deep Swamp maroons built post-in-ground living structures with raised floors laid upon horizontally laid floor joists. Walls were either waddle and daub or mud chinking between horizontal logs. The labor and planning required to construct a house like this was considerable. Large holes had to be dug to accommodate structural posts that were between 20–30 centimeters in diameter (approx. 7–12 inches), posts which themselves had to be cut from standing hardwood trees. Maroons dug trenches around the perimeter of the houses, and gathered and prepared the plants and clay necessary to construct weather-tight walls.[47] Burnt clay discovered in soils associated with architectural features is also indicative of intentional soil hardening for structural stability.[48] Overall, documentary and archaeological evidence suggests that Deep Swamp maroon structures were erected, strengthened, repaired, and used throughout a two-century era.[49]

Certainly, level and dry ground was prioritized for housing, but in the case that the most desirable areas of an island were already occupied, maroons utilized alternative architectural approaches. On swampy ground, maroons built houses elevated on stilts or even in the trees. Even on higher knolls, elevated houses were not superfluous, and most were raised some distance above the ground as a protection against occasional flooding and rodents. The space also helped circulate the air in the warm months, and when enclosed with dirt around the edges, insulated the house when it was colder.[50] It was also the case that maroons built homes on sloping terrain during the periods of densest population when more desirable land was already taken.[51]

According to multiple accounts, maroons built roads in the deepest parts of the swamp, near their settlements, but not running far towards the dangerous outer parts of the swamp. The approach to the village was by a faint trail virtually impossible to follow without guidance. As these trails converged closer to the village, there might be a well-kept-up dirt road, with trees carefully blazed and logs, worked into shape by axe, laid side by side over the frequent wet portions.[52]

The Deep Swamp maroon diet was quite nutritious and offered residents a great variety of foodstuffs. They raised small livestock in pens near their houses, and kept gardens on the elevated drier land of their settlements which allowed them to live, as one observer noted, "in security and plenty."[53] Swamp soils are generally deficient in nitrogen, but manure from their chickens or other animal waste could have been used as a fertilizer. Wood ashes would have counteracted soil acidity.[54] An acre of land planted with corn could yield forty bushels at harvest, and sown as it usually was along with peas and beans (with other crops like squashes, gourds, sunflowers, and melons at the margins), a small area could yield many calories.[55] Most of these foods could be dried and easily stored for the winter. Sweet potatoes were also harvested in the colder months. Dismal Swamp beekeepers maintained hives throughout the swamp. The seeds of the blue lupine flower were edible, grapes were plentiful in season, and flour and ultimately coarse bread could be produced from certain swamp reeds, which an outsider declared to be a "fair substitute" for wheat. Their remoteness allowed an extensive husbandry that would have been impossible to hide nearer the swamp's edge.[56]

Also available to the Deep Swamp maroon table were opossum and raccoon, venison, wild pig goat and beef, duck and other fowl, squirrels, otter, beaver, bear, turtle, and even alligator. Game moved into the cooler and damper areas in the swamp in the summer, and essentially into the hands of maroon hunters.[57] Fishing parties also frequently traveled with their bark or dugout canoes to Lake Drummond, the 3,000-acre central feature of the swamp that "thronged with fish."[58] The animal bones discovered in the Deep Swamp archaeological digs indicate a heavy reliance on fish and perhaps snakes among interior maroons.[59]

Like the Fringe raiders, interior maroons were relatively well-armed, though for defensive rather than offensive purposes. Several documentary sources place pistols, rifles, and long guns in the hands of Deep Swamp maroons.[60] Osman, one of the few interior maroons actually witnessed by a white observer, was armed with such a gun.[61] A former maroon in 1863 listed two guns among his possessions.[62] Another source remarked that "they, in different ways, not unfrequently, manage to obtain fire arms and ammunition, which places them in quite independent circumstances."[63] The GDSLS has discovered British and French gunflints in archaeological digs, used almost to the point of disappearance. Flints and shot were discovered in what may have been ammunition caches within the maroon structure the GDSLS believes to be a fort or defensive structure on a higher-elevation swamp site.[64]

Though their level of armament would have supported it, it seems most likely that Deep Swamp maroons would have seldom if ever sent out raiding parties to the outside. Deep Swamp maroons had the luxury of self-sufficiency. Moreover, any potential haul resulting from such a raid would only have been brought back to their community with considerable difficulty and at a steep cost. These communities were often miles from the nearest point of potential contact with the outside, an expanse that might take an entire day or more to cross. This worked to their advantage as a barrier to outside intrusion, yet would have made the transport of any plunder worth taking quite onerous, not to mention the loss of days of crucial labor-hours that could not be spared. The artifact assemblage of the GDSLS Deep Swamp excavations shows a near-total absence of mass-produced or outside world materials; they relied almost entirely on items sourced within the swamp itself.[65] Firearms would have been potentially the most precious items a community possessed, and they would have been treated with the utmost of care, repaired whenever possible, and never lost or discarded. The near-microscopic remnants of gunflints themselves utilized down to the last possible firing, in fact, represent a significant portion of the outside world materials located in the Deep Swamp excavations.

Isolation and protection by nature also facilitated the development of families within the depths of the swamp. A few enslaved people originally absconded with their families in tow.[66] This, of course, would have been rare, like it was with all self-emancipators. Maroons, though, often met and married spouses in the swamp, and they had children there as well.[67] Eventually, there were residents of the inner swamp who had never experienced life outside the Dismal and indeed some who would reach the end of their days having never set foot on solid ground outside the swamp or seen a white face.[68] There is evidence to suggest that kinship was the main organizational force in the deep swamp maroon communities. Authority among these maroons was most often earned over time through the development of strong kin affinities rather than military prowess or pre-maroon status.[69] The archaeological record also suggests that the longer-established kin groups among Deep Swamp maroons occupied the areas of highest elevation while less-desirable plots, sloped land for example, was utilized as the kin group expanded generationally or as newcomers were accepted in.[70]

It is no wonder that these maroons went to great lengths to remain fast in their isolation. Entrance to the deep swamp settlements was strictly controlled. Even the smallest bits of information about the settlements were tightly guarded.[71] Moreover, paths to and from the deep swamp settlements were concealed as much as possible. Multiple sources mention secretive pathways through the swamp and over boggy or wet terrain marked only by "notches cut on trees" with false trails and dead ends as added precautions.[72] It was common knowledge that any attempt by an outsider to venture near an interior maroon settlement would entail great danger if he were discovered in the attempt.[73] Dismal Swamp maroons in the deep interior also appear to have extensively "vetted" potential recruits. Questions would be asked of the newcomers without revealing the locations of the communities, or newcomers on the swamp's borders seeking entrance to the interior might be observed for days or even weeks before they were invited to join a settled community.[74]

Interior maroons so zealously guarded their isolation and secrecy that, with very few exceptions, they would do without some good or item rather than venture out of the Deep Swamp recesses to get it. Because of the scarcity of mass-produced goods from outside the swamp, maroons also utilized discarded prehistoric Indigenous tools and artifacts whenever they were available. The swamp had been a favored hunting ground of pre-contact Indigenous groups, and artifacts from that occupation, including arrowheads, ceramics, and stone knives, occasionally surfaced at some deep swamp locations.[75] The immense care with which they were repaired and their very longevity show that they were highly prized items not easy to replace. The fact that more than 75 percent of all stone flakes recovered from deep swamp excavations were small tertiary and microdebitage flakes suggest a constant reworking of already ancient tools.[76] In fact, the majority of materials recovered from historical contexts by archaeologists have been very small in size, less than one half of a centimeter at their widest, suggesting a community ethos and normative requirement that materials stay in use. When they could be found in the ground, fashioned out of animal bones, or obtained through some risky contact with the outside world, maroons recycled such tools almost into disappearance.[77] Deep Swamp maroons even incorporated pieces of Native American ceramics dated 1200–800 B.C. into their home construction to strengthen and shore up organic materials.[78]

It is interesting to note that even though the use of recycled lithic tool and Indigenous ceramics was common at the "nameless" site, prehistoric soil strata there do not contain correspondingly high concentrations of those artifacts. This is likely due to the site being so isolated as to have had only irregular and non-intensive occupation by Native Americans. Thus, the artifacts utilized by the maroons of the "nameless" site had to have been brought in from elsewhere. Documentary sources suggest that at other Deep

Swamp locations, such artifacts were in fact plentiful. The maroons of the "nameless" site, then, could have possibly "mined" other swamp locations for these artifacts themselves. However, considering the evidence of continuous dense habitation even at the lower, less desirable elevations at the "nameless" site, other locations in the swamp that had been suitable for intensive use by pre-contact Native Americans would have also likely been at a premium for maroon settlement later and thus not available for their own excavations. It seems more likely that these artifacts entered the "nameless" community through a trade network among Deep Swamp maroon communities.

Reliance on other "scission" communities would have been safer from a security standpoint and most consistent with the community ethos of Deep Swamp maroons. Lacking access to useful inorganic materials on their own island, "nameless" community maroons would have likely offered what they did have in relative abundance, items of their own organic material culture.[79] Some Deep Swamp maroons were skilled craftsmen, and one of the rare primary sources we have that offers a small glimpse into swamp life shows that maroons often produced items, especially those made of organic materials, in greater numbers than would have been necessary for personal use.[80] These would have easily become part of the circulation of materials within what archaeologist Daniel Sayers calls the "metacommunity" of interior maroon settlements, a system of reciprocal exchange.[81]

The end of the eighteenth century witnessed a revolution in the swamp that significantly impacted the lives of both Fringe and Deep Swamp maroons. The digging of canals by small armies of enslaved workers and the rise of the lumbering and shingling industries within the swamp forced a fundamental reconfiguration of the Dismal Swamp landscape and reorientation of life for many maroons. Deep swamp communities had once been separated from the outside world by miles of near-impenetrable swampland. Navigating that expanse would have taken hours for even the most skilled swamper, and the Great Dismal itself was the most faithful and diligent protector the maroons had. However, canals brought the outside world into the depths of the interior, sometimes even directly into a Deep Swamp Maroon settlement.[82] What had once been isolated might now be exposed, and an "industrial revolution" within the swamp forced dramatic changes for many Great Dismal Swamp maroons.

In 1763, George Washington and several business partners chartered the Adventurers to Drain the Great Dismal Swamp. Their corporate name highlighted but one of their goals—the businessmen also hoped to extract lumber, shingles, and other wood products from the swamp and transform what had long been considered a "dismal" wasteland into a productive landscape. The company owned 40,000 acres in the Virginia side of the swamp (including Lake Drummond), and sponsored the digging of the Washington Ditch, a four-mile canal that ran from the western edge of the swamp to the central lake. The work was to be done by fifty-four enslaved Africans, "company slaves," whose numbers were constantly diminished through death or desertion and required constant resupply.[83] Their hand-dug canal effectively bisected the western half of the swamp and became the first significant encroachment into the interior, marking the start of a canal boom as more of the interior landscape was bought and divided among other companies. The 22-mile long Dismal Swamp Canal, dug with enslaved labor from 1784 to 1805, ran the north-south length of the swamp and connected the Chesapeake Bay with Albemarle Sound, and importantly, the swamp interior and the outside world.

On the banks of these canals were camps of enslaved workers. These would have initially housed the hundreds of canal diggers under the close supervision of an overseer, but with the rise of lumbering in the swamp, they would have served as the home base for enslaved people compelled to do that type of work. However, in order for these enslaved workers to harvest the wood of the Great Dismal, they would have to venture into the virgin swamp itself, far away from their settlements. These workers were called shingle "gitters." Typically, starting in early February, companies of bondsmen, under the loose supervision of a driver, were sent to the swamp with several months' worth of pork, flour, and cornmeal. They built huts on high ground or over piles of shingle shavings and lived there until the end of June. The wilderness offered them a modicum of freedom not found on the plantations. They fished, hunted, and worked at their own pace. Their only requirement was to produce a certain quantity of shingles at the end of the season, and any production beyond their "task" was generally rewarded with cash or additional supplies. Moses Grandy, an enslaved man hired out to the Great Dismal Swamp Land Company for a year to cart lumber through the swamp, appreciated the deal. "I had plenty to eat and plenty of clothes," he remembered. "I was so overjoyed at the change, that I then thought I would not have left the place to go to heaven." He eventually saved up enough money to purchase his freedom. Enslaved workers sometimes considered swamp work, apart from the brutal canal-digging itself, as a sort of privileged position that allowed them a degree of freedom, distance from slave traders, and closeness to family. Predictably, of course, as shingle slaves penetrated deeper into the swamp's recesses to cut down trees to make shingles and barrel staves, some seized the opportunity to free themselves.[84]

In addition to the shingle "gitters" who might become maroons, there were maroons who actually worked in the timber camps to sustain themselves. This third maroon group, Liminal maroons, were men and women who intentionally and regularly kept a foot in the outside world and settled into another form of permanent swamp life in which they had very little need to remain undetected. The enslaved workers and these maroons often knew each other well, and were, in the words of one former swamp slave, "quite intimate" with each other. Evidence of a declining deep swamp population after 1800 suggests that many of these men and women had migrated from the swamp's interior.[85] Others marooned to the Great Dismal Swamp specifically for the opportunity to avail themselves of a life that avoided the terrors of both the plantation and life on the run. The lure of a life of relative freedom drew fugitive slaves from Virginia, North Carolina, and beyond to the swamp.[86]

An important aspect of the "intimate" relationships between maroons and enslaved workers is reflected in the description of the slaves as shingle "gitters" instead of either shingle-makers or shingle-cutters. This title implies the worker, rather than cutting his shingles in the camp and under the eyes of the company, went into the undeveloped swamp and "got" them. Their "task" each week was to bring in approximately 400 shingles, and just as the task system functioned in the Carolina Lowcountry, the requirement was based on the productivity expected of a prime hand over a full week's worth of days. In the Dismal Swamp, this quota was expected to offset expenses and recoup the price of the enslaved worker, who was often hired from his or her owner by the season.[87] A week's task generally took five days to complete.[88] However, when the shingles were counted, it was often the case that the number of shingles produced by a company of shingle slaves far exceeded the number of enslaved workers on the roll multiplied by the maximum productivity of a worker.[89] In the official records of the Great Dismal Swamp Land Company, there is no commentary or conjecture about how this occurred; shingles are simply tallied for individual slaves.[90]

The solution to the mystery is found in the testimony of maroons and others "in the know." "Gitters" who were largely free to their own devices, whether motivated by personal gain or by goodwill towards fellow victims of oppression, often became the employers of Dismal Swamp maroons. On counting days, they did not just bring in the shingles they had produced themselves but also those of maroon subcontractors. The workers who brought in these swollen loads would be paid per piece for their overage (often as much as three times the amount necessary for their own subsistence, or 24,000 shingles), then return to their swamp camps to divide the earnings.[91] For his service as a front and the danger to which he exposed himself, the "gitter" kept a part of his payment for the maroons' labor and paid the balance to the hidden workers. Maroons could expect to earn food, clothing, powder and bullets, or as much as two dollars a month for their labor.[92]

The corporate interests would have undoubtedly been aware of these arrangements; otherwise tasks would have been revised upward. However, the aiding and abetting of "fugitives" or using maroon labor was a crime that carried severe penalties, thus the company's silence regarding the maroons' presence in the swamp. The closest company accounts come to acknowledging their very profitable arrangements are occasional and ambiguous notations such as "extra lightering & other work done by hands this month," and tabulations for anonymous workers appear alongside others who are named.[93] Regardless, everybody benefited from this arrangement. The workload of the "gitter" might be lightened, and maroons were able to earn an income without leaving the safety of the swamp. With their proceeds from shingle-making, maroons may have emulated the practices of their enslaved coworkers. Those maroons still lived an unfree life, and with that realization, the enduring specter of their continued status as property. Two dollars a month would not have added up quickly, but maroons may have taken notice of slaves like their potential "employer" Moses Grandy, who had "got into a fair way of buying myself" through his canal labor.[94] And, managers and foremen of the Land Company closed their eyes in accord with judiciously unwritten company policy. The maroons were, it was understood, the best shingle-cutters (if not "gitters") available.[95]

The Civil War, particularly the arrival of Union gunboats in Norfolk in 1862, marked the beginning of the end of the Great Dismal Swamp maroon colonies. As the war raged around them, the already organized maroon raiding bands on the fringe, as well as many Deep Swamp and Liminal maroons, joined white Unionists and contrabands in a guerrilla war to disrupt Confederate power in areas surrounding the swamp, most often on the North Carolina side.[96] Many maroons who left the swamp to fight did not become regulars in the Union Army, but rather maintained their status as guerillas in the region. Dismal Swamp guerillas helped provision Union forces with beef and corn obtained in their plantation raids. Perhaps as important, dozens of maroons emerged from the swamp and served as scouts necessary for passage through the swamp.[97] Moreover, maroon fighters already busy "spread[ing] terror over the land," in the words of a North Carolina woman, loosely joined forces with the Confederate deserter Jack Fairless and his "Wingfield Buffaloes."[98]

From their base on the North Carolina edge of the Great Dismal, guerrilla bands set off on regular campaigns into northeastern North Carolina, both to plunder and make good on their explicit pledge to "clear the country of every slave." And, when the war ended, nearly all of the maroons quietly emerged from the swamp and then soon disappeared again, this time into the bustle of a world where slavery no longer existed. But now they traded one set of dangers and uncertainties for another. Bears and rattlesnakes were no longer a constant threat to their safety, but many now-former maroons were a bit skittish on the outside after so many years in hiding. They had to learn how to deal with a child that had never seen a white face, how to retrain one's feet to tread upon solid dry ground, how to live alongside those who had once sent snarling bloodhounds into the swamp after their trail. They would have to wrestle with the still-ambiguous meaning of freedom, their place in Reconstruction governments, and later, a Jim Crow world that all too closely resembled slavery times.

Indeed, as many white Virginians embraced the romantic notion of a Lost Cause of antebellum days and rolled back the gains African Americans had won during the Reconstruction years, the memory of the Dismal-as-refuge remained strong in the local black community, especially among former swampers. James Bland drew on the Dismal Swamp nostalgia in the lyrics to his famous 1878 song "Carry Me Back to Old Virginny," where a former bondsman longs to return "to the old Dismal Swamp." "Uncle" Bob Garry, born to maroon parents in the swamp around 1820, and who estimated himself in 1903 to be "de oldest swamper in de world," longed to return to his former Dismal Swamp home. He was "mighty lonesome" living in the outside world. Garry shared that lonesomeness and uncertainty with many other former maroons, some of whom, sources suggest, returned to their lives as maroons, no longer "fugitives" from slavery, but intent on living out their days in the only secure and safe place they had ever known, the Great Dismal Swamp.[99]

Notes

1. Edmund Jackson, "The Virginia Maroons," in *The Liberty Bell, By the Friends of Freedom* (n.p., 1852), 146.

2. Herbert Aptheker, *American Negro Slave Revolts* (New York: International Publishers, 1983), 151.

3. See, for example, Richard Price, *Maroon Societies: Rebel Slave Communities in the Americas* (Baltimore: Johns Hopkins University Press, 1996); Richard Price, *The Guiana Maroons: A Historical and Bibliographical Introduction* (Baltimore: Johns Hopkins University Press, 1976); Wim Hoogbergen, *The Boni Maroon Wars in Suriname* (Leiden: E. J. Brill, 1990); Carla Lewis Gotlieb, *The Mother of Us All: A History of Queen Nanny, Leader of the Windward Jamaican Maroons* (Trenton: African World Press, 2000); Mavis

Campbell, *The Maroons of Jamaica, 1655–1796* (Trenton: African World Press, 1988); Kenneth Bilby, *True Born Maroons* (Gainesville: University Press of Florida, 2008); *Out of the House of Bondage: Runaways, Resistance, and Marronage in Africa and the New World*, ed. Gad Heuman (London: Frank Cass, 1986).

    4. See Kevin Mulroy, *Freedom on the Border: The Seminole Maroons of Florida, the Indian Territory, Coahuila, and Texas* (Lubbock: Texas Tech University Press, 1993); Nathaniel Millette, *The Maroons of Prospect Bluff and their Quest for Freedom in the Atlantic World* (Gainesville: University Press of Florida, 2013).

    5. Michael Mullin, *Africa in America: Slave Acculturation and Resistance in the American South and the British Caribbean, 1736–1831* (Urbana: University of Illinois Press, 1992), 61.

    6. Eugene D. Genovese, *From Rebellion to Revolution: Afro-American Slave Revolts in the Making of the Modern World* (Baton Rouge: Louisiana State University Press, 1979), 69, 77.

    7. John Hope Franklin and Loren Schweninger, *Runaway Slaves: Rebels on the Plantation* (New York: Oxford University Press, 2000), 86.

    8. Philip D. Morgan, *Slave Counterpoint: Black Culture in the Eighteenth-Century Chesapeake & Lowcountry* (Chapel Hill: University of North Carolina Press, 1998), 449–50.

    9. Alvin O. Thompson *Flight to Freedom: African Runaways and Maroons in the Americas* (Kingston: University of the West Indies Press, 2006).

    10. Sylviane Diouf, *Slavery's Exiles: The Story of the American Maroons* (New York: New York University Press, 2014). Diouf attempts to expand scholars' understanding of the phenomenon of marronage from the simplistic binary of *petit* and *grand* marronage (the former truancy of just a few days, the latter an escape and attempt to hid meant to be permanent) to what she terms "the maroon landscape," that takes specificity of place more fully into account.

    11. See Tommy Bogger, "Maroons and Laborers in the Great Dismal Swamp," in *Readings in Black and White: Lower Tidewater Virginia*, ed. Jane H. Kobelski (Portsmouth, VA: Portsmouth Public Library, 1982), 1–8; I published the first extended essay on the Great Dismal Swamp maroons in 2008. This was more of an exploratory piece, and it drew primarily on published sources. Admittedly, my conceptual framework contained significant flaws; my limited knowledge of the swamp itself, particularly its geography, produced an overly simplistic analysis of maroon life in the swamp. Moreover, large gaps in my documentary research (gaps that still exist to some extent, but which I am now able to bridge through a more interdisciplinary approach) forced an overreliance on conjecture which was ultimately the roadblock that frustrated my pursuance of the Dismal Swamp project. See J. Brent Morris, "'Running Servants and All Others': The Diverse and Elusive Maroons of the Great Dismal Swamp," in *Voices from Within the Veil: African Americans and the Experience of Democracy*, ed. Alexander et al. (Cambridge Scholars Press, 2008), 85–112; Ted Maris-Wolf's 2013 article, "Hidden in Plain Sight: Maroon Life and Labor in Virginia's Dismal Swamp," *Slavery and Abolition* 34, no. 3, 446–64, looks only at one small group of Dismal Swamp maroons, those most closely connected to the industrial logging/canal economy of the early 1820s—that is, the most easily accessible in the documentary record. His analysis of Dismal Swamp maroon life is at odds with the overwhelming weight of new documentary and archaeological evidence.

    12. Donald R. Whitehead. "Developmental and Environmental History of the Dismal Swamp," *Ecological Monographs* 42, no. 3 (Summer 1972), 301–302

    13. William Byrd, "Description of the Dismal Swamp," reprinted in *Columbian Magazine*, April 1789.

    14. Ibid.; Crayon, "Dismal Swamp," 448–50; J. F. D. Smythe, *A Tour in the United States of America* (London: G. Robinson, 1784), 234–36.

15. See Edward Bottoms and Floyd Painter, "Evidence of Aboriginal Utilization of the Bola in the Dismal Swamp Area," in *The Great Dismal Swamp*, ed. Paul W. Kirk (Charlottesville: University of Virginia Press, 1979), 44–56; Peter C. Stewart, "Man and the Swamp: The Historical Dimension," ibid., 57–58.

16. Hugo Prosper Leaming, *Hidden Americans* (New York: Routledge, 1995), 3–142, passim; Mildred Campbell, "Social Origins of Some Early Americans," in *Seventeenth-Century America: Essays in Colonial History*, ed. James Morton Smith (New York: Norton, 1959), 69–82.

17. There is strong archaeological evidence that points to a steady occupation of the Great Dismal Swamp from the early seventeenth century. The GDSLS is able to date soils associated with several of the larger cultural features through Optically Stimulated Luminescence, a laboratory dating method not commonly used in historical archaeological contexts, but necessary in our case due to the relative lack of dateable mass-produced artifacts. See Sayers, *Desolate Place for a Defiant People*, 172.

18. Herbert Aptheker, *American Negro Slave Revolts* (New York: International Publishers, 1943), 169.

19. Byrd, *History of the Dividing Line* (Petersburg: Edmund and Julian C. Ruffin, 1841), 13–17; On Byrd and Jamaica see Diouf, *Slavery's Exiles*, 25.

20. See Cecelski, *Waterman's Song*, 16, 227–28, n37–39.

21. See Aptheker, *American Negro Slave Revolts*, 231; "From a Norfolk Paper of May 23: More About Negroes," *New York Herald*, June 2, 1802; *Raleigh Register*, June 6, 1802; James Hugo Johnson, *Race Relations in Virginia & Miscegenation in the South, 1776–1860* (Amherst: UMASS Press, 1970), 34–36; *Eastern Herald*, June 7, 1802; Aptheker, *Slave Revolts*, 231; Cecelski, *Waterman's Song*, 129; *New York Herald*, June 2, 1802; Diouf, *Slavery's Exiles*, 260–61. See also Egerton, *Gabriel's Rebellion*, 119–23, 127–31, 145.

22. Higginson, "Nat Turner's Insurrection," in *The Atlantic*, August 1861; Johnson, *Tales from Old Carolina*, 159; Aptheker, *American Negro Slave Rebellions*, 307–308; Arnold, *Dismal Swamp and Lake Drummond*, 21–23.

23. See Olmsted, *Journey in the Seaboard Slave States*, 159–61.

24. Crayon, "In the Dismal Swamp," 451–55; R. P. Fouts, *Registration of Slaves to Work in the Great Dismal Swamp, Gates County, North Carolina, 1847–1861* (Cocoa, Florida: GenRec Books, 1995); see "An Act to provide for the apprehension of runaway slaves in the great Dismal Swamp and for other purposes," in *Laws of the State of North Carolina, Passed by the General Assembly . . . 1847* (Raleigh: Thomas J. Lemay, 1847), 109–113.

25. Olmsted, 159–61; J. Brent Morris, "Life in the Swamp," *New York Times*, October 13, 2013, https://opinionater.blogs.nytimes.com/2013/10/19/life-in-the-swamp/, accessed October 13, 2013.

26. J. Brent Morris, "The Importance of Marronage in the Study of North American Slave Resistance," paper given at the 2012 Meeting of the South Carolina Historical Association.

27. The central goal of the GDSLS has been to recover interpretable archaeological information about pre-Civil War swamp communities that may exist in Great Dismal Swamp National Wildlife Refuge. The GDSLS undertook archaeological fieldwork in 2003–2006 and more recently in 2009–2013. This represents the first extensive archaeological research to ever take place in the Refuge or historical boundaries of the Great Dismal Swamp. I came onto the project as historian in 2009, and participated in the second phase of fieldwork. After 2010, our work benefited from a three-year National Endowment for the Humanities "We the People" research grant. To date, we have generated one of the largest archaeological

and historical datasets on marginalized communities in North America, including the most detailed and expansive body of materials related to maroon communities currently available in North America. The archaeological fieldwork, my continued archival research, and the utilization of new technology (LIDAR [Light Detection and Ranging imaging] and geophysics [ground-penetrating radar and electroresistivity]) have conclusively demonstrated the existence of maroon communities/settlements throughout the swamp.

The results of much of the archaeological fieldwork have been published by GDSLS Director Daniel O. Sayers (archaeologist, American University) as *A Desolate Place for a Defiant People: The Archaeology of Maroons, Indigenous Americans, and Enslaved Laborers in the Great Dismal Swamp* (Gainesville: University Press of Florida, 2014).

28. Sayers, *A Desolate Place for a Defiant People*, 172.

29. Graham Callaway, "Identifying Mesic Island Locations in the Great Dismal Swamp: Applied Cartography and GIS," unpublished research report submitted to the Great Dismal Swamp Landscape Study, 2010.

30. *The Great Dismal Swamp Landscape Study: The Final Results of Intensive Excavations at Several Sites in the Great Dismal Swamp National Wildlife Refuge, North Carolina and Virginia, 2003–2006*. GDSLS Report No. 2, submitted to United States Fish and Wildlife Service, Region 5, Hadley, Massachusetts. Also, more than half of the historic swamp is now drained, cleared, and developed, so we're looking at a fraction of what may have once existed as far as settlements go.

31. Wrote Edmund Jackson: "An intelligent merchant . . . estimated the value of slave property lost in the swamp at one and a half million dollars. This, at the usual rate of slave valuation, would give near 40,000 as the population of the swamp." Jackson, "The Virginia Maroons," 149.

32. Frederick Douglass, *My Bondage My Freedom* (New York: Miller, Orton, & Mulligan, 1855), 436; see Frederick Douglass, "The Heroic Slave," in *Autographs for Freedom*, ed. Julia Griffiths (Cleveland: John P. Jewett, 1853), 174–239.

33. See Edmund Jackson, "The Virginia Maroons," *The Liberty Bell by Friends of Freedom* (n.p., 1852), 149–150; William C. Nell, *The Colored Patriots of the American Revolution* (Boston, 1855), 229; "The Dismal Swamp," *Frederick Douglass' Paper*, March 11, 1859;

34. Sayers, *Desolate Place for a Defiant People*, 344.

35. GDSLS Director Daniel Sayers chose the "nameless site" (no capitalization) in order to avoid applying a name to the site that would stick. In the event that at some point an actual historically used name for the site emerges, the "nameless site" can be jettisoned rather easily.

36. Ibid., 167, 211.

37. See "The Dismal Swamp," *Frederick Douglass' Paper*, March 11, 1859.

38. The Great Dismal Swamp was recognized in 2003 as a landmark on the National Park Service National Underground Railroad Network to Freedom.

39. William Siebert, *The Underground Railroad from Slavery to Freedom* (New York: MacMillan, 1898), 25; Redpath, *The Roving Editor*, 245; "The Dismal Swamp," *Frederick Douglass' Paper*, March 11, 1859; H. Cowles Atwater, *Incidents of a Southern Tour; or the South as Seen with Northern Eyes* (Boston, 1857), 46.

40. John Patterson Green, *Recollections of the Inhabitants, Localities, Superstitions, and Kuklux Outrages of the Carolinas* (Cleveland, 1880), 72.

41. Davis, *The Great Dismal Swamp*, 61; Jackson, "The Virginia Maroons," 145; *State v. Bill (a slave)*, 6 Jones N.C. 34, December 1858, in *Judicial Cases Concerning American Slavery and the Negro*, vol. II, ed. Helen Tunnicliff Catterall (Washington, 1929), 218–19.

42. "A Yankee Tutor in the Old South," 56.

43. William Caswell to Thomas Burke, September 4, 1781, in *The State Records of North Carolina*, vol. XXII, ed. Walter Clark (Goldsboro, NC: Nask Brothers, 1907), 592–93.

44. Atwater, *Incidents of a Southern Tour*, 50; "Social Conditions in the Colonies," *Century Magazine*, October 1884, 865.

45. Robert Arnold, *The Dismal Swamp and Lake Drummond: Early Recollections and Vivid Portrayal of Amusing Scenes* (Norfolk, 1888), 7.

46. Alexander Hunter, "Through the Dismal Swamp," *Potter's American Monthly* (July 1881), 1; Jackson, "The Virginia Maroons," 145.

47. Sayers, *Desolate Place for a Defiant People*, 168–69, 173, 179, 211.

48. Sayers, *Desolate Place for a Defiant People*, 201.

49. Ibid., 170–75.

50. "Life in the Swamp," *Lorain County (Ohio) News*, September 19, 1863; *The Friend; A Religious and Literary Journal*, November 23, 1867; Sayers, *Desolate Place for a Defiant People*, 176; Belinda Hurmence, *We Lived in a Little Cabin in the Yard: Personal Accounts of Slavery in Virginia* (Winston-Salem: John F. Blair, 2000), 16.

51. Sayers, *Desolate Place for a Defiant People*, 175.

52. *The Annual Review and History of Literature for 1807*, vol. VI (London, 1808), 44; *The Terrific Register, or, Record of Crimes, Judgments, Providences, and Calamities*, vol. II (London, 1825), 130.

53. Schoepf, *Travels in the Confederation*, 100.

54. Kirby, *Poquosin*, xii–xiii.

55. Diouf, *Slavery's Exiles*, 143; "Pompey's Secret," *The Catholic World*, vol. XXXI, no. 4 (July 1880), 548; *Liberator*, September 11, 1863; Jackson, "The Virginia Maroons," *The Liberty Bell by Friends of Freedom* (n.p., 1852), 145; Johann David Schoepf, *Travels in the Confederation, 1783–1784*, trans. Alfred J. Morrison (Philadelphia, 1911), 100.

56. "Pompey's Secret," *The Catholic World* XXXI, no. 4 (July 1880), 548; *Liberator*, September 11, 1863; Jackson, "The Virginia Maroons," *The Liberty Bell by Friends of Freedom* (n.p., 1852), 145; Johann David Schoepf, *Travels in the Confederation, 1783–1784*, trans. Alfred J. Morrison (Philadelphia, 1911), 100.

57. Frederick Street, "In the Dismal Swamp," *Frank Leslie's Popular Monthly* LV, no. 5 (March 1903), 530; H. Cowles Atwater, *Incidents of a Southern Tour; or the South as Seen with Northern Eyes* (Boston, 1857), 50; "Life in the Swamp," *Lorain County (Ohio) News*, September 19, 1863; "The Dismal Swamp," *Frederick Douglass' Paper*, March 11, 1859; Schoepf, *Travels in the Confederation*, 100.

58. "Some Account of the Great Dismal Swamp," *The Literary Magazine and American Register* III, no. 18 (March 1805), 171; *Scientific American*, October 5, 1895, 220.

59. Sayers, *Desolate Place for a Defiant People*, 197; "The Copy-Book," *Southern Literary Messenger*, January 1838, 25; "The Dismal Swamp," *Frederick Douglass' Paper*, March 11, 1859.

60. "Eliphaz" to "Br. Stevens," February 8, 1848, in *Zion's Herald and Wesleyan Journal*, February 23, 1848; March 31, 1848.

61. David Hunter Strother, "In the Dismal Swamp," *Harper's Monthly* 13, no. 73 (June 1856).

62. "Life in the Swamp," *Lorain County (Ohio) News*, September 19, 1863.

63. H. Cowles Atwater, *Incidents of a Southern Tour; or the South as Seen with Northern Eyes* (Boston, 1857), 50.

64. Sayers, *Desolate Place for a Defiant People*, 193–94.

65. 94.5 percent of the artifact assemblage represents swamp available materials, while 5.5 percent represents outside world materials like glass, iron, lead, and clay pipe fragments. Sayers, *Desolate Place for a Defiant People*, 189.

66. "Sketches in Color," *Putnam's Magazine*, December 1869, 742.

67. Olmsted, *Seaboard Slave States*, 159–61; One woman was believed to have given birth to at least eleven children while resident in the swamp. *Boston Daily Mail*, n.d., in Henry Clapp, *The Pioneer* (Lynn: J. B. Tolman, 1846), 76.

68. Winslow, "The Dismal Swamp," 170; "Life in the Swamp," *Lorain County (Ohio) News*, September 19, 1863.

69. "Dismal Swamp on Display," *Rising Son*, December 22, 1906.

70. Sayers, *Desolate Place for a Defiant People*, 231–32.

71. Jackson, "The Virginia Maroons," 146–47.

72. *The Annual review and History of Literature for 1807*, vol. VI (London, 1808), 44; *The Terrific Register, or, Record of Crimes, Judgments, Providences, and Calamities*, vol. II (London, 1825), 130.

73. David Hunter Strother, "In the Dismal Swamp," *Harper's Monthly* 13, no. 73 (June 1856), 452.

74. Edmund Jackson, "The Virginia Maroons," *The Liberty Bell by Friends of Freedom* (n.p., 1852), 146; William C. Nell, *The Colored Patriots of the American Revolution* (Boston, 1855), 228; Crayon, "In the Dismal Swamp," *Harper's Monthly* 13, no. 73 (June 1856), 452; Thompson, *The Negro's Flight from American Slavery to British Freedom* (London, 1849), 12–13; *The Annual Review and History of Literature for 1807*, vol. VI (London, 1808), 44; *The Terrific Register, or, Record of Crimes, Judgments, Providences, and Calamities*, vol. II (London, 1825), 130.

75. "Dismal Swamp," *Southern Literary Messenger*, January, 1838, 25; William Kreutzer, *Notes and Observations Made During Four Years of Service with the Ninety-Eighth N.Y. Volunteers in the War of 1861* (Philadelphia, 1878), 168. Several projectile points were recovered in different historical contexts that point to reuse and modification of older tools for use in the scission community or communities. A modified Morrow Mountain Stemmed, Type II point (Archaic type, 5,000–3,500 BP) recovered by the GDSLS clearly demonstrates a historical reworking of one side of the original point into a knife or scraper. Sayers, *Desolate Place for a Defiant People*, 178, 204–207.

76. Sayers, *Desolate Place for a Defiant People*, 178–79.

77. "In the Dismal Swamp," *Frederick Douglass' Paper*, March 11, 1859; Sayers, *Desolate Place for a Defiant People*, 190.

78. Sayers, *Desolate Place for a Defiant People*, 198–99.

79. Ibid., 224–25.

80. Account book of William Aitchison and James Parker, 1763–1804, University of Virginia Special Collections, MSS12992, 51.

81. Sayers, *Desolate Place for a Defiant People*, 225–26.

82. Ibid., 245.

83. Charles Royster, *The Fabulous History of the Dismal Swamp Company: A Story of George Washington's Time* (New York: Knopf Doubleday, 1999), 147.

84. "Eliphaz" to "Br. Stevens," February 8, 1848, in *Zion's Herald and Wesleyan Journal*, February 23, 1848; *North Star*, March 31, 1848; "The Dismal Swamp," *Forest and Stream*, January 13, 1876; Frederick Street, "In the Dismal Swamp," *Frank Leslie's Popular Monthly* LV,

no. 5 (March 1903), 530; Moses Grandy, *Narrative of the Life of Moses Grandy: Late a Slave in the United States of America* (London, 1843), 25–45.

85. Sayers, *Desolate Place for a Defiant People*, 180–82.

86. Runaway notices advertised for swampers like Aaron, "a shingle weaver, on the Virginia side of the Dismal," Dave, whose master believed that he had probably run away to "work in the Shingle Swamp," and Diver, "a good sawyer" lurking "near the shingle-Swamp." Edenton *Herald of Freedom*, March 27, 1799, *The Edenton Gazette and North Carolina General*, November 11, 1828, in *Stealing a Little Freedom*, 196, 343, 383. The Land Company itself had a hard time keeping tabs on its own slaves. Jack and Venus, "who worked in the Dismal Swamp for about two years," under John Washington were advertised as runaways in 1771. *Virginia Gazette*, December 5, 1771, in *Runaway Slave Advertisements*, 105.

87. Olmsted, *Seaboard Slave States*, 153–54.

88. Edmund Ruffin, "Observations Made During an Excursion to the Dismal Swamp," *Farmer's Register*, January 1, 1837, 518.

89. Letters from F. Hall to Son, January 16, 1818, January 22, 1819, Dismal Swamp Land Company Records, Duke University Library, quoted in Leaming, *Hidden Americans*, 281.

90. Frederick Street, "In the Dismal Swamp," *Frank Leslie's Popular Monthly* LV, no. 5 (March 1903), 530; "The Dismal Swamp," *Frederick Douglass' Paper*, March 11, 1859; Strother, "In the Dismal Swamp," 451

91. Strother, "In the Dismal Swamp," 451; Winslow, "The Dismal Swamp," 170.

92. Frederick L. Olmstead, "The South, #13," *New York Daily Times*, April 23, 1853; Street, "In the Dismal Swamp," 40; Redpath, *The Roving Editor*, 243.

93. Dismal Swamp Land Company Records, October 1860 and August 1860, quoted in Edward Maris-Wolf, *Between Slavery and Freedom: African Americans in the Great Dismal Swamp, 1763–1863*, unpublished MA thesis (Anthropology, College of William and Mary, 2002), 104.

94. Grandy, *Narrative*, 25; see also Howard, *In the Shadow of the Pines*, 76.

95. "The Dismal Swamp," *Frederick Douglass' Paper*, March 11, 1859; Strother, "In the Dismal Swamp," 451

96. See A. Burnside to H. B. Stanton, March 21, 1862, in *The War of the Rebellion*, vol. VII (Washington, DC: Government Printing Office, 1865), 812.

97. "An Adventure in the Dismal Swamp," *The Cosmopolitan*, April 1886, 99.

98. See *Savannah Republican*, March 29, 1863; Edwin W. Stone, *Rhode Island in the Rebellion* (Providence: George H. Whitney, 1864), 851; Kirby, *Poquosin*, 181–94.

99. "The Dismal Swamp," *Monmouth Inquirer*, January 22, 1903; Morris, "Running Servants," 95–97; J. Brent Morris, "Life in the Swamp," *New York Times*, October 19, 2013.

Secondary Source Bibliography

"An Act to provide for the apprehension of runaway slaves in the great Dismal Swamp and for other purposes." In *Laws of the State of North Carolina, Passed by the General Assembly . . . 1847*. Raleigh: Thomas J. Lemay, 1847.
Aptheker, Herbert. *American Negro Slave Revolts*. New York: International Publishers, 1943.
Aptheker, Herbert. *American Negro Slave Revolts*. New York: International Publishers, 1983.
Arnold, Robert. *The Dismal Swamp and Lake Drummond, Early recollections, Vivid portrayal of Amusing Scenes*. Norfolk: Evening Telegram Print, 1888.

Atwater, H. Cowles. *Incidents of a Southern Tour; or the South as Seen with Northern Eyes.* Boston: J. P. Magee, 1857.

Bilby, Kenneth. *True Born Maroons.* Gainesville: University Press of Florida, 2008.

Bogger, Tommy. "Maroons and Laborers in the Great Dismal Swamp." In *Readings in Black and White: Lower Tidewater Virginia.* Edited by Jane H. Kobelski, 1–8. Portsmouth, VA: Portsmouth Public Library, 1982.

Bottoms, Edward, and Floyd Painter. "Evidence of Aboriginal Utilization of the Bola in the Dismal Swamp Area." In *The Great Dismal Swamp.* Edited by Paul W. Kirk, 44–56. Charlottesville: University of Virginia Press, 1979.

Byrd, William. "Description of the Dismal Swamp." Reprinted in *Columbian Magazine,* April 1789.

Byrd, William, II. *History of the Dividing Line Betwixt Virginia and North Carolina.* Petersburg: Edmund and Julian C. Ruffin, 1841.

Callaway, Graham. "Identifying Mesic Island Locations in the Great Dismal Swamp: Applied Cartography and GIS." Unpublished research report submitted to the Great Dismal Swamp Landscape Study, 2010.

Campbell, Mavis. *The Maroons of Jamaica, 1655–1796.* Trenton: African World Press, 1988.

Campbell, Mildred. "Social Origins of Some Early Americans." In *Seventeenth-Century America: Essays in Colonial History.* Edited by James Morton Smith, 69–82. New York: Norton, 1959.

Cecelski, David S. *The Waterman's Song: Slavery and Freedom in Maritime North Carolina.* Chapel Hill: University of North Carolina Press, 2001.

Diouf, Sylviane. *Slavery's Exiles: The Story of the American Maroons.* New York: New York University Press, 2014.

Dismal Swamp Land Company Records, October 1860 and August 1860. Quoted in Edward Maris-Wolf. *Between Slavery and Freedom: African Americans in the Great Dismal Swamp, 1763–1863.* Unpublished MA thesis, Anthropology, College of William and Mary, 2002, 104

Douglass, Frederick. "The Heroic Slave." In *Autographs for Freedom.* Edited by Julia Griffiths, 174–239. Cleveland: John P. Jewett & Company, 1853.

Douglass, Frederick. *My Bondage My Freedom.* New York: Miller, Orton, & Mulligan, 1855.

Egerton, Douglas R. *Gabriel's Rebellion: The Virginia Slave Conspiracies of 1800 and 1802.* Chapel Hill: University of North Carolina Press, 1993.

Fouts, R. P. *Registration of Slaves to Work in the Great Dismal Swamp, Gates County, North Carolina, 1847–1861.* Cocoa, FL: GenRec Books, 1995.

Franklin, John Hope, and Loren Schweninger. *Runaway Slaves: Rebels on the Plantation.* New York: Oxford University Press, 2000.

Genovese, Eugene D. *From Rebellion to Revolution: Afro-American Slave Revolts in the Making of the Modern World.* Baton Rouge: Louisiana State University Press, 1979.

Gotlieb, Carla Lewis. *The Mother of Us All: A History of Queen Nanny, Leader of the Windward Jamaican Maroons.* Trenton: African World Press, 2000.

The Great Dismal Swamp Landscape Study: The Final Results of Intensive Excavations at Several Sites in the Great Dismal Swamp National Wildlife Refuge, North Carolina and Virginia, 2003–2006. GDSLS Report No. 2, submitted to United States Fish and Wildlife Service, Region 5, Hadley, Massachusetts.

Green, John Patterson. *Recollections of the Inhabitants, Localities, Superstitions, and Kuklux Outrages of the Carolinas.* Cleveland, 1880.

Hoogbergen, Wim. *The Boni Maroon Wars in Suriname*. Leiden: E. J. Brill, 1990.
Howard, John Hamilton. *In the Shadow of the Pines: A Tale of Tidewater Virginia*. New York: Eaton and Mains, 1906.
Hunter, Alexander. "Through the Dismal Swamp." *Potter's American Monthly* (July 1881): 1.
Hurmence, Belinda. *We Lived in a Little Cabin in the Yard: Personal Accounts of Slavery in Virginia*. Winston-Salem: John F. Blair, 2000.
Kirby, Jack T. *Poquosin: A Study of Rural Landscape and Society*. Chapel Hill: University of North Carolina Press, 1995.
Jackson, Edmund. "The Virginia Maroons." In *The Liberty Bell, By the Friends of Freedom*. n.p., 1852.
Johnson, F. Roy. *Tales from Old Carolina*. Johnson Publishing, 1965.
Johnson, James Hugo. *Race Relations in Virginia & Miscegenation in the South, 1776–1860*. Amherst: University of Massachusetts Press, 1970.
Leaming, Hugo Prosper. *Hidden Americans*. New York: Routledge, 1995.
Maris-Wolf, Ted. "Hidden in Plain Sight: Maroon Life and Labor in Virginia's Dismal Swamp." *Slavery and Abolition* 34, no. 3 (2013): 446–64.
Millette, Nathaniel. *The Maroons of Prospect Bluff and their Quest for Freedom in the Atlantic World*. Gainesville: University Press of Florida, 2013.
Morgan, Philip D. *Slave Counterpoint: Black Culture in the Eighteenth-Century Chesapeake & Lowcountry*. Chapel Hill: University of North Carolina Press, 1998.
Morris, J. Brent. "The Importance of Marronage in the Study of North American Slave Resistance." Paper presented at the 2012 Meeting of the South Carolina Historical Association, 2012.
Morris, J. Brent. "'Running Servants and All Others': The Diverse and Elusive Maroons of the Great Dismal Swamp." In *Voices from Within the Veil: African Americans and the Experience of Democracy*. Edited by Alexander et al., 85–112. Newcastle upon Tyne, Cambridge: Cambridge Scholars Press, 2008.
Mullin, Michael. *Africa in America: Slave Acculturation and Resistance in the American South and the British Caribbean, 1736–1831*. Urbana: University of Illinois Press, 1992.
Mulroy, Kevin. *Freedom on the Border: The Seminole Maroons of Florida, the Indian Territory, Coahuila, and Texas*. Lubbock: Texas Tech University Press, 1993.
Nell, William C. *The Colored Patriots of the American Revolution*. Boston, 1855.
Olmsted, Frederick Law. *A Journey in the Seaboard Slave States; With Remarks on Their Economy*. New York: Dix and Edwards, 1856.
Out of the House of Bondage: Runaways, Resistance, and Marronage in Africa and the New World. Edited by Gad Heuman. London: Frank Cass, 1986.
Price, Richard. *Maroon Societies: Rebel Slave Communities in the Americas*. Baltimore: Johns Hopkins University Press, 1996.
Price, Richard. *The Guiana Maroons: A Historical and Bibliographical Introduction*. Baltimore: Johns Hopkins University Press, 1976.
Redpath, James. *The Roving Editor: Or, Talks with Slaves in the Southern States*. New York: A. B. Burdick, 1859.
Royster, Charles. *The Fabulous History of the Dismal Swamp Company: A Story of George Washington's Time*. New York: Knopf Doubleday, 1999.
Sayers, Daniel O. *Desolate Place for a Defiant People: The Archaeology of Maroons, Indigenous Americans, and Enslaved Laborers in the Great Dismal Swamp*. Gainesville: University Press of Florida, 2014.

Schöpf, Johann David. *Travels in the Confederation*. Translated by Alfred J. Morrison. Philadelphia: William J. Campbell, 1911.
Siebert, William. *The Underground Railroad from Slavery to Freedom*. New York: MacMillan, 1898.
Smythe, J. F. D. *A Tour in the United States of America*. London: G. Robinson, 1784.
Stewart, Peter C. "Man and the Swamp: The Historical Dimension." In *The Great Dismal Swamp*. Edited by Paul W. Kirk, 57–58. Charlottesville: University of Virginia Press, 1979.
Thompson, Alvin O. *Flight to Freedom: African Runaways and Maroons in the Americas*. Kingston: University of the West Indies Press, 2006.
Whitehead, Donald R. "Developmental and Environmental History of the Dismal Swamp." *Ecological Monographs* 42, no. 3 (Summer 1972): 301–302.

Chapter Two

Belonging and Alienation: Gullah Jack and Some Maroon Dimensions of the "Denmark Vesey Conspiracy"

James O'Neil Spady

A group of black Charlestonians came very close to commencing an insurrection in 1822 (Egerton and Paquette 2017; Spady 2011).[1] Their plan can be summarized quickly from the most credible evidence: a small band would steal (or make) bladed weapons and use them in a surprise attack in the dead of night. The first goal would be to capture firearms from public and private arsenals. Then, joined by countryside slaves, they would march through the city killing and recruiting until they had burned, hacked, and shot their way to freedom. Some said they would kill whites indiscriminately whether adult or child, man or woman. Some swore to kill any black people who refused to join them. If their surprise assault succeeded, the insurgents would have had several strategic opportunities to choose from. Some said they would take the country from the whites—a revolutionary course of action. Others said they would commandeer a ship and escape to Haiti or perhaps somewhere in Africa. A third possibility was to retreat into the countryside as a maroon community. Whatever their plans, many rebels likely would have been trapped on the Charleston peninsula, forced to barricade themselves and confront a ferocious white counterattack. Among the insurrectionary leaders was an African-born "conjuror" named Gullah Jack, who had significant social ties in town and countryside and whom some believed was virtually invulnerable to the whites. This chapter considers this plan as a marronage in the making, and Gullah Jack as one of its leaders (Kennedy and Parker 1822, 20, 56; "Examination of George" 1822; "Examination of [Name Redacted]" 1822; "Examination of Joe" 1822).[2]

For a generation, maroon communities have been widely understood among scholars to be one of several modes of resistance to enslavement in the Americas. During the 1970s, Gerald Mullin (*Flight and Rebellion*), Richard Price (*Maroon Societies*), and Eugene Genovese (*From Rebellion to Revolution*) showed that maroon events could be a significant part of African and African American resistance to slavery (Price 1973, 4–5; Mullin 1972; Genovese 1979). Their scholarship was founded in earlier work by Herbert Aptheker and others, and it has significantly enhanced debates on slave resistance "from the bottom, up." The dominant definition of marronage (running away into inhospitable areas to form semi-autonomous communities) emphasizes spatial movement as a strategy of resistance. Maroons resist slavers without necessarily destroying slavery. They escape. They create space for communities of belonging that are nearly out of the reach of their former masters. Such mass escapes, scholars have held, threaten the slaving society by withholding labor and facilitating further flight by still more slaves. They therefore strike at the stability of the system even though slavery persists. Their incidence in the US was greater than historians have recognized until recently (Diouf 2014, 1, 2, and 4–5; Fick 1992). Nonetheless, this emphasis on rural spaces and bodily escape from plantations into the hidden, inaccessible, backcountry obscures instructive parallels with insurrectionary conspiracies.

We understand the "Denmark Vesey" conspiracy's planners better if we consider their actions in light of marronage. Although they were primarily based in town, the 1822 planners used rural and plantation spaces. At least some of the planners had flight from slavery as their main objective, though they intended to use ships. Their decision to create space within the city for insurrectionary talk was an expression of a psychic marronage. Such talk presupposes a decision to withdraw cooperation with the slavers' demand that they accept domination meekly and obediently. Without such a change of will, no insurrectionary talk would have occurred. Without illicit discussions about rebellion, collaboration and armed rebellion could not have followed. The discussion was a rebellion-in-process within the system of relations of power the planners inhabited. Furthermore, conspiracies for flight, insurrection, and marronage all had illicit discussions and the psychic marronage that preceded them in common. Maroons might be thought of as rebels who discuss retreat before they perhaps fight the master, whereas insurrectionists discuss fighting before they perhaps flee the master. The 1822 Charleston planners did not just engage in "loose talk" or merely generate "rumors." Instead, they escaped into momentarily appropriated urban spaces in a shop or behind trees to urge each other to decisive and deadly resistance on behalf of the claim that they belonged to the class of "men" (Wade 1964, 160). Maroons trapped in an urban place, the 1822 planners created spaces of belonging in which to trust each other with illegal organizing against the alienation of enslavement.

Reading the Archive

The scholarship on the 1822 events has tended to focus on the town dimensions almost exclusively, and it has heavily emphasized the role of Vesey himself. Maroon dimensions, rural spaces, women's testimony, and figures such as Gullah Jack have remained in the background. And there has been a debate over the integrity of the records ever since 2001, when Michael Johnson attacked the archive of the "Denmark Vesey" trials as a conspiracy by white Charlestonians. In essence, Johnson argued that the slaves that testified against others were motivated to win their freedom by naming names. He also argued that the prisoners had the opportunity to falsify testimony when they were jailed collectively or in pairs. For these and other reasons, the trials were a farce and their records are a fraud (Johnson 2001). Most scholars have rejected the most radical of Johnson's conclusions: that there was no black antislavery conspiracy and that whites conspired to fake the record. Douglas Egerton and Robert Paquette have offered an exhaustively thorough volume of documents relevant to the events that should allay any doubt that the record is entirely fraudulent (Egerton and Paquette 2017). But there is still no consensus as to how extensive and immanent an insurrection might have been, how many of the accused were actually involved, and what might actually have been the details of the plan (Paquette 2004, 293, 327 nn. 6–11). Contributing to the latter debate is the main purpose of this chapter. I argue for a new method of interpretation and describe some of the findings it helps reveal, and I will focus specifically on Gullah Jack and some of his near associates. Some of Johnson's arguments influenced the approach: rumor and confinement probably affected the nature of testimony as the summer wore on. But there is no evidence that all the slaves' testimony was coordinated, coerced, or deceptive. No evidence shows that all the witnesses spoke with the intent to win manumission by getting friends and acquaintances hanged on false charges. Instead, the method shows why a portion of the testimony was highly credible (Spady 2011) and how to distinguish a credible context from a dubious context.[3]

We also need to read the credible testimony differently, and I am drawing cues from Ann Laura Stoler, Giorgio Agamben, and others (Hyde 2014; Fiskesjö 2012; Stoler 2009, 2002; Agamben 1998; Scott 1992). The archive itself was a discourse on the truth of not only the uprising but also of the nature and dynamics of the slave community. It has elisions, distortions, and agendas, and it can and should be read "along the archival grain" (Stoler 2009, 1–4; 2002, 94). My approach is based in a careful assessment of the materiality of the records, carefully examining paper, ink, and handwriting for the "story" of the surviving materials. Doing so will help describe the documents as a social artifact. It also helps identify the uncontroversial relationships and information recorded in the testimony. The records show us who was related to whom, who was a close intimate of whom, who owned whom, and who lived or worked near whom. Those relationships matter for how they testified, and they should matter to historians trying to understand why they said what they said. It is not a project of this research to state definitively what the subjective intentions of the accused were. But we have a duty to speculate using clearly stated methods for discerning credibility. We have an ethical responsibility to these deceased, enslaved, and free black people: in the Charleston black community—and in many other communities—they have been hallowed as heroes of liberation by local tradition. It was a struggle for the Charleston community to win public representation and respect for the community memory of these men as would-be liberators. If we now render the documents of the trial as mere rhetoric—refusing to engage core questions of what actually happened and why—we implicitly trivialize that struggle and the community memory underpinning it. And we chip away at the decedents' reputations: they become snitches and people of craven self-interest, or else abject victims of despotic power. At the same time, we must not falsely convict people in death, colluding with racist white judges worried about saving themselves from the possibility of a black revolution.

To address these ethical duties and historiographical requirements, I built (with research assistants) an index of all persons who appear in the three known versions of the trial records and the capacities in which they appear.[4] We mapped the strength of the social connections among key individuals. We assessed the nature of their testimony, discerning hearsay from what was personally experienced. I have begun to build a new narrative of the events based on the most credible testimony by noting correspondences and differences between the various statements. The method for discerning the credibility of testimony centers on five points that suggest how relations of power bore upon the agonizing theater of testimony, where everyone knew that capital punishment was possible:

1. How early was the testimony given? Before the guard was alerted? Before Monday Gell and Charles Drayton were jailed together?
2. Was testimony given voluntarily (or at least by individuals never imprisoned)?
3. Was testimony potentially self-incriminating, such as a confession to being willing to join the insurrection if there was "force enough"?
4. Did the witness have an intimate bond of loyalty or affection with the accused (student/teacher, close friend, or family)?
5. Did a white owner/lawyer witness the testimony, endorse the testimony, or cross-examine the witness on behalf of the defendant?

Applying these tests to a reading of the archive has created three categories of credible testimony: (1) core, (2) corroborating, and (3) background testimony. To be allowed to contribute core facts to the narrative of the insurrectionary planning, such as who was involved and what was being planned, all the testimony had to pass at least four of these five credibility tests. There is every reason to accept, categorically, testimony from individuals who were not imprisoned or coerced, who had close relationships of affection with those they accused, and whose testimony was witnessed by people with the privilege and power to have taken the court to task if it lied about the facts in order to falsely affirm a nonexistent uprising and destroy property in chattel slaves. The latter is important. The state could compensate masters for the loss of their slaves by execution for insurrection, but that incurred a significant public expense. In fact, the costs of compensation for all the executed and transported slaves might well have rivaled the entire annual outlay for state-wide public schools in 1822. It was dangerous for the court to falsify records that attached such liability to the state.

A second category of evidence is "corroborating testimony." Corroborating testimony of the core statements should be credible if the conditions of testimony meet two or more of the tests above. This testimony is used to strengthen core facts and add details to the core narrative. It also helps establish the scale and reveal the dynamics of the uprising's social network. Statements that meet few of these credibility tests can only be used as "background testimony," which is the third and last category of credible evidence. "Background testimony" can only be used to expand or confirm the detail of uncontroversial facts, such as names of places or people, and other incidental information. Any statements in the background category that contradict corroborated or core testimony are used only to describe disagreements and factions among the planners and the black community at large.

A newly nuanced understanding of the archive emerges when we read it "against the grain" in this way. The method allows an understanding of Gullah Jack's role as a central organizer belonging simultaneously in his African origins and the Carolina slave community—urban and rural. This chapter reports that finding.

Gullah Jack as Maroon Leader

The court suffered more from fear, outrage, and racism than from mendacity and turpitude. After hesitating when the first evidence of an imminent uprising emerged, the white authorities moved decisively only when a second highly credible report shocked them into more drastic actions. Once they had begun arresting people, they soon concluded that there must have been a main instigator. Why, exactly, they made this conclusion so quickly is not entirely clear, but there were suggestions of key organizers in the most credible early reports. One person described a man who fit the description of Gullah Jack. But the court did not learn the names of these central figures immediately. The court was probably prejudicially certain that such a plot required an original instigator. Someone must have "poisoned and embittered their minds against the white population," as the court put it. This assumption was consequential. Some of the statements of the enslaved under interrogation suggest the possibility that the court asked leading questions about individuals. For example, one witness seemed to answer an implied question when he said, "I know Rolla, belonging to Mr. Bennett," as if he had perhaps just been asked if he knows him (*Official Report* 1822, 24.). Several statements from the slaves who testified have this form, as Michael Johnson has pointed out.

The court was searching for an overall leader, and after some days of interrogations they concluded that Denmark Vesey was it. Vesey was a prominent person in the planning. But because of the court's assumptions and possibly leading questions, we cannot be certain that Vesey was quite the sole leader-instigator the court imagined. In the court's *Official Report*, Gullah Jack is named approximately eighty times while Denmark Vesey is mentioned over 260 times (Kennedy and Parker 1822, passim). But in the most credible testimony (a smaller subset of the whole), witnesses identified Gullah Jack as a prominent planner more often than Vesey. That does not make Jack more important. It suggests that we should look more closely at the sources and dynamics of Gullah Jack's influence, both in the community and in the uprising planning. The reasons for Vesey and Jack's influence were partly about their individual abilities and partly about their social relationships. The court could not appreciate these relationships fully. Instead, they argued—assumed, really—that the enslaved were manipulated. Vesey became the sole instigator in their minds because he professed the religion they thought true and powerful, he had charisma, he was educated, and he was a free man. His existence was probably discomforting at the least, and offensive at the worst. By contrast, the court's denunciation of Gullah Jack as a diabolical savage dismisses him as pathetic because of his religion and his spiritual practices (Kennedy and Parker 1822, 179).

Despite dismissing Jack, the court treatment of him as a diabolical agent shows its desire to identify something they could believe had polluted the slave community from the outside. In sentencing Jack to die, the court emphasized his individual agency as a uniquely talented beguiler. He was "not satisfied with resorting to natural and ordinary means," the court declared. Rather, he deployed "the most disgusting mummery and superstition" and represented himself "as invulnerable." Mocking claims that he "could neither be taken nor destroyed" and that his comrades "would be invincible" too, the court's sentence played up his role at the expense of a serious consideration of the intelligence and resentment that the men who joined him felt. Jack must have been a corrupter "of the ignorant and credulous." Surely, they declared, his techniques "produce no other emotion in the minds of the intelligent and enlightened, but contempt and disgust." Confidently, the court declared that the "airy spectres" he had "conjured" had been "chased away by the superior light of Truth." Again, with emphasis upon him as an individual—rather than one part of a social community—they condemn him to be "consigned to the cold and silent grave" in which "all the Powers of Darkness cannot rescue you." The court then turns to "conjure" him in a sort of spiritual grappling. They offer him the comfort of clergy whose power he certainly did not recognize in the hope of learning more details of people involved. "Unburthen your guilty conscience" they suggest. "Neglect not the opportunity" (Kennedy and Parker 1822, 179). But Jack kept silent. By his silence, he kept his power and he hid a community of belonging that was moving toward attacking slavery by killing indiscriminately, burning the city to the ground, and taking their families and friends with them out of slavery. In other words, he protected a maroon community in the making.

The court's vision of Jack seen in its sentencing statement uses a rhetoric of barbarity, darkness, and eschatological finality. As such it is reminiscent of Aphra Behn's 1689 novel of a maroon event, *Oroonoko*. The title character is a duplicitously captured prince from the Gold Coast (now Ghana) brought to Surinam as a slave. Oroonoko incites the slaves in his midst to rebellion.

But he faces reluctance from other slaves who declare that fear for their families gives them pause about the risks of rebellion. Oroonoko responds by inciting them to value their honor above their continued enslavement—or the enslavement of their families. He calls on them to find courage and manhood. It is the model of leadership that the 1822 court in Charleston fantasized about, in which a charismatic and persuasive individual motivates otherwise docile slaves to rebellion. Like the 1822 court in Charleston, Aphra Behn could not, apparently, conceive of an agency for rebellion among the common enslaved population. She did not develop her novel's sub-theme on the social dynamics of rebellion among the enslaved, traces of which are seen in the reservations about safety and family that the enslaved express to Oroonoko. Slavery itself is almost normalized in her novel. The central conflict of the plot is white duplicity in enslaving noble personages, such as Oroonoko and his wife Amoinda. Treated as slaves, these two rebelled like nobles nonetheless. We do not learn much or come to sympathize with the humanity of the general population of the enslaved. When they get motivated, it is by Oroonoko's agency, not their own (Lipking, ed., 1997, 52–54). The 1822 Charleston court likewise had difficulty recognizing the conflicted and dynamic social network that alternately supported the insurrection planners and then doubted them. The court could not really see the agency of the enslaved and instead searched for the Oroonokos among them.

Gullah Jack was a remarkable person, with unique ability, but he was only one leader in a social process. He did not claim to possess an absolute supernatural command of the enslaved, as the court claimed. If he had possessed such power, perhaps none would have betrayed him to the hangman. Gullah Jack knew he was not a magical overlord. His power and prestige was borne of his history, which featured a common enslavement story that began in betrayal and led him to integration in the slave community in his distinctive way. For Jack, slavery's effort to alienate his body from his will had begun in Africa. He was an adult when he was enslaved in 1805 and sold in East Africa to a US slave ship. His ethnicity and nativity has not yet been conclusively identified. Records indicate he was from a place called "M'Choolay Moreema," but that appears to be a much-corrupted transliteration of an African name. The real site has not yet been conclusively identified (Shafer 2013, 80–81). He was a "doctor" or "conjuror" before he was enslaved. He likely spoke a Bantu language of the Niger-Congo family, a large linguistic grouping extending from East to West across the center of the continent (Olson 1996, 70). His struggle against enslavement commenced immediately. Jack managed to bring his conjure bag onto the slaving vessel, an object of immense importance to him. He presumably still had it when he was sold on-ship in the Charleston,

South Carolina, harbor in 1806. During all his life as a slave he kept it, or perhaps replacements for it that he made as needed or desired.[5]

The fact that he was able to keep his medicine bag, with its implements of conjure, certainly would have suggested to Jack that his methods could protect him in his new world of slavers. It must have been some comfort to realize that he might still use knowledge he already possessed. It clearly helped confirm him as "a doctor Negro" in Charleston's slave community. Former slaves and the children of former slaves interviewed in the early twentieth century sometimes referred to such "conjure bags" when interviewed by researchers. Conjure bags were often for injuring people, or causing distress or bad luck. But there were protective charms, too, including cat bones and other animal parts and plants. As one woman, Liza Basden of Harris Neck, Georgia, told interviewers, lots of people carried charms for protection. Even in the early twentieth century, these charms could closely resemble what Gullah Jack had carried with him. As Basden reportedly said, "mos of the folks carry sumpm fuh pruhtection." They might collect hair, nails, graveyard dirt, cloth, or string, and "tie em all up in a lill bag." The bag might be worn around the ankle, wrist, or neck. And Gullah Jack was not the only slave to have arrived wearing such objects. One black family in Georgia had kept a carved stone fig that they said an ancestor had brought from Santo Domingo (Johnson 1940, 25, 102, 124–25). William Wells Brown also remembered a conjurer from his years of enslavement before 1834. According to Brown, the slaves understood Dinky to be "his own massa." Dinky was in his fifties in the 1820s or 1830s and had healing, protective, and second-sight abilities. He made talismans and used "goofer dust" for protection. No one on the plantation could remember Dinky working. And he came and went as he pleased, getting respect and even awe from slaves and whites alike (Brown 1880, 68–82).

Thus, Jack's conjure bag and the replacements for it he certainly made over time, helped him demonstrate the skills that built his reputation. Tactical, strategic, and assertive is the image of Jack that emerges from the credible trial testimony—a key leader of a closely allied group of African and Gullah slaves. One might expect that he became a powerful spiritual presence among the African-born. But he was more a part of the Gullah community in the region—native Carolina-born people with a language that was a composite of West African languages and English. This reputation was emblematic of the social belonging he found among some of the enslaved. Although whites regarded his knowledge of conjure as savage superstition, blacks who understood paid attention. And though some of the evangelical Christians in the black community were suspicious of him, for some of the enslaved he was a person of significance. His doctoring skills had recovered for him the distinctive role he once had in Central Africa. He belonged again, on terms that would have made some sense to him. Little in the testimony echoed the court's portrayal of Jack as a fearful "necromancer" ("Examination of [Name Redacted]" 1822; "Examination of Joe" 1822; "Examination of George" 1822; *Official Report* 1822, 20, 89, 105). The court simply could not see Jack as a leader of a subversive social process welling-up within a community with members who had accepted Gullah Jack as a resource.[6]

Jack and his friends and acquaintances had other reasons for faith in his powers, too. By the 1820s, Jack had been wearing unusually long whiskers for years. They were so important to his identity that his master knew he could use the threat of cutting them as leverage in his relationship with his talented and unusual slave. But the fact that his master never cut them, and never took his charms, might have suggested to Jack and others that he in fact had power in this slave society. Frederick Douglass relates a story from his own enslavement that helps illuminate. A "root" that another slave gave him, Douglass suggested, seemed to have protected him against the slave breaker and brought him the power to "become a man" through resistance (Douglass, 72).

The slave community had agreed to and—perhaps had created—at least two aliases for Jack. "Gullah Jack" was his most common name. The name was a reference to the African-derived, American-born culture of the rural enslaved community in the lowcountry. It suggests he was strongly associated with these communities, despite his urban residence. The name suggests a significant reputation—at least among town slaves—for association with the Gullahs. He was also called, however, "Cooter Jack." Cooter was a common name for a swamp turtle in the lower south and the word was also akin to "kuta," which occurs in some of the Niger-Congo family languages, of which class of languages Jack's native tongue was a part. The word "kuta" is found in Swahili, which was the most common language in the region of East Central Africa from which Jack was trafficked. In Swahili, "kuta" can mean "find" or "come across." Both translations would work well as a description of Jack, a collector of crab claws and other items for conjure bags and the like. The name also suggests possible confirmation of his first master's claim that Jack originally spoke an "Angolan" language. As John K. Thornton has argued, American slavers frequently used Angola as the label for a large cultural region (Thornton 1998 [1992], 85–105; 1991, 1101–13). Both names for Jack strongly suggest ties to rural Carolina slaves, even though he never worked a plantation and spent his entire sixteen years as a Carolina slave living in Charleston. Court records show that there were Gullah-speaking slaves in

Charleston with whom he was close. To build such a reputation, Jack must have been outgoing and forceful in his social interactions. But some portion of the community must also have viewed him as a person who mattered.[7]

The slave community participated in creating Gullah Jack. His spiritual power summoned the courage of some and palliated the conscience of others. This African-born man of unknown birth name who was renamed "Jack" against his will became a "Gullah" because the community accepted him as such. He apparently learned to speak the Gullah language. They empowered him as much as he led them. Just as there were social dimensions to his identity formation in South Carolina, there were also social dimensions to Gullah resistance as a community. It was not a magical deception that Jack practiced; it was rather the ritual they knew and, at least in part, believed in. Resistance to the brutality, indignity, and exploitation of slavery was shaped by these relations of power as much as between the slaves and the masters.

Jack's ritual practices were an option for solace—like Christianity—but black Charlestonians had witnessed actual departures from slavery, too. In the fall of 1821, James Creighton—a free man of color—had taken a few Carolina slaves and free people to West African colonies of Britain and the US. Colonization, well-known to some moderate antislavery advocates in the 1820s, sought to free black people and return them to Africa. Sierra Leone and Liberia were the main locations. And the Charleston court in 1822 would hear testimony that Denmark Vesey had considered going, but had chosen to stay so that, in words the court attributed to Vesey, he might "see what he could do" for his fellow black Charlestonians (Official Report 1822, 87–88; "Examination of Frank, a negro man belonging to Mr. Ferguson" 1822; *City Gazette & Commercial Daily Advertiser* October 3, 1821, February 2, 1822, August 7, 1822, and August 14, 1822). Others had left, but it was probably a bitter and daunting freedom, acquired as a master's favor and representing separation from family or at least friends and one's home for a foreign country.[8] By contrast, maroon communities take freedom as a right, not at the whim of a master. And they take family with them—as well as any friends willing to risk the endeavor, regardless of a master's asserted property rights. The experience of the 1821 colonization departures to Sierra Leone were clearly in the community memory in 1822 as the uprising planning progressed.

In 1822, urban hideouts-in-plain-sight appeared and disappeared moment-to-moment at Gullah Jack's, Monday Gell's, and Denmark Vesey's whenever slaves turned from lawful activities to illegal conversations about plans. In an instant, three men talking shop could become three men illegally inciting rebellion, punishable by death. Such flash meetings, furtive and fleeting, must have often accompanied marronage events, as the would-be escapees

Freetown, Sierra Leone, ca. 1803, to which James Creighton sailed with African Americans. Thomas Winterbottom, *Account of the Native Africans in the Neighbourhood of Sierra Leone* ... (London: Whittingham, 1803), frontispiece.

identified allies and established plans. In Charleston in 1822, such conversations might have generated a full-scale marronage had a significant body of slaves fled to the regional swamps and forests to which maroons in the region often resorted. The shared activities of these sites were directly linked to rural spaces in the surrounding parishes through the families and friendship networks of the men involved. It is clear they had rural links via family and friends living nearer to Stono, south of Charleston. And other connections linked the urban people to rural communities along the neck north of town. Bulkley's farm outside the city saw nighttime meetings in which plantation slaves and town slaves met. Several organizers seemed especially close to Gullah Jack—namely, Peter Poyas, Harry Haig, and Tom Russell. Each time the men from town—or others from the plantations—snuck off in order to gather at night in the woods or in town, their actions were the equivalent of running away. Were a patrol to find them, individually or in a group, the punishment could be severe. A night curfew prohibited such movements by the enslaved. If a patrol had learned what the men were discussing, the punishment could have been death.[9]

The plan called for small groups of slaves to capture important sites. Most urgently, they wished to capture the city arsenal on June 16, probably using a small core of fighters armed only with spears made by one of the planners. The attack would commence at about midnight or early in the morning,

Bulkley's Farm was near the center of this image, where King Street and Meeting Street merge into one road headed northward along the neck in this early nineteenth-century map detail. South Carolina Historical Society.

after the city guard was dismissed for the night. In the weeks before the date, Gullah Jack distributed ritually prepared foods—parched corn and groundnuts—for the rebels to consume as their only food on the morning of the insurrection. The people in the coastal, rural parishes and swampy islands surrounding Charleston had been contacted, using family and friendship networks of trust to keep the secret. Organizers insisted they would have force enough, including help from the countryside. Investigators were never clear how many total people were committed to the insurrection and how many had only casually expressed a tepid support, offering to join when the rebels "passed by" and only if they were numerous enough. Perhaps the "real" number was unknown even to the planners. And perhaps it does not really matter. After all, the insurrection in the North Province of Saint Domingue in 1791 had only dozens, perhaps hundreds of initial adherents. What mattered in Saint Domingue was how the insurrection caught on as plantations began to burn. Rumors of substantial numbers of conspirators and of their intent had circulated and were regarded casually by the planners in Saint Domingue. The organizers and their nearest collaborators seemed to expect that at least some of the enslaved men they approached would already have heard about the possible insurrection ("Examination of [Name Redacted]" 1822).

By the late spring of 1822, in Charleston rumors were spreading among some of the enslaved that "the blacks were going to try to take the country from the whites." Indeed, in the records, several men declare that they had heard something of the rising, but that they were not part of it. Of course, if they were actually a part of the plan, they would not likely admit it to the court. But even if they were involved, these conversations depict how they learned of the plan: a man approaches and furtively asks "what's the news" and obliquely alludes to a discord or interruption in the relationships between white and black to break out soon. Even if the conversation breaks off right away and is never restarted, the seed of a rumor has possibly been planted. In fact, the planners of the rising could have expected that rumors might precede them and that it could work to their benefit. Their goal was personal discretion rather than absolute secrecy. They had no choice but to suggest the plan to people, if they wished to recruit people quickly when the fighting broke out. Unlucky choices about whom to approach led to their betrayal. Trouble started as some who knew of the plan shared it with others, in dangerously public places. Fatefully, William Paul and another man, Peter Prioleau, briefly discussed the possible insurrection with each other at the Charleston waterfront. By itself this was something the records show multiple men doing. But this time one of the men, Peter, got spooked and informed the white authorities ("Examination of Mr. John Paul's Negro Man William" 1822). Despite this dangerous misfire, spreading the news was nonetheless a tactic. Marronage and insurrection are inherently dangerous. There was little choice for the organizers. When recruits worried about how many slaves would join, rumors might have helped assure them that many people knew the secret and that, on the night of the uprising, there would be force enough. The real number of committed rebels might have remained small, but rumors suggesting thousands were prepared to fight might have been self-fulfilling.[10]

It was a violent and dangerous plan, and it was controversial among the slaves. Several slaves in credible testimony condemned or criticized the plan when informed of it. They disagreed about the feasibility of the plan and morality of the violence. Evidence of the factionalism is one of the most important and rare virtues of the court records of the 1822 plan. Often, records from maroon or insurrectionary events allow only a superficial view of the rebels' activities. For example, from 1765 into the late 1780s, a maroon camp on the Savannah River watershed periodically drew organized military excursions against it, as masters tried to stamp out the community. But there is nothing in the resulting records to suggest the movements of the enslaved. We learn nothing of the people involved, their ideologies, their social process, and their family connections and other loyalties (*Gazette of the State of Georgia* April 26, May 10, May 17, 1787).[11]

Comparison of an incident in *The Narrative of the Life of Frederick Douglass* is instructive. Douglass offered a rich portrait of the decision-making and planning process of a marronage he attempted. Douglass's approach to planning his marronage was similar in some respects to the Charleston planners of 1822. Still in his teens, he decided to attain his freedom. But like Denmark Vesey, who felt he should not colonize to Africa but stay in Charleston to see what could be done for the enslaved people, Douglass also had strong feelings for his fellows. He wrote "my fellow slaves were dear to me [and] I was anxious to have them participate with me in this." He therefore began "with prudence" to seek how they felt and what they believed about "their condition." He gradually developed a plan while convincing his friends that slavery was a gross injustice. He chose which slaves to approach first, and when he found people ready to act if a reasonable opportunity arose, he focused on them. His terms were about gendered manhood, much like the Charleston planners. Writes Douglass, "I talked to them about our want of manhood if we submitted to our enslavement without at least one noble effort to be free." They met frequently in secret, "the odds were fearful," and there was often "shrinking." Every contingency seemed to promise pain, injury, capture, or death. These fears stalled the plan. It "was a doubtful liberty at best, and almost certain death." His final group of four or five men included two men who were related to him. But they were betrayed by one of their own. These social dynamics in Douglass's experience closely parallel the Charleston uprising. In Charleston thirteen years earlier, there had also been gendered incitements to manliness, a sense of failure being more likely than success, a need to convince others of the feasibility, entrenched ideological disagreement about the plan, and betrayal by a trusted friend (Douglass, 96–102).[12]

In 1822, slaves in Charleston sometimes showed such fear for their own lives and concern for the well-being of friends and relatives. Six enslaved women are named in the court proceedings (and more are mentioned without being named). Prudence Bussacre, Doll Perry, Lydia "Liddy" Perry, and Sally Howard testified under credible conditions. None of these women were arrested. Some of the women testified against their own relatives and declared they had feared for the consequences of the planning. Others testified in the defense of relatives and acquaintances who were subsequently convicted—without becoming suspects themselves. This latter testimony was interpreted by the court as partly incriminating against the accused as it confirmed suspicious movements, even though the women reported innocent, ordinary activities by the men. Yet, their testimony was also allowed to soften the convicted men's sentences to transportation out of the United States.

The women could have easily invented false stories in an effort to curry favor with the court. But their stories often incriminated loved ones. Other women tried to exonerate the accused. Their testimony has rarely drawn the attention of historians. Their statements reveal concerns that the men shared as they stood before the court and decided whether to name names. They appear to have feared the court, the insurrection talk itself, the death and destruction an insurrection would bring ("Prudence belonging to Mr. Bussacre Examined" 1822; "Doll Perry on behalf of the Prisoner" 1822; "Lydia Agrippa's Mother" 1822; "A Negro woman belonging to Mr. Alexr Howard" 1822; "Examination of [Name Redacted]" 1822; "Examination of Joe" 1822).[13]

Fears forced the men to demand to know how large the army was, what weaponry was in hand, and how further weapons would be acquired. Suffering and alienation as slaves was not enough to motivate some of the people to risk death and injury to themselves and loved ones; they wanted reassurance about the goal and how it would be attained. If slavery itself was a key driving force motivating resistance, it does not appear to have often been how the rebels were explicitly motivated. They knew a desire for freedom through a gendered discourse of manly affection and belonging: they were "bosom friends" or "intimate friends" who "always worked together." Some appear plausibly to have been motivated by the desire to defend themselves, friends, or family. This was a desire for forms of belonging that resonated regardless of whether the men were African, Gullah, or town-dwelling hired-out slaves—regardless even of whether they were already free in this slaving and colonizing society in the way Denmark Vesey or Saby Gaillard were free ("Prudence . . . Examined" 1822; "Examination of George" 1822; "Examination of [Name Redacted]" 1822).[14]

Slaves testified that there were meetings at Gullah Jack's and at other public and private places in Charleston for planning and recruitment. Men would also gather at Monday Gell's shop in order to do lawful business as well as to discuss the uprising. Such talk of insurrection would have been forbidden for slaves, especially in meetings unsupervised by whites, and slaves knew this. One white man, James Mall, testified that he had heard Gullah Jack and Tom Russell frequently speak Gullah. Other meetings were held secretly. Their talk was not an "inchoate crime," as Carrie Hyde has argued (Hyde 2014, 26). Their talk was an actual crime. The law of conspiracy that applied to slaves, the Negro Act of 1740 (with 1751 revisions), ordered that slaves "suffer death" for being an accomplice or an abettor to insurrection, even if the plans never came to fruition. If a court felt "merciful," it might merely execute one of the conspirators and flog the rest. Moreover, incitement of others just to run away could draw the same harsh penalties. Given how often slaves ran away, the harshness of the Negro Act was probably known painfully well in the community. That is why some witnesses told the authorities that they reproached people who talked to them about the rising. It is why some said they fled lest they be construed as part of the plan. It might have contributed to the decision of Peter Prioleau or George Wilson to reveal the plot; knowledge of such a plot exposed one to the accusation of abetting the plot. Slaves were the quintessential example of a being whom the state could easily declare outlawed and mercilessly punish. Gullah Jack and his co-planners' meetings and discussions were risky acts of resistance, not possible acts of resistance.[15]

And they discussed insurrection often. Charles Drayton, Harry Haig, John Horry, George Vanderhorst, and others discussed the insurrection at Gullah Jack's, in random street locations, at the City Market, in rural secret meetings, at Monday Gell's shop, and elsewhere in town and out of town. Monday was an African-born man, reputedly of Igbo ethnicity. And he was reportedly in charge of a group of Igbos expected to coordinate an attack. Individuals identified weapons they thought they could get access to, such as a master's sword or gun. Few claimed any weapons to be in their actual possession. A white witness, James Mall, declared that he personally saw Tom Russell making a foot-long knife from a file, saying Tom was an edged toolmaker. They therefore had a real but limited capacity to produce a few edged weapons to use in a surprise, nighttime assault on the whites' known weapons stores. As the uprising plans became known to the white authorities, desperation set in, with some men making panicked declarations of fear that cohorts would betray them ("James Mall, a white man sworn for the Prisoner" 1822; "Prudence belonging to Mr. Bussacre Examined" 1822; "Examination of George a negro belonging to Mr. Wilson" 1822; "Examination of [Name Redacted]" 1822; "Examination of Joe, a negro man belonging to Mr. LaRoche" 1822). The slaves understood that they lived in what Agamben would describe as a state of exception; they could easily become a fair target for punitive violence as "savages" or "barbarians." Therefore, although fearful that some would talk, they sat on their hands, knowing whites would give no quarter if they spoke up and believing community loyalties would protect them. For some, it was a fateful mistake, for they were named.

The trial records' portraits of the fears and desires of both slavers and enslaved map the relations of power between masters and various individual slaves and their factions. The uprising was a psychic marronage, not reducible to the heroic effort of a single leader. White fantasies of insurrection are part of the complexity, but cannot be allowed to obscure the slaves' own visions of what to do and how to do it. The slaves were divided, and they jostled with each other over proper action, while some of them prepared to fight their masters. There were recently arrived Africans from different regions, and there were Carolina-born slaves of urban, plantation, and Gullah backgrounds. There were men and women who were devoted members of Christian churches. And there were men and women devoted to the various spiritual traditions that had made the crossing from Africa. There were also individuals not committed to any religion in particular. There were rural slaves and urban. There were people committed to instigating revolutionary violence, others willing only to join a successful wave of rebellion. There were wild and contradictory stories of vast numbers of conspirators circulating to encourage the intimidated. And there were those opposed to violence as either too risky or a mortal sin. It was people of that last category who betrayed the uprising in the end. Since many "conspiracies" for marronage or insurrection were betrayed in quite the way the 1822 uprising was, the Vesey events' records might suggest the power dynamics and processes of many town-based uprisings.

Jack knew his vulnerability. He knew the likelihood of betrayal. He declared to a cohort that his "cullah" could protect him from whites but could not protect him from the betrayal of his own people. Jack had been a doctor in Central Africa, betrayed to slavers by his own people. Like other maroon communities, in which hybrids of West and Central African beliefs and practices created a distinct African feel, the Central African Jack had won respect from West Africans and Gullah people. Facing betrayal again in 1822 in this new community, he spoke painfully from memory and profound alienation: he believed he could not protect himself from the "treachery" of his "own color." Whites had been weaker. They had been unable to take his implements from him throughout the slaving process, and his master had threatened but never actually shaved his symbolic beard and mustache. To be delivered into the hands of the whites required other Africans' collusion with them.

Ultimately, on the scaffold, Jack physically struggled against a white power that his doctoring skills suddenly failed to hold at bay: whites had again found the power to destroy his body when they could no longer feel guaranteed in their control of his will in the slave community. He had emerged as a maroon leader, and they had caught him. With their scaffold, slave owners completed a betrayal begun in 1805 by Jack's original enslavers, who likely were other Africans in his home region. He left behind in Charleston black organizers who had a variety of plans for what they would have attempted had they broken open the doors to slavery's arsenal. All seem to have been motivated by personal, family, and community ties first and foremost; for these men, it was about gender, about their manhood. But none of the slaves could have controlled events after the moment they seized guns and powder from the city guard. We too will never know what would have followed. But that we get to see the psychical process of rebellion through this remarkable and troubling trial record is uniquely valuable. We must interpret it, and we must address core questions of what actually happened.

Conclusion

A maroon theme runs through the archive of the Denmark Vesey affair. Alienated in a sharply exploitative society, some black Carolinians sought a sense of belonging with each other that could only be provided through rebellion and escape. Their modes of escape from the surveillance of whites had some social-cultural similarities with marronage that are instructive for understanding the insurrectionary plan. For some, belonging meant escape into a spiritually potent Christianity housed in an autonomous black church as free of white intrusion as possible. For others in the Charleston black community, belonging was apparently not possible without colonization out of Carolina to Sierra Leone or Liberia in West Africa. And a final group retreated into Monday Gell's shop or Denmark Vesey's home or corners of public places outdoors to plan insurrection and flight from the city.[16]

To date, the 1822 events have been treated by historians primarily as conspiracy. A white court interdicted, investigated, and punished an "insurrectionary conspiracy." Considered as conspiracy, the story becomes one of planning and defeat at an inchoate state. Yet, skeptically reading along the grain of the white court's archive by reopening questions of credibility without silencing black Charleston's critical voice offers a different narrative: the planners expected men to flee their plantations and domestic servants' quarters as runaways. Their insurrection would have started with unlawful travel. Some of the planners personally expected to flee in a mass marronage to Haiti or elsewhere. Still more simply talked about "taking the country from the whites" as in a revolution. If these slaves could speak and typologize their own actions, the results would have been quite different than what the white court prosecuted as conspiracy.

"Conspiracy" carries the stigma of illegality, as whites saw the actions of the enslaved. Yet, these outcomes all emerged from psychic marronages in the slave community—moments when people decided to speak with each other about asserting themselves fully and uncompromisingly. Too much focus on success or failure would fail to analyze the slaves' actions fully. The talk that Gullah Jack and others engaged in together was the necessary opening stage of any uprising of any type. Given that they were starting in the heart of a relatively stable slave society, their plans were less likely to succeed than the gathering of slaves at Bois-Caiman in the North Province of Saint Domingue in the summer of 1791. At that time, Saint Domingue had already become unstable as factionalism from the French Revolution affected the colony. But the Charleston uprising nonetheless shared some of the African and maroon dimensions that were present at the start of the Haitian Revolution. Focusing on the political story alone will relegate the documents to a sequence of events that denies the slaves themselves full subjectivity in their rebellion and its fate. It is to make the events solely a way station between the American Revolution and the US Civil War, part of a narrative of the progress and paradoxes of American liberty.[17]

Thinking about the talk as akin to marronage helps bring forward a new narrative of the 1822 Charleston uprising, one that has greater emphasis upon Jack and a variety of his associates. Based on the testimony of women as well as men, this story focuses more on finding space for social relationships of close affection and rivalry, African spirituality, and black Carolinians' creole Gullah culture. It is less concerned with the size of an insurrectionary army or the content of a single revolutionary ideology.[18] We know what Vesey's revolution was alleged to look like: an Old Testament and libertarian revolt against liberty's nemesis (slavery and slavers). But do we know what Jack's African and Gullah revolution would have looked like? It was commencing as a maroon revolution, calling rural slaves to come into town for reinforcements and envisioning spiritual protection for their assertion of the courage to assuage the pain and address the needs of enslaved friends and family. Vesey and the urban slaves closest to him had little or no connection with many of these rural people. Though he too was in town, Jack's revolution involved a psychic marronage in urban spaces closely allied to nighttime, brief physical marronages in the countryside with rural slaves. Its most powerful expressions were ceremonies at Bulkley's farm outside the city, where town-dwelling spiritual apprentices of Jack met rural Gullah slaves. In short, if Vesey's revolution can be compared to the American Revolution in its national story of working out the complexities and contradictions of liberty, Gullah Jack's revolution might be compared to the Haitian Revolution and its African-creole national story of self-emancipation and identity. Together, both visions—and more—offer a nuanced story of African American antislavery in the heart of the colonizing and slaving society that Carolina was in the early nineteenth century.

Notes

1. Despite debate about the nature of the archive of the "Denmark Vesey Slave Conspiracy," credibly given testimony suggests a real conspiracy of some kind. However, this chapter is primarily about the psychic marronage occurring within the minds and social relations of the black community in 1822. And I am interested in what the records have to say about how Gullah Jack and others fit within those social networks and relations of power. For the debate about the Denmark Vesey trial records, see Michael Johnson, "Denmark Vesey and his Co-conspirators," *WMQ* (2001), Douglas Egerton, *He Shall go Out Free* (2004), Appendix 2: "Denmark Vesey and the Historians," 233–52; Robert Paquette, "From Rebellion to Revisionism: The Continuing Debate About the Denmark Vesey Affair," *Journal of the Historical Society*, vol. 4 (Fall 2004), 291–334; Paquette and Egerton, "Of Facts and Fables: New Light on the Denmark Vesey Affair," *The South Carolina Historical Magazine*, vol. 105 (2004), 8–48.

2. For the court's use of the word "insurgents" to describe the planners, see Lionel Kennedy and Thomas Parker, *An Official Report of the Trials of Sundry Negroes, Charged with an Attempt to Raise an Insurrection in the State of South Carolina . . .* (Charleston, 1822), 20, 28, 31, 32, 33, 38, 39, 40, 41, 44, 52, 54, 56; "Examination of George a negro belonging to Mr. Wilson," "Examination of [Name Redacted]"; and "Examination of Joe, a negro man belonging to Mr. LaRoche," Governor's Message, Enclosure B, Court Proceedings and Testimony Regarding the Denmark Vesey Rebellion, House of Representatives Copy, South Carolina Department of Archives and History, http://www.archivesindex.sc.gov/ (hereafter cited as SCDAH online). Literature scholars interested in the conspiracy continue to debate the veracity of the archive of the 1822 events. Historians seem to be reaching a consensus that some version of the events were "real" as reported, though which details might be factual or fabrication is still a source of debate. See James O'Neil Spady, "Power and Confession," *William and Mary Quarterly* (2011); Joseph Kelly, *America's Longest Siege: Charleston, Slavery, and the Slow March toward Civil War* (New York, 2013); Carrie Hyde, "Novelistic Evidence: The Denmark Vesey Conspiracy and Possibilistic History," *American Literary History*, vol. 27 (2014), 26–55. See also John Saillant, "Before 1822: Anti-Black Attacks on Charleston Methodist Churches from 1786 to Denmark Vesey's Execution," *Common-place.org* 16, no. 2 (2015); Tracy Keith Flemming, "Denmark Vesey: An Atlantic Perspective," *Journal of Pan African Studies* 7, no. 4 (2014); Philip F. Rubio, "'Though He Had a White Face, He Was a Negro in Heart': Examining the White Men Convicted of Supporting the 1822 Denmark Vesey Slave Insurrection Conspiracy," *South Carolina Historical Magazine* 113, no. 1 (January 2012), 50–67; Douglas Egerton, *He Shall Go Out Free* (2004), appendix 2: "Denmark Vesey and the Historians," 233–52; Robert Paquette, "From Rebellion to Revisionism: The Continuing Debate About the Denmark Vesey Affair," *Journal of the Historical Society*, vol. 4 (Fall 2004), 291–334; Paquette and Egerton, "Of Facts and Fables: New Light on the Denmark Vesey Affair," *South Carolina Historical Magazine*, vol. 105 (2004), 8–48; Jordan Lewis Reed, "American Jacobins: American Revolutionary Radicalism in the Era of the Civil War" (PhD dissertation, University of Massachusetts at Amherst, 2009), 55 n35, 61–66.

3. Spady, "Power and Confession," *WMQ*, vol. 68 (2011): 287–304; Michael P. Johnson, "Denmark Vesey and His Co-Conspirators," *William and Mary Quarterly*, 3rd series, 58, no. 4 (October 2001), 915–76; Robert L. Paquette, "From Rebellion to Revisionism: The Continuing Debate about the Denmark Vesey Affair," *Journal of the Historical Society* 4, no.

3 (Fall 2004): 291–334. For an abstract of Michael P. Johnson's success with some media and other scholars, ibid., 293, 327 nn. 6–11. See also Paquette and Egerton, "Of Facts and Fables: New Light on the Denmark Vesey Affair," *South Carolina Historical Magazine* 105, no. 1 (January 2004): 8–48.

4. Douglas Egerton and Robert A. Paquette, *The Denmark Vesey Affair: A Documentary History* (Gainesville: University Press of Florida, 2017), also have an index in their newly released and massive volume of documents on the Vesey events. But their index is different than mine in two important respects: first, it does not include the House copy of the transcripts or James Hamilton's published narrative; and, second, it is not designed to differentiate the roles people played in the court proceedings (accused, witness, confession, and etc.) in a way that supports a graphic social network map.

5. An excellent exploration of Jack's possible origins is in Daniel L. Schafer's (2013) book. Shafer believes Jack may have been of Ndonde, Ngingo, or Makua ethnicity, based on a Charleston newspaper ad that announced the arrival of the *Gustavia's* cargo in 1806: pp. 80–81.

6. "Examination of [Name Redacted]," "Examination of Joe, a negro man belonging to Mr. LaRoche," and "Examination of George a negro belonging to Mr. Wilson," Governor's Message, Enclosure B, SCDAH online. Similar assertions about fear are made regarding Denmark Vesey, reflecting the economy of fear through which the masters understood their relationship with their enslaved people: *Official Report*, 20, 89, 105.

7. For translation of "cooter" as "kuta" and as meaning "come across" or "find" in English, see "Kuta," *Glosbe Swahili-English Dictionary*, accessed September 20, 2017, https://en.glosbe.com/sw/en/kuta; "Kuta," *Online Swahili-English Dictionary*, http://africanlanguages.com/swahili/, accessed September 20, 2017. This usage of "cooter" in the trial record predates Merriam-Webster's earliest known usage for "cooter" by ten years. Merriam-Webster defines "cooter" as a word for several species of freshwater turtles that live in the Southern USA: "Cooter," *Merriam-Webster Dictionary*, accessed September 20, 2017, https://www.merriam-webster.com/dictionary/cooter.

8. *Official Report*, 87–88; "Examination of Frank, a negro man belonging to Mr. Ferguson," Governor's Message, Enclosure B, SCDAH online; *City Gazette & Commercial Daily Advertiser*, October 3, 1821, February 2, 1822, August 7, 1822, and August 14, 1822.

9. For Bulkley's farm location, see John Potter to Langdon Cheves, Charleston, July 15, 1822, Langdon Cheves Papers, South Carolina Historical Society.

10. William's testimony is of the corroborating and background variety, as I am defining those terms in this research. William's overall testimony is of lesser credibility because he was imprisoned for so long, with good reason to fear for his life. And he perhaps does make up a false story when he claims that Peter (the informant who had reported him) was actually the one to raise the question of an insurrection. Why lie? Perhaps because William's meeting was in a public place and there might have been witnesses to the alleged conversation. Even if nobody could hear the content of their conversation, he and Peter might at least have been seen. What was said is just a matter of William's word against Peter's word. If William can convince the court that Peter might have been the instigator and otherwise confess only that he knew of the plot but did not join and did not recruit, then he might survive. But ironically, such a set of lies (if they are lies) would confirm some basic facts—for example, that he did meet Peter on the wharf and they did talk about an uprising in somewhat coded language. William's lie thus suggests that he realizes he can persuasively deny neither the reality of the conspiracy nor the fact of his conversation on the wharf with Peter. Knowing that, he denied that he was the instigator of the conversation about rebellion

because instigation could be construed as a capital crime carrying the death penalty under South Carolina law. Because some of his factual claims are confirmed in other testimony and because nothing he says about basic facts is contradicted by highly credible "core" testimony, I use William's statements as "corroborating" and "background" testimony.

11. It found its way into newspaper reports in 1787, at the moment officials were succeeding in breaking up the camp. "Savannah April 26," *Gazette of the State of Georgia*, April 26, 1787: a battle between runaways and South Carolina militia and Catawba Indians; "Savannah May 10," *Gazette of the State of Georgia*, May 10, 1787: attack upon a maroon camp in Patton's Swamp by South Carolina and Georgia militia and fifteen Catawbas; "Savannah, May 17," *Gazette of the State of Georgia*, May 17, 1787: maroon camp near Savannah was broken up and runaways were surrendering daily. The African Church was long thought, incorrectly, to be an A.M.E. affiliated congregation, but John Saillant has recently observed that there is no primary evidence to support this belief. The violence against the African Church in 1822 reflects a deeper history of local white violence against black Methodists. Saillant, "Before 1822: Anti-Black Attacks on Charleston Methodist Churches from 1786 to Denmark Vesey's Execution," *Common-place.org*, 16, no. 2 (2015), http://common-place.org/book/before-1822-anti-black-attacks-on-charleston-methodist-churches-from-1786-to-denmark-veseys-execution/; Diouf, *Slavery's Exiles: The Story of the American Maroons* (New York: NYU Press, 2014), 1, 2, 4–5. Diouf, of course, focuses specifically on backcountry maroons and specifically refuses the kind of "maroon" thought experiment I am engaging in this chapter. But Diouf also pushes us to move beyond "petit" and "grand" marronage and reconceive what marronage might be. Diouf proposes "borderland maroons" and "hinterland maroons" instead. My main interest is in the recovery of the social process that preceded marronage, as that seems to be at least one tactic that the 1822 uprising planners may have been contemplating given their rural contacts and plans to flee the city after burning it.

12. Similarly, but with less descriptive detail, Jacob Stroyer describes the social dimensions of running away in his post-war account of his life as a slave in the 1850s as a boy. Nonetheless, Stroyer's story confirms the social process, in general: *My Life in the South* (Salem, MA, 1885), 64–66.

13. "Prudence belonging to Mr. Bussacre Examined," "Doll Perry on behalf of the Prisoner," "Lydia Agrippa's Mother," "A Negro woman belonging to Mr. Alexr Howard," "Examination of [Name Redacted]," and "Examination of Joe, a negro man belonging to Mr. LaRoche," Governor's Message, Enclosure B, SCDAH online.

14. Spady, "Power and Confession," 294: "Rolla Bennett, Joe LaRoche, and another of the witnesses against Rolla—a man called only Sambo in the records—were related by marriage or kinship with a woman named Amaretta. Sambo was her brother. Joe LaRoche was her former husband. She was married to Rolla Bennett at the time of the trials." Further examinations of three of Thomas Bennett's slaves (Peter, March, and Sampson) on Rolla's behalf took place on June 22, 1822, and helped substantiate larger family and friendship networks around Rolla and Joe.

15. As the South Carolina Negro Act of 1740 (revised 1751) put it: "every slave who shall raise or attempt to raise an insurrection" or "entice any slave to run away" shall be guilty of a felony and "suffer death" along with his or her "accomplices, aiders, and abettors" (as quoted in *Official Report*, xiii) See also David McCord, ed., *The Statutes at Large of South Carolina, Volume 7, Containing the Acts Relating to Charleston, Courts, Slaves, and Rivers* (Columbia, SC, 1840), 397–417 (especially sections XVI, XXXVI, and XLIII); and Thomas D. Morris, *Southern Slavery and the Law, 1619–1860* (Chapel Hill: University of

North Carolina Press, 2004), 272–73. "Prudence belonging to Mr. Bussacre Examined," "Examination of George a negro belonging to Mr. Wilson," "Examination of [Name Redacted]," and "Examination of Joe, a negro man belonging to Mr. LaRoche," Governor's Message, Enclosure B, SCDAH online.

16. James Creighton, a free black resident of Charleston, ferried Afro-Carolinians from Charleston to Sierra Leone in 1821. Britain's Freetown, in Sierra Leone, was already struggling with lots of growth and few resources. Early reports from the colony to London show large numbers of slaves arriving in the colony. One report claimed approximately 20,000 "liberated Africans" had been deposited into the colony between 1812 and 1825, with the rate continuing to increase. Yet resources and infrastructure were lacking. See *Abstract Statement of Expenditures, Papers Relating to the Colony of Sierra Leone* (London, 1830), 4–5; Major General Turner to Earl Bathurst, Sierra Leone, January 25, 1826, 6–7.

Liberia launched a little later than the Sierra Leone project, but it also featured a colonial rhetoric in its founding logic. And African American colonials contended with an ironic suspicion from their former masters that they were not, as a people, fully to be trusted with a colonial project. It was similar to the reticence in the British reports. Both programs featured a phased and patronizing process of attaining freedom in the colony. A group of 142 African Americans arrived at Cape Mesurado in 1827 from Georgia. They were immediately entered into a disciplinary plan for their adjustment to freedom. The US agent reported on his process for getting them off the public support rolls as quickly as possible. After six months, "all the adults" were to receive land. And after a year they will be "admitted to the privileges of colonial settlers" if they prove worthy "of the civil rights attaching to landed property in the colony." See United States Agency for Recaptured Africans on the Coast of Africa, *Recaptured Africans: Letter from the Secretary of the Navy . . . Aug 28, 1827 . . .* (Washington, DC, 1828), 5.

17. Ranjit Guha argued a generation ago that the subjective positions of rebels and insurrectionists were obscured by the narrative of national liberty, see Ed White, *The Backcountry and the City: Colonization and Conflict in Early America* (Minneapolis: University of Minnesota Press, 2005), 2.

18. Intimacy has been a theme in the scholarship on the Vesey events before, see William Freehling, "Denmark Vesey's Anti-Paternalistic Reality," in *The Reintegration of American History* (New York: Oxford University Press, 1994), 34–58. But to return to it in the way proposed here is to move beyond Vesey, and is to ask more nuanced questions about power in the relationships of the various factions of whites, African Americans, and Africans involved in the events—men and women. For another approach to slave rebellion fixed on "intimate-level" human relationships, see Michael Nicholls, *Whispers of Rebellion: Narrating Gabriel's Conspiracy* (Charlottesville: University of Virginia Press, 2012). In Nicholls's account, it is a neighborhood called "the Brook . . . framed by a watershed north of Richmond" that is the focal point of the "physical and human connections these men had with other parts of central Virginia" (see 11).

Secondary Source Bibliography

Behn, Aphra. *Oroonoko: An Authoritative Text, Historical Background, Criticism*. Johanna Lipking, ed. New York, 1997.
Diouf, Sylviane. *Slavery's Exiles: The Story of the American Maroons*. New York: New York University Press, 2014.

Egerton, Douglas R. *He Shall Go Out Free: The Lives of Denmark Vesey*. Lanham, Maryland: Rowman & Littlefield Publishers, 2004.

Egerton, Douglas, and Robert A. Paquette, *The Denmark Vesey Affair: A Documentary History*. Gainesville: University Press of Florida, 2017.

Flemming, Tracy Keith. "Denmark Vesey: An Atlantic Perspective." *Journal of Pan African Studies* 7, no. 4 (2014): 7–114.

Fick, Carolyn E. *The Making of Haiti: The Saint Domingue Revolution from below*. Nashville: University of Tennessee Press, 1990.

Freehling, William. "Denmark Vesey's Anti-Paternalistic Reality." In *The Reintegration of American History*, 34–58. New York, 1994.

Hyde, Carrie. "Novelistic Evidence: the Denmark Vesey Conspiracy and Possibilistic History." *American Literary History* 27 (2014): 26–55.

Johnson, Guy B. *Drums and Shadows: Survival Studies among the Georgia Coastal Negroes*. Athens: University of Georgia, 1940.

Johnson, Michael. "Denmark Vesey and his Co-conspirators." *William and Mary Quarterly* 58, no. 4 (2001): 915–76.

Kelly, Joseph. *America's Longest Siege: Charleston, Slavery, and the Slow March toward Civil War*. New York: The Overlook Press, 2013.

Morris, Thomas D. *Southern Slavery and the Law, 1619–1860*. Chapel Hill: University of North Carolina Press, 2004.

Nicholls, Michael. *Whispers of Rebellion: Narrating Gabriel's Conspiracy*. Charlottesville, VA: University of Virginia Press, 2012.

Olson, James S. *The Peoples of Africa: An Ethnohistorical Dictionary*. Westport, CT: Greenwood, 1996.

Paquette, Robert. "From Rebellion to Revisionism: The Continuing Debate About the Denmark Vesey Affair." *Journal of the Historical Society*, vol. 4 (Fall 2004): 291–334.

Paquette, Robert, and Douglas R. Egerton. "Of Facts and Fables: New Light on the Denmark Vesey Affair." *South Carolina Historical Magazine*, vol. 105 (2004), 8–48.

Reed, Jordan Lewis. "American Jacobins: American Revolutionary Radicalism in the Era of the Civil War." PhD dissertation, University of Massachusetts at Amherst, 2009.

Rubio, Philip F. "'Though He Had a White Face, He Was a Negro in Heart': Examining the White Men Convicted of Supporting the 1822 Denmark Vesey Slave Insurrection Conspiracy." *South Carolina Historical Magazine* 113, no. 1 (January 2012): 50–67.

Saillant, John. "Before 1822: Anti-Black Attacks on Charleston Methodist Churches from 1786 to Denmark Vesey's Execution." *Common-place.org* 16, no. 2 (2015), http://common-place.org/book/before-1822-anti-black-attacks-on-charleston-methodist-churches-from-1786-to-denmark-veseys-execution/.

Schafer, Daniel L. *Zephaniah Kingsley Jr. and the Atlantic World: Slave Trader, Plantation Owner, Emancipator*. Gainesville: University Press of Florida, 2013.

Spady, James O'Neil. "Power and Confession: On the Credibility of the Earliest Reports of the Denmark Vesey Slave Conspiracy." *William and Mary Quarterly* 68, no. 2 (2011): 287–304.

Thornton, John K. *Africa and Africans in the Making of the Atlantic World*. Cambridge: Cambridge University Press, 1998 [1992].

White, Edward. *The Backcountry and the City: Colonization and Conflict in Early America*. Minneapolis: University of Minnesota Press, 2005.

Chapter Three

"We Will Never Surrender!": Quilombos, Their Descendants, and the Struggle for Land and Rights in Brazil's Ribeira

Edward Shore

Aurico Dias is a farmer and activist from São Pedro, one of eighty-eight rural Afro-Brazilian communities descended from fugitive slaves known as *quilombos* that call the Atlantic Forest of São Paulo state and neighboring Paraná their home. Two hundred years ago, Dias's ancestors escaped the gold mines and rice plantations that dotted the landscape of the Vale do Ribeira (Ribeira Valley), joining scores of maroon communities of fugitive slaves throughout the Americas. During the 1990s, Dias and his neighbors pressed for land and federal benefits under Article 68, a constitutional provision that granted legal recognition and territorial rights to *remanescentes de quilombos* (quilombo descendants) in 1988 on the centenary of abolition. While 165 communities in Brazil have received titles from the government, more than 6,000, including São Pedro, still await full certification of their lands (Comissão Pró-Índio n.d.). Like their ancestors, they face threats to their livelihoods, this time from the intrusion of cattle ranchers, mining companies, and forest rangers. "Brazil waited almost 500 years to recognize quilombos," Dias told me in a 2015 oral history.[1] "Now it feels like we will have to wait another 500 years for our government to enforce its own laws."

This chapter traces the historical evolution of rural black communities in the Vale do Ribeira that have mobilized for legal recognition and territorial rights as remanescentes de quilombos under Article 68. Drawing from oral history, ecclesiastical documentation, and NGO archives, I contend that escaped slaves and their descendants appealed to history, ecology, and the law to challenge their territorial dispossession decades prior to the enactment of the Quilombo Law. My analysis of the grassroots activism of maroons and their descendants has both historiographical and political implications. By emphasizing rural Afro-Brazilians' long-standing tradition of engaging with the state and of transmitting historical struggles across generations, this chapter emphasizes a historical agency that is often overlooked. Further, I challenge the allegations of Article 68's opponents, who have attempted to discredit remanescentes by dismissing their territorial claims as the fabrication of outside agitators (Farfán-Santos 2016). Although the legal frameworks may have been supplied to these communities by outsiders, the narratives they have channeled had been transmitted for generations.

First, I revisit Flávio dos Santos Gomes's revisionist thesis about the nature of historical quilombos in Brazil (Gomes 2016; 2015). Early historians described quilombos as an attempt by fugitive slaves to recreate Africa on the other side of the Atlantic through the formation of autonomous and geographically isolated communities dedicated to the overthrow of the slave plantation system (Carneiro 1966; Rodrigues 1933; Freitas 2004; Do Nascimento 1980; Kent 1965; Moura 1972). Their model was the 10,000-strong Quilombo dos Palmares (1600–95), whose armies of fugitive slaves, led by the warrior-king Zumbi, battled Portuguese troops in the arid hinterlands of the Brazilian Northeast. Revisionists argued that Palmares was the exception rather than the rule (Reis and Gomes 2016; Schwartz 1992; De Almeida 2011; Barboza 1993, 60–62). Most quilombos in Brazil, they claimed, were quite small. Although geographical location was critical for their survival, rebel slaves often inhabited areas that were not totally isolated from arable land and small villages (Gomes 2016, 232; Schwartz, 108).

Gomes introduced the concept of the *campo negro* (black countryside) to refute the conventional wisdom that quilombos existed in isolation from the world of slavery (Gomes 2015; Ramos 2016). The campo negro represented a physical and metaphysical space produced and reproduced by maroons, plantation slaves, self-liberated blacks (*libertos*), and other subaltern groups living on the margins of rural society (Gomes 2016, 232–38). His 1995 essay, "Quilombos of Rio de Janeiro in the Nineteenth Century," revealed that runaway slaves forged relationships and extensive commercial linkages with merchants, plantation slaves, and even planters residing in the Iguaçu lowlands near Guanabara Bay. Gomes argues these contacts shielded maroon communities from the onslaught of slave hunters and allowed them to maintain autonomy (Gomes 2016, 238).

Many quilombos remained firmly embedded within the dominant socioeconomic institutions of colonial and nineteenth-century Brazil, much as their descendants maintained ties with political activists, government agents, and commercial middlemen during the twentieth and twenty-first centuries. However, I argue that revisionists have underestimated the degree to which ancestral knowledge of forest ecosystems and mastery of complex landscapes contributed to the survival of maroon communities in such remote regions of Brazil as the Vale do Ribeira. This chapter analyzes the cultural ecology of fugitive slaves and their descendants to demonstrate the material and symbolic foundations of freedom, matters that remain at the heart of contemporary conflicts over land, resources, and social justice in the region today.

Second, this study revisits Richard Price's 1998 article, "Scrapping Maroon History: Brazil's Promise, Suriname's Shame," which questioned the historical links between slave-era maroons in Brazil and their post-1988 descendants. Price argued that remanescentes de quilombos in Brazil differed from the Saramaka of Suriname—a maroon population he had long studied—in one major respect: few of the Afro-Brazilian communities that mobilized for land and legal recognition in accordance with Article 68 included the actual descendants of maroons (Price 1998, 238; 2002). He wrote: "Despite the existence of hundreds of maroon communities in Brazil during the era of slavery, present-day Brazil is not home to the kind of maroon communities—with clear historical continuities to slave era rebel communities and with deep historical conscious and semi-independent political organization—that still flourish in other parts of the Americas (Jamaica, Suriname, French Guiana, and Colombia)" (1998, 237–38).

Price listed three factors that accounted for this contrast. First, Brazil's ruling classes appeared "singularly successful" in destroying the country's hundreds (or more likely thousands) of fugitive slave settlements (Price 1998, 237). Second, the vast majority of quilombos blended into the surrounding population in the decades preceding abolition, absorbed by an emerging black peasantry that included free blacks and plantation slaves.[2] And third, remanescentes de quilombos were no longer required to authenticate their descent from historical maroon communities to obtain legal recognition and territorial rights under Brazilian law.

Price is also correct in pointing to a historical mosaic of Afro-Brazilian experiences in the countryside. Several communities that are today recognized by the government as remanescentes de quilombos, including Pacoval in the lower Amazon rainforest, were settled by refugees fleeing quilombos that were destroyed by the Brazilian military near the end of the slave era (Funes 2016). Other remanescentes traced their origins to gifts of land from ex-masters, purchases of land by former slaves, or land grants to slaves from religious orders (*terras de santo*) (Centro de Cultura Negra do Maranhão 2002; Almeida 2011, 43).

Indeed, the legal definition of remanescente de quilombo has evolved since 1988. In a surprising twist, the Brazilian government no longer required that communities provide historical evidence attesting to their maroon ancestry (Arruti 2006; French 2009; O'Dwyer 2002; Chagas 2001; Farfán-Santos 2016). Today, the government recognizes rural black communities that live on a subsistence level and whose identities derive from their ancestral ties to the land and to their resistance to oppression.

However, in the Atlantic Forest of São Paulo state and neighboring Paraná, eighty-eight rural black communities descended from fugitive slaves and libertos managed to endure into the present day. Their survival is in part the result of geographical isolation and mastery of forest ecosystems that allowed for the social reproduction of Afro-descendant communities with historical origins in slavery and marronage, as well as social networks of support. Yet it also derives from the fact that since the nineteenth century, maroon descendants have demonstrated "clear historical continuities to slave-era rebel communities" (Price 1998, 238). Contrary to Price's assertion that remanescentes de quilombos "lacked a deep historical consciousness," this chapter shows how the communities of the Ribeira Valley harbored historical memories and even legal claims predating emancipation to challenge territorial dispossession prior to the Quilombo Law.[3] This study aims to link the histories of quilombo communities *before* 1888 to those made by their descendants *after* Article 68 in 1988. Where possible, it seeks to "see like a quilombo," rather than a state (Scott 1998).

Rebel Slaves in the Vale do Ribeira

The Vale do Ribeira is situated between two of Brazil's largest cities—São Paulo and Curitiba—covering 1.7 million hectares between the Atlantic Ocean and the Serra do Mar (Bim 2012, 19; Dos Santos and Tatto 2008). Bathed by the mighty Ribeira de Iguape River, the region is characterized by an extensive network of rivers and tributaries that crisscross the emerald landscape. The area features a tropical monsoon climate and heavy annual rainfall (Dos Santos and Tatto 2008, 8–9). Described by conservationists as

"São Paulo's Amazon," the Ribeira Valley also preserves the largest remaining concentration of the Atlantic Forest in Brazil, which covers approximately 60 percent of its territory (Resende 2002, 18).[4]

Prior to the Portuguese arrival, the Atlantic Forest, or Mata Atlântica, was one of the largest tropical rainforests on the planet, covering 150 million hectares (Dean 1995). The Mata Atlântica hosts a wide range of ecosystems, including rainforests, seasonal forests, mountain woodlands, grasslands, savannas, and mangrove forests (Da Fonseca 2005; Ribeiro et al. 2009). These environments have favored species endemism and diversity, earning the Vale do Ribeira a UNESCO designation as a "major biodiversity hotspot" (Dos Santos and Tatto 2008, 8–9).

Adventurers, settlers, and fortune hunters (*bandeirantes*) arrived in the Ribeira Valley in search of gold, silver, and Indians to enslave during the sixteenth century. In 1531, the Portuguese explorer Martim Afonso de Sousa established the coastal city of Cananéia, regarded as Brazil's oldest city, which emerged as an outpost for Portuguese expeditions to the Rio de La Plata (Dos Santos and Tatto 2008, 8–9). The Ribeira Valley quickly earned a reputation for vice, banditry, and lawlessness. The discovery of alluvial gold on the banks of the Ribeira de Iguape River lured prospectors (*garimpeiros*) to the region during the mid-seventeenth century. São Paulo's first wave of West African slaves arrived as laborers for the emerging gold rush (Carril 1995, 55).

Almost as soon as they arrived, slaves began plotting their escape. In February 1782, Martin Lopes Lobo de Saldanha, the governor of São Paulo Captaincy, ordered authorities to marshal "bush captains" (*capitães de mato*) to hunt fugitive slaves in the Ribeira Valley. "It has been brought to my attention that *negros* working in the foothill mines continue to escape into the woods, inflicting unspeakable losses upon their masters," he wrote (Arruti 2003, 50).[5] "I command the council, as soon as it receives this letter, to dispatch a regiment of bush captains, who will be properly compensated by their masters" (50).

Mountains, forests, rivers, waterfalls, caverns, and abysses provided safe haven to rebel slaves (Oliveira, Stucchi, et al. 2000, 61). Captives escaped the mines with such frequency that prospectors named local streams, waterfalls, and mountain ranges after quilombos. Fugitives demonstrated remarkable resourcefulness, raising temporary, clandestine settlements in the Serra do Penedo mountains or near river banks that subsisted on hunting, farming, fishing, and foraging (Arruti 2003, 50). Escaped slaves continued to pan for gold while in hiding, and local authorities referred to runaways as *lavradores d'ouro*, or "gold farmers" (Rath 1856, 25). Runaways traded with their neighbors and formed various relationships with settlers and the small free population of color on the frontier.

Authorities lacked the manpower and resources to stanch the rash of desertions in the Vale do Ribeira.[6] Further, gold deposits exhausted by the 1790s, causing many prospectors to abandon the region (Vieira, Stucchi, et al. 1998). The Ribeira Valley descended into chaos as garimpeiros clashed over control of the last productive mines (Rath 1856, 25). Slaves seized the opportunity to purchase their freedom with gold acquired from their labor, a common practice associated with Brazil's mining-slave complex at the turn of the nineteenth century (Vieira, Stucchi, et al. 1998, 10–12; Karasch 1999, 154). Many slaves were abandoned by their masters (Vieira, Stucchi, et al., 19–20). Still others escaped to the sanctuary of the highland rainforests.

Carlos Rath, a German-born geographer who traveled to the Vale do Ribeira decades later in 1855, wrote: "The gold miners who lived there killed each other off and that is why the whites disappeared and the blacks remain near the Guaporunduva [sic] River, Anhanguera [sic], the Serra do Quilombo [mountains] etc., to this day. The slaves escaped these tragic places filled with dark memories. The Serra do Quilombo was, for a certain time, a hideout for a number of slaves, all of whom were miners that killed their masters in the fields near Pilões and Sant'Anna [sic], and who found asylum in the mountains."[7] The collapse of the mining economy triggered white flight, blazing a path to freedom for the enslaved (Vieira, Stucchi, et al., 14).

Ivaporunduva and the Emergence of the "Black Countryside"

Fugitive slaves and free persons congregated in Ivaporunduva, the region's oldest remanescente de quilombo community, during the early decades of the nineteenth century (Barboza 1993, 24; Dos Santos and Tatto 2008, 10). Arraial d'Ivaporunduva (Camp Ivaporunduva) was a thriving boomtown during the mid-eighteenth century, located alongside the Ribeira de Iguape River 55 kilometers west from the center of Xiririca (Vieira, Stucchi, et al. 1998, 12–13; Dos Santos and Tatto 2008, 93). The name Ivaporunduva signifies "river of abundant fruit" (*rio de muito vaporu*), a reference to the lush riparian forests and thick jungle vegetation that covers the landscape (Vieira, Stucchi, et al., 12). Ethnographer Guilherme dos Santos Barboza estimates that two hundred people occupied Ivaporunduva during the gold rush and that the majority were African slaves.[8] The population of Ivaporunduva shrunk by half following the exhaustion of fluvial deposits during the 1790s (Barboza interview 2015). Those who remained were predominately Afro-descendants.

Joanna Maria was a native of Minas Gerais and the widow of a Portuguese miner, João Marinho. She was Ivaporunduva's largest slave owner (Vieira,

Stucchi, et al. 1998, 12–13). Her slaves included members of the Marinho, Furquim, Pupo, Pereira, Machado, Moraes, and Da Costa families, surnames that remain common in Ivaporunduva and neighboring remanescente communities today (Barboza 1993, 61). Bondsmen panned for gold and tended to provision grounds called *roças*. Joanna Maria emancipated her slaves and gave them lands before her death at the age of ninety in April 1802 (61).

During the nineteenth century, settlers in the Vale do Ribeira turned to the production of rice for export to Rio de Janeiro and Santos following the decline of mining. The emergence of the rice economy signaled the arrival of new captives, who toiled on rice plantations in the wetlands of Iguape and Xiririca. There were fifty-four landowners and 255 slaves in Xiririca in 1801. By 1836, there were 102 landowners and 523 slaves, an increase of 87 percent and 105 percent, respectively (Valentin 2012, 171). The share of African-born slaves in Xiririca increased as well, from 8 percent to 30 percent of the enslaved population (167). Planters annually exported 120,000 bushels of rice to Rio de Janeiro by 1856.[9]

The boom afforded new opportunities to black subsistence farmers in Ivaporunduva. They traversed the Ribeira de Iguape River by canoe to trade surplus crops for hard currency and material goods at outposts that dotted the shoreline. The expanding marketplace fostered social interactions between farmers in Ivaporunduva, free persons of color, and plantation slaves, who found safe haven in the remote riverside village. Bernardo Furquim, an African-born fugitive slave, arrived in Ivaporunduva from Campinas with his wives, Coadi and Rosa Machado, during the 1830s (Carvalho 2007). Gregório Marinho, a slave who toiled on the Caiacanga Plantation in Xiririca, escaped to Ivaporunduva during the 1840s (Arruda 2003, 15). Ivaporunduva occupied the nexus of the campo negro (black countryside) in the Vale do Ribeira, a vast network of social and commercial relationships that bound together maroons, free persons of color, and plantation slaves during the nineteenth century (Gomes 2016, 238–39).

In 1791, the Chapel of Our Lady of the Black Rosary (Capela da Nossa Senhora do Rosário Preto) was built in Ivaporunduva by Joanna Maria's slaves. Scholars have studied how baptism and membership in religious confraternities (*irmandades*) catalyzed the formation of kinship ties that helped Afro-descendants to traverse the precarious boundary between freedom and enslavement in nineteenth-century Brazil.[10] The same was true in Ivaporunduva, where the Brotherhood of Our Lady of the Black Rosary raised funds for manumission and administered religious rites and sacraments to slaves and free persons (Kishimoto et al. 2015, 19; Reis 2013, 39–41, 51; Ramos 2016, 148–50).

José Francisco de Mendonça, a Franciscan friar in Xiririca, traveled to Ivaporunduva to perform hundreds of baptisms between 1817 and 1828 (Nossa Senhora da Guia Baptismal Records, 1817–28). The majority of baptisms involved the offspring of "*pardos livres*" (free persons of mixed ancestry) and "*pretos livres*" (free blacks). Newborn slaves and African-born adult captives received the sacrament of baptism at Nossa Senhora do Rosário Preto as well. The careful selection of godparents allowed rural Afro-Brazilians to expand their networks of kinship and solidarity. *Compadrio* (godparentage) acted as self-defense against slave hunters, cruel overseers, and local landowners. For instance, José Marinho and Esmaria da França chose two associates of their former master, Joanna Maria, to be godparents to their infant son, Francisco, in 1817. Perhaps José Marinho and Esmaria de França sought to curry the favor of local rice planters against bush captains who preyed upon former slaves lacking manumission papers in the Ribeira Valley (Luz 2013, 26).

Free persons in Ivaporunduva also chose plantation slaves as godparents. Theodino da Costa and his wife, Catharina da Costa, were the former slaves of Manoel Bento Dias, a rice planter from Xiririca. They selected Manoel Morato and Florinda Dias, both slaves of Dias, as the godparents of their son, Fabiano, in April 1818. By doing so, Theodino and Catharina da Costa formalized the relationships they established with other slaves on the plantation. In the process, the couple strengthened the social and commercial links that tied Ivaporunduva to the enslaved population in the Xiririca lowlands. Ivaporunduva remained embedded within the dominant socioeconomic and religious institutions of nineteenth-century Brazil, much as their descendants maintained ties with political activists, government agents, and commercial middlemen during the twentieth and twenty-first centuries.

Still, the Vale do Ribeira remained historically inaccessible and vulnerable. Floods submerged entire plantations in the lowlands in 1807, 1809, 1826, 1833, and 1858 (Paes 2014, 53). "How tragic it was to watch as the people tried to escape in their canoes with all their earthly possessions, searching for higher ground, only to discover that the [flood] waters had gotten there first," a Catholic priest in Xiririca wrote to the Bishop of São Paulo in 1809.[11] The standing water attracted mosquitoes and rats, spreading disease. "The excessive rains brought millions of rats who destroyed everything," Carlos Rath wrote in 1856. "Rats, sparrows, pigeons, and lizards all brought plagues. Their presence here is dangerous and often fatal to the workers, especially the slaves" (53).

Annual exports of rice to Rio de Janeiro plummeted from 160,000 bushels in 1857 to 70,000 bushels after a devastating flood in 1858 and never recovered to previous levels (Cúria Metropolitana cited in Paes 2014, 55). To make matters worse, mudslides destroyed the Valo Grande Canal, built to facilitate the passage of steamboats transporting rice from Xiririca to Iguape during the late 1830s. By 1876, large ships could no longer access the canal due to the accumulation of thick sediment and debris, which severed regional trade with Santos and Rio de Janeiro (55). Without canals, railroads, or dependable roads, economic growth in the Vale do Ribeira lagged far behind the rest of São Paulo and the coffee-rich Paraíba River Valley, in particular (56).

Locals had little choice but to traverse the Ribeira de Iguape River by raft or canoe, a perilous proposition. João Martins da Silva, a farmer from the village of Juquiá in the Baixada Ribeira, complained to the bishop of São Paulo of the dangers of traveling to Xiririca to attend Sunday Mass. "I risk my soul as a parishioner of Xiririca, not only because the parish is so far away but [also] because navigating the river is costly and extremely difficult, particularly when the [flood] waters flow from the mountaintops and empty into the river."[12]

Shipwrecks and drownings occurred with such frequency that officials in São Paulo encountered difficulties in filling administrative positions in the Ribeira Valley with qualified candidates. In 1846, Joaquim de Moura Rolim of Iporanga rejected an appointment to become inspector of schools in Xiririca. "I would need to travel thirty leagues in a single day from my farm in Iporanga just to reach the village of Xiririca. The return [voyage] would take two-and-a-half days and it is extremely dangerous. I would risk my life, as well as the lives of my slaves [cativos] in the journey" (cited in Paes 2014, 46). While posing obstacles to planters and local authorities, the Ribeira de Iguape River and its myriad tributaries formed a superhighway for fugitive slaves, who risked their lives in pursuit of freedom.

Gregório Marinho and the quilombo of Pedro Cubas

Few details exist about the life and times of Gregório Marinho, the founding father of Pedro Cubas, a quilombo community formed near Ivaporunduva during the mid-nineteenth century. According to oral history, Gregório Marinho toiled as a slave in the fields of the Caiacanga, the largest rice plantation in the municipality of Xiririca. He escaped Caiacanga by canoe and reached the sanctuary of Ivaporunduva during the 1840s (Vieira, Stucchi, et al. 1998, 12–13). His name first appears in the historical record in 1849 when he and his wife, Felicia, baptized their daughter, Rosa, at the Chapel of Our Lady of the Black Rosary in Ivaporunduva (Casa Paróquial de Eldorado 1813–98). According to the baptismal registry, Marinho resided with his family near Múndeo Creek, one of twenty-six streams that cross the community of Ivaporunduva (Casa Paróquia de Eldorado 1813–98). Marinho's brother, Vicente, also resided in Ivaporunduva with his wife, Maria Antonia, and their son, Generoso (Vieira, Stucchi, et al. 1998, 12–13). The Marinhos were small farmers who planted beans, rice, cassava, corn, yams, sweet potatoes, and sugar cane on family owned garden plots in the Atlantic Forest.

Gregório Marinho's story then took a surprising turn. In 1856, he purchased a small farm (*sitio*) named Catas Altas from his former master, Miguel Antonio Jorge, for the price of 600 mil-réis (Vieira, Stucchi, et al., 1998, 12–13). Catas Altas was situated on the banks of the Pedro Cubas and Ivaporunduvinha Rivers approximately 34 kilometers west from the center of Xiririca (Dos Santos and Tatto 2008, 55–57). The 40-acre farm consisted of garden plots, a house for grinding manioc flour, and a rice mill. In 1857, Vicente Marinho purchased a property named Pai Romão near his brother's farm at the confluence of the Pedro Cubas and Penteado Rivers (Vieira, Stucchi, et al. 1998, 12–13). The circumstances surrounding the Marinho family's purchase of Catas Altas and Pai Romão remain unclear, but their story reveals several clues about the nature of rural Afro-Brazilian communities descended from fugitive slaves in the Vale do Ribeira during the nineteenth century.

First, Afro-descendants capitalized upon the collapse of the rice economy to expand their territorial control during the 1850s and 1860s. Historian Agnaldo Valentin explained how floods, in addition to the rising costs of slaves following the cessation of the Atlantic slave trade, devastated small- and medium-sized planters, who represented the majority of property owners in the Ribeira Valley (Valentin 2012, 169, 55). Racked by debt, planters mitigated their losses by selling their farms and slaves. By the 1870s, many small- and medium-sized planters had abandoned the Ribeira Valley, leaving behind a trail of vacant lands (*terras devolutas*) in the lowland rainforests of Xiririca and Iporanga. Free blacks and fugitive slaves settled these lands, which are today recognized by the Brazilian government as remanescentes de quilombos: Pedro Cubas, Pedro Cubas de Cima, São Pedro, Sapatu, Nhunguara, André Lopes, Maria Rosa, Porto Velho, Praia Grande, and Pilões (Dos Santos and Tatto 2008, 10–11).

Second, fugitive slaves like Gregório Marinho settled remote areas crossed by rivers and covered by dense forests. The two-day journey from Xiririca to Pedro Cubas by canoe was dangerous due to strong currents and whitewater rapids on the Ribeira de Iguape River.[13] To this day, the quilombo is accessible only by boat or by ferry, which departs from the village of Batatal (Dos Santos and Tatto 2008, 10–11). Heavy rains during the summer months

(January–March) cause the river to swell and the ferry often ceases to operate. Inaccessibility thus protected quilombos like Pedro Cubas during the final decades of slavery in Brazil. A resident of Pedro Cubas told anthropologists in 1998: "In those days, the masters gave their slaves holidays. The slaves escaped during the holidays, heading for the woods and making camp here next to the river, where they joined other people. More people escaped and joined them on the shores that they called Gregório Marinho Beach. That is how the first generation [of maroons] arrived. They started to communicate with the people of Ivaporunduva, where there were also many slaves. That's how the community [Pedro Cubas] grew."[14]

Isolation nurtured the expansion of the campo negro because it compelled Afro-Brazilian farmers to collaborate in order to survive. Smallholders like Gregório and Vicente Marinho cleared thickets in the Atlantic Forest to cultivate roças, which they maintained collectively with neighboring families: the Pupos, Pereiras, Da Costas, and Furquims (Arruda 2003, 38–40). Relying upon family labor and the *mutirão* (collective work), the Marinhos planted rice, beans, and cassava and exchanged surplus crops with their neighbors. Solidarity—cemented through marriage, compadrio, and collective work—proved necessary for survival in the hinterlands. "Our ancestors used to plant rice, beans, and corn, and they raised pigs and other animals. They used to occupy the foothills near the Peixe River, over there by the Penteado River, and all around here, really," a resident of Pedro Cubas remembered. "Everything was spread out. The people never just lived in one *bairro* [village/neighborhood]. The people married and then they would move to wherever the father-in-law lived. The people would go to live with their in-laws. It was always like that."[15]

Third, the Marinho story reveals that fugitive slaves sought official legitimation of their territorial possessions. The rapid expansion of the coffee-plantation complex in rural São Paulo ushered reforms of Brazil's traditional land and labor practices (Da Costa 2000, 78). The Land Law of 1850 attempted to rationalize landownership in the backlands and to create a free labor market by restricting smallholders' and squatters' (*posseiros*) access to land. The legislation prohibited the acquisition of vacant public lands through any means but purchase and outlawed traditional practices of acquiring land: *posse* (squatting) and *sesmarias* (royal land grants) (79). Although the Land Law of 1850 allowed posseiros to legitimize their possession of terras devolutas, they could do so only after surveying the land and paying taxes (79). In essence, the Land Law of 1850 invalidated the territorial claims of poor farmers, paving the way for the expansion of commercial agriculture in the Brazilian frontier. Yet Gregório and Vicente Marinho acquired

Catas Altas and Pai Romão through purchase and registered their plots at notarial offices (*cartórios*) in Xiririca in 1856, 1857, and 1861 (Casa Paróquia 1813–98). Decades later, their descendants brandished these deeds to defend their communities against the onslaught of government-sponsored projects to develop the Vale do Ribeira.

The Heirs of Gregório Marinho (1937–70)

Developers in São Paulo city aimed to transform the Ribeira Valley during the early twentieth century. Beginning in the 1930s, the state government of São Paulo provided 50,000 hectares of land to Japanese immigrant farm workers in the municipalities of Registro, Sete Barras, and Pariquera-Açú in the Baixada Ribeira (Sampaio and Furlan 1993). Each family received 24 hectares to cultivate rice and tea, as well as technical assistance and education (Sampaio and Furlan). In the Lower Ribeira, the state government of São Paulo transformed terras devolutas into commercial enterprises for the cultivation of bananas and tea. In the mountainous Upper Ribeira, where mechanized agriculture was difficult, the government converted public lands for cattle ranching and mineral exploration (Adams, Munari, et al. 2012). The city council of Xiririca renamed the city Eldorado in an effort to court investment in lead- and silver-mining in 1948 (Dos Santos and Tatto 2008, 8). The enclosure campaign on the Ribeira frontier embroiled poor communities descended from slaves in legal battles over the rightful ownership of land and natural resources that continue to this day.

Ruy Baptista Pereira, an attorney for the São Paulo State Land Commission, wrote to Manoel Carlos da Costa Leite, the county judge in Xiririca, in April 1937 (Equipe de Articulação e Assessoria às Comunidades Negras, hereafter EAACONE 1937, 1–2). Pereira urged Leite to convene a hearing to resolve the legal status of vacant public lands in Xiririca county within sixty days. He also demanded that squatters appear in Xiririca court with proof of legal title to their plots (EAACONE, 1–2). Developers in São Paulo city had coveted 1,900 acres of "virgin forest land" that nestled the Ribeira de Iguape River between Xiririca and Iporanga. "This land is ideal for cultivating fruits and grains," Pereira wrote. "The lands are bathed by the streams that empty into the Ivaporunduvinha, Penteado, and Pedro Cubas Rivers. There are no known inhabitants in this area" (EAACONE, 1–2).

In fact, state planners had known about the presence of farming communities descended from slaves since at the least the turn of the twentieth century. In 1912, the geographer Edmundo Krug described his two-day journey by canoe from Xiririca to Ivaporunduva in an article that appeared in *Revista do Instituto Histórico e Geográfico de São Paulo* (1912).[16] Krug visited neighboring communities as well, noting Pedro Cubas's origins as a quilombo. "In one of the plantations in the region, I think it is called Pedro Cubas, if my memory serves me correctly, gold can still be found. The place was named after a slave, who, after learning from his master the art of combat, managed to escape and established residence there" (Krug 1912, 32).

The São Paulo State Land Commission pressed forward with plans to privatize 1,900 acres in the river lands despite, or more likely *because of*, the presence of poor farmers descended from slaves. Government officials vilified Afro-Brazilian peasants as obstacles to capitalist development in the Ribeira Valley, just as elites had demonized their ancestors for controlling the landscape in ways that challenged the mines and plantations central to Brazil's nineteenth-century economy. However, state officials underestimated the backlash that enclosure would inflame in the countryside. A poor farmer named José Silvério da Costa challenged the São Paulo State Land Commission's plans to seize his land in Xiririca court.

Few details exist about José Silvério da Costa's life. He was born in Pedro Cubas on June 30, 1895, the son of Bras Morato da Costa and Silvina Silvério da Costa (Casa Paróquia 1813–98). He married Edwiges Maria da Conceição, the maternal grandmother of Antonio Benedito Jorge, a prominent activist in Quilombo Pedro Cubas today (Arruda 2003, 18). He inherited two properties—Catas Altas and Pai Romão—that were located in what is today Quilombo Pedro Cubas de Cima.[17] Like the majority of rural Brazilians in the 1930s, Da Costa was illiterate and likely never attended school.[18] Yet he was also litigious, later demonstrating keen awareness of Brazilian property law. His refusal to relinquish his farms led to a protracted battle with the state government of São Paulo that culminated with Pedro Cubas and Pedro Cubas de Cima's recognition as *comunidades remanescentes de quilombos* decades after his death.

In March 1938, São Paulo State Land Commission tried to evict José Silvério da Costa from Catas Altas and Pai Romão, alleging the farms were located on vacant state-owned lands, or *terras devolutas*.[19] The land commission's attorney, Ruy Baptista Pereira, invoked the Land Act of 1850 and the Republican Constitution of 1891 to defend the state government's authority to place *terras devolutas* up for auction to private bidders.[20] Pereira assumed that José Silvério da Costa, like many poor farmers in Brazil, lacked legal title to his land. However, Da Costa arrived in Xiririca court with a deed that belonged to Gregório Marinho, the fugitive slave who settled Catas Altas in 1856. Da Costa asked the judge to rescind the order of eviction on behalf of his family and neighbors, described by the court as the "unnamed heirs of Gregório Marinho."[21]

Furious, Pereira challenged the veracity of José Silvério da Costa and his neighbors: "All this talk about Gregório Marinho was brought up by the attorney representing José Silvério da Costa and the 'OTHERS,' who aren't even related to each other! These people claim to be descendants of Gregório, who owned these lands. But how can this be true if Gregório was never the proprietor of the lands in this perimeter? ... Did José Silvério da Costa bring proof of a title in his [own] name? No. Did he demonstrate that he was the heir of Gregório Marinho? No. Did he prove that Gregório was even the owner of these lands? No. Your honor, he [José Silvério da Costa] doesn't have title. He does not have possession [*posse*]. He cannot be recognized as the proprietor of the land in question."[22]

Pereira's tactics were effective. He calculated that the defendants lacked documentation to substantiate their descent from Gregório Marinho. The Constitution of 1891 mandated civil registries of births, deaths, and marriages where previously only ecclesiastical registries had existed (Fraga 2016, xxi).[23] In the Ribeira Valley, where the presence of state institutions was historically weak, church marriages and common-law marriages prevailed. Although José Silvério da Costa and Edwiges Maria da Conceição were married in the Catholic Church, they were not *legally* married because they never recorded their marriage in a civil registry (French 2009, 44–45; Fraga, xv). Pereira seized upon the couple's failure to legalize their marriage to cast doubt upon their relation to Gregório Marinho and to disqualify their claims to Catas Altas. This stratagem foreshadowed how landowners challenged the veracity of rural communities' claims to maroon ancestry in Brazil in the aftermath of Article 68.[24]

The São Paulo State Land Commission opposed José Silvério da Costa's territorial claims on a technicality. Under Decree 6473/1938, which regulated the privatization of terras devolutas in São Paulo state, squatters could be recognized as legal proprietors if they demonstrated "uninterrupted dominion" of the land for a period of at least thirty years, a condition known in Brazil as *usucapião* (adverse possession) (Governo do Estado de São Paulo 1938). The law also required that squatters provide the State Treasury of São Paulo and the Judiciary Section of the São Paulo Land and Colonization Board with "justification" (*justificação*) of their dominion (Governo do Estado). Justification obliged squatters to survey the land themselves and to conduct an inventory of the property, which included the dates of occupation, the legal names of all occupants, the type and quantity of crops and livestock, the projected costs of improvements, and an estimate of the property's market value (Governo do Estado). Da Costa and his neighbors failed to demonstrate long-term dominion of Catas Altas, Pereira argued, because the 1861 deed belonged to Gregório Marinho and no one else. Nor could farmers in Pedro Cubas fulfill the obligations of justificação due to their "absolute lack of financial resources."[25]

In 1940, a judge ordered the eviction of José Silvério da Costa and the heirs of Gregório Marinho from Catas Altas. The farmers protested the court's decision. Their public defense attorney, Haroldo de Barros Cardoso, wrote a scathing letter to the Xiririca magistrate. "It seems unbelievable to me that the state of São Paulo would strain so hard to deny a Brazilian family the right to defend the lands [upon which] they have worked so hard."[26] In August 1941, Da Costa and his neighbors appealed the court's decision.[27] For the next thirty years, the case of the *State Treasury of São Paulo v. José Silvério da Costa and Unnamed Heirs of Gregório Marinho* stalled in the São Paulo State Court of Appeals, the byproduct of a Brazilian legal system that intended to perpetuate rather than resolve conflicts over land.[28]

What insights into quilombos' histories and legacies can we draw from the legal battle between the government of São Paulo and the heirs of Gregório Marinho? First, poor farmers descended from runaway slaves used historical memory and legal claims predating emancipation to challenge territorial dispossession decades prior to the enactment of Article 68 (De la Torre 2012, 34). A growing body of scholarship has examined how slaves and free persons throughout the Americas invoked laws, jurisprudence, and legal culture to demand better treatment, freedom, and inclusion (Scott 1988; De la Fuente 2004; Fraga 2016; Chalhoub 1990, 2011; Grinberg 2002). However, these studies have focused disproportionately on cities despite the fact that slavery in Latin America was a predominately rural phenomenon. In a similar vein, research of Afro-Brazilian political activism in the twentieth century has focused on cities like Rio de Janeiro, São Paulo, and Salvador while largely ignoring the countryside (see e.g., Alberto 2011; Andrews 1991; Butler 1998; Hanchard 1998; Twine 1998; Burdick 1998; Sansone 2003). Few researchers—with the notable exception of Walter Fraga (2016), Hebe de Castro (1995), and Oscar de la Torre (2012)—have investigated *rural* Afro-Brazilians' legal struggles for land after the abolition of slavery in 1888. This is because scholars have generally assumed that rural communities descended from escaped slaves lacked the juridical basis—charters, treaties, deeds—to stake claim to territorial rights until *after* the enactment of Article 68 in 1988.

The case of José Silvério da Costa and the heirs of Gregório Marinho challenges the conventional wisdom that descendants of maroons transitioned into a rural peasantry wracked by poverty but devoid of racial and historical consciousness. Afro-Brazilian farmers in Pedro Cubas were meticulous record keepers, preserving ancestral deeds that attested to their status as legitimate proprietors. They were not alone. All throughout the Vale do Ribeira, poor farmers descended from slaves faced the threat of eviction. Like Da Costa, they appeared in court with titles that belonged to their ancestors—maroons, slaves, and self-liberated blacks—who resided in Ivaporunduva, Pedro Cubas, and the surrounding area during the nineteenth century. For instance, smallholders in Ivaporunduva claimed to be heirs of Salvador Pupo, one of Joanna Maria's former slaves ("Discriminação de Terras do 11 Perímetro" 1942). In August 1943, they furnished Salvador Pupo's 1842 deed to substantiate their long-term dominion ("Discriminação"). Another family in Ivaporunduva provided the court with an 1872 deed that belonged to José Meira Marinho, a relative of Gregório and Vicente Marinho ("Discriminação"). These circumstances indicate that rural Afro-Brazilians living in the Vale do Ribeira had perceived their rights to land as stemming from their descent from the original founders of these communities (Rappaport 1994, 31).[29]

These circumstances further suggest that rural Afro-Brazilians nurtured a collective history that they would use for legal and political battles. The descendants of fugitive slaves who faced eviction emphasized the continuous occupation of the land by families with the same surnames: Marinho, Furquim, Meira, Costa, Pupo, Vieira, Pedroso, Moraes, Araújo, Machado, Pereira, Santos, and Silva. Each of these surnames traced their origins to the original settlers of Ivaporunduva, which also included fugitive slaves Gregório Marinho and Bernardo Furquim. Xiririca court documents revealed the identities of the "unnamed heirs" of Gregório Marinho in 1963: Virgilio Silvério da Costa, Antonia Silvério da Costa, Tomé Santana da Costa, Isabela Cecilia da Costa, Sebastião Furquim, Antonia Meira, Honorato Silvério, Dulmás Silvério, Porfirio João Lourenço, Paula Antonia, and Arminda Maria da Gloria.[30] By establishing a link between themselves and their ancestors whose names appeared in the nineteenth-century deeds, the defendants demonstrated the importance of the intergenerational transmission of historical knowledge in the campo negro.

If rural Afro-Brazilians in the Vale do Ribeira did not consistently embrace quilombo-descendant identities against outsiders until after the enactment of Article 68 in 1988, we might ask: what incentives existed for Afro-descendants to claim maroon ancestry publicly during the 1930s and 1940s? The Brazilian government did not offer any kind of restitution to quilombo descendants. Further, the enduring stigma of slavery led many to conceal their enslaved pasts, compounded by their disparagement as "hicks" (Gomes 2015: 22; Fraga 2016, xiii). Indeed, Afro-Brazilians in the Vale do Ribeira confronted racial prejudice. Renato Queiróz, an anthropologist who conducted ethnographic research in Ivaporunduva during the 1970s, observed how lighter-skinned, urban denizens discriminated against the darker-skinned peoples in the countryside: "They called them 'people from the boonies,' 'people with six fingers on each hand,' 'people who don't work,' 'those that speak [Portuguese] differently.' . . . Hicks [*caipiras*] and *negros*, a double stigma, a difficult and painful reflection of our urban, industrial, Brazilian society that exploits the poor, peasants, and people of color" (1983, 26, English translation by the author).

Admittedly, the Pedro Cubas and Ivaporunduva communities' allusions to maroon history during the early decades of the twentieth century were telegraphic, especially when compared to the Saramaka Maroons of Suriname, the subject of Richard Price's historical ethnography, *First-Time* (2002). Nevertheless, José Silvério da Costa and his associates defended their longstanding occupation of the river lands by appealing to genealogical memory and by brandishing nineteenth-century documentation that belonged to a fugitive slave. Contrary to the notion that remanescentes de quilombos of Brazil "lacked the clear historical continuities to slave-era rebel communities" and the "deep historical consciousness of resistance to slavery that still flourish[es] in other parts of the Americas," the descendants of Gregório Marinho demonstrated both over the course of the twentieth century (Price 2002, 238).

Conclusions

What happened to the descendants of Gregório Marinho? José Silvério da Costa died during the 1970s. Da Costa's widow, Edwiges Maria da Conceição, and their children remained on the family farms (Arruda 2003, 18). Cesar Ferreira, a resident of Pedro Cubas de Cima, inherited part of Catas Altas. He granted permission to the Curitiba-based mining company, Eli, to mine for lead and bauxite on the shores of the Pedro Cubas River. During the 1980s, Abel Bernardino de Santos, an investor from Jundiaí, evicted the descendants of José Silvério da Costa and Edwiges Maria da Conceição from Catas Altas and Pai Romão (18). Residents told anthropologists in 2002, "He [Abel Bernardino de Santos] invaded and seized the land through force, with armed thugs [*capangas*]. They burned houses to the ground and there were deaths. Many people sold their lands out of fear. Dito Chapéu [a resident] was evicted more than once, and so were Antonio Benedito Jorge and Adão

Rolim Dias" (18). As of 2018, farmers in Pedro Cubas and Pedro Cubas de Cima are still fighting to reclaim their ancestral lands.

The expulsion of quilombo descendants coincided with an array of government projects to colonize the Vale do Ribeira during the 1970s and 1980s. The expansion of the BR-116 Federal Highway, which linked São Paulo to Curitiba, and the creation of SP State Road 165, which connected Eldorado (formerly Xiririca) to Iporanga, produced a speculative bubble in the region (Dos Santos and Tatto 2008, 8–9). The arrival of cattle ranchers, banana farmers, and mining companies led to violent clashes with small farmers, which included the descendants of quilombos. In 1982, Carlitos da Silva, a community activist from what is today Quilombo São Pedro and a descendant of fugitive slave Bernardo Furquim, was assassinated by thugs working for Francisco Tibúrcio, a rancher from São Paulo.[31] The creation of state parks and enactment of environmental restrictions on subsistence farming in the Atlantic Forest also posed challenges to maroon descendants, whose livelihoods came under attack (Adams, Munari, et al. 2012). In 1989, the proposed construction of four hydroelectric dams—Tijuco Alto, Batatal, Itaóca, and Funil-threatened to flood 11,000 hectares of rainforest and submerge five communities descended from escaped slaves that occupy the banks of the Ribeira de Iguape River: Praia Grande, André Lopes, Nhunguara, Sapatu, and Ivaporunduva (Pinto 2014, 10–11).

The dam proposal proved a catalyst for Afro-Brazilian political mobilization in the Vale do Ribeira during the 1990s. The descendants of maroons gained the support of new allies—left-wing politicians, urban black activists, conservationists, and progressive Catholics—who backed their fight against territorial dispossession. Maria Sueli Berlanga and Ângela Biagioni, Sisters of Jesus the Good Shepherd nuns (shepherdesses, or *pastorinhas*), founded MOAB (Movimentos dos Ameaçados por Barragens, Movement of Those Threatened by Dams) in Eldorado. The nuns helped to organize rural black communities in opposition to the dams while pursuing legal action against the state government of São Paulo. In 1991, MOAB coordinated a "consciousness-raising campaign" to educate rural black communities about Article 68 and its implications.[32]

Afro-descendant farmers and fishermen in communities like Ivaporunduva, São Pedro, and Pedro Cubas, supported by MOAB, demanded legal recognition and territorial rights as "remanescentes de quilombos" during the early 1990s. They transformed a historical memory of exploitation into a moral appeal and legal claim to pressure the Brazilian government to recognize their dominion of ancestral lands based on resistance to slavery. At town hall meetings and public demonstrations in São Paulo, Curitiba, and Brasília, the descendants of Gregório Marinho linked their contemporary battles for territorial autonomy to their ancestors' struggle for freedom. A protest song, "Por quê o negro mora lá?" ("Why does the *negro* live out there?"), composed by Dona Jovita Furquim de França of São Pedro, displays how these historical legacies of resistance to slavery and white supremacy continue to shape maroon identities in the twenty-first century: "Why does the *negro* live out there? Why does the *negro* live out there? / They are wise black folk, the descendants of wise black folks, and that's why they *still* live there. / We are people of the *quilombo* and we carry on our shoulders the marks of slavery. / That's why we are fighting this war to defend our lands, and we will never surrender! / No, we will never surrender! / Why do black folk live out there? Why do black folk live out there? / We are black warriors who trust in our Lord, who comes to our aid in this battle to defend our lands."[33]

Like their ancestors, rural Afro-Brazilians in the Vale do Ribeira have also taken action through the courts to defend their lands. In 1994, Ivaporunduva became the first community to sue the Brazilian government for its failure to apply Article 68. The lawsuit was overseen by Sr. Michael Mary Nolan, an American nun and attorney working for the Archdiocesan Human Rights Commission of São Paulo, and Luiz Eduardo Greenhalgh, a human rights lawyer and activisit with the Workers' Party (Partido dos Trabalhadores, or PT).[34] The attorneys commissioned Guilherme dos Santos Barboza, an Afro-Brazilian ethnographer, to publish an anthropological study of Ivaporunduva, Praia Grande, and Pilões, which traced these communities' origins to Joanna Maria's former bondsmen and escaped slaves. Each member of the community of Ivaporunduva signed the pleading, the first of its kind in Brazil (Barboza interview, 2015). Their action to sue the Brazilian government for its failure to bestow federal benefits and collective rights to land in accordance with Article 68 marked a sea change in rural black politics in the Vale do Ribeira. As this chapter has demonstrated, the perseverance of quilombos and their descendants rested on agro-ecological mastery, social networks, and historical memories of resistance to slavery. The courtroom furnished another venue for struggle.

The 1994 lawsuit had a significant impact. On November 20, 1997, in commemorating Black Consciousness Day, President Fernando Henrique Cardoso granted collective land titles to Ivaporunduva and six other remanescentes de quilombos in Brazil (Pinto 2014, 27–28).[35] In São Paulo, Governor Mario Covas charged the São Paulo Institute of Agrarian Reform (ITESP) with certifying and titling remanescentes de quilombos that occupied vacant state-owned lands in 1996. Pedro Cubas, São Pedro, Maria Rosa, Pilões, and Galvão obtained collective titles to part of their ancestral lands by 2003. That same year, President Luiz Inácio Lula da Silva issued Decree 4.887/2003, which entrusted the Palmares Cultural Foundation with overseeing the anthropological certification of rural black communities as remanescentes de quilombos and charged INCRA, the land reform agency, with titling quilombola lands (Farfán-Santos 2016, 112–13).

Several of the descendants of José Silvério da Costa who were evicted during the 1980s returned to the region during the early 2000s (Arruda 2003, 18–19). Pai Romão, Vicente Marinho's old farm, is included in the Pedro Cubas deed. However, Catas Altas, the farm that belonged to Gregório Marinho and his heir, José Silvério da Costa, is excluded from the deed. Today, a São Paulo-based rancher occupies Catas Altas. Farmers in Pedro Cubas and neighboring Pedro Cubas de Cima have urged state officials to expel the rancher from Catas Altas, but to no avail.

The ongoing fight to reclaim Catas Altas highlights the challenges that many remanescentes de quilombos in Brazil still face nearly three decades after ratification of Article 68. Although eighty-eight communities in the Ribeira Valley have petitioned for legal recognition as remanescentes de quilombos, just forty-seven communities have obtained certification from the Palmares Cultural Foundation, a branch of the Ministry of Culture tasked with preservation of Afro-Brazilian cultural heritage.[36] Only Ivaporunduva has obtained a full title to its territory. Where remanescentes de quilombos claim private land—which is the case in Pedro Cubas and Pedro Cubas de Cima—the Brazilian government must indemnify the landowner. INCRA, the federal agency in charge of titling quilombola lands and compensating landowners, has rarely moved forward with such cases. In fact, only fifteen remanescentes de quilombos in Brazil fully occupy their lands. For the descendants of Gregório Marinho, the struggle for land and rights continues.

Notes

1. Interview with Aurico Dias, Quilombo São Pedro, March 12, 2015.

2. On formation of the black peasantry in Brazil see Stuart Schwartz, *Slaves, Peasants, and Rebels: Reconsidering Brazilian Slavery* (Urbana and Chicago: University of Illinois Press, 1992); Walter Fraga, *Crossroads of Freedom: Slaves and Freed People in Bahia, Brazil, 1870–1910* (Durham: Duke University Press, 2016); Flávio dos Santos Gomes, *Mocambos e quilombos: Uma história do campesinato negro no Brasil* (São Paulo: Claroenigma, 2015); and Hebe Maria Mattos de Castro, *Das cores do silêncio: Os significados da liberdade no Sudeste escravista, Brasil século XIX* (Rio de Janeiro: Arquivo Nacional, 1995).

(1995).

3. See Oscar de la Torre, "'The Land Is Ours and We Are Free to Do All That We Want': Quilombos and Black Rural Protest in Amazonia, Brazil, 1917–1929," *Latin Americanist* 56,

no. 4 (December): De la Torre also examined how descendants of maroons involved in land and labor disputes in the lower Amazon "imaginatively combined references to their past as maroons with claims of being the owners of the lands where they lived on the basis of custom," 34.

4. Ecologists estimate that only 7 percent of the original Atlantic Forest survives today. Approximately 21 percent of that remaining forest is located in the Ribeira Valley. See also Ribeiro, Metzger, et al. (2009, 1141–53).

5. Arquivo Público do Estado de São Paulo (AESP), Documento 4, "Para a Câmara da Vila de Apiahy," vol. 83, p. 71. Source cited in Arruti (2003, 50).

6. For analysis of maroon communities and their participation in colonial mining economies in Brazil, see Carlos Magno Guimarães, "Mining, Quilombos, and Palmares: Minas Gerais in the Eighteenth Century," in *Freedom by a Thread: The History of Quilombos in Brazil*, ed. João José Reis and Flávio dos Santos Gomes (New York: Diasporic Africa Press, 2016), 120–42.

7. Arquivo do Equipe de Articulação e Assesoria às Comunidades Negras do Vale do Ribeira (hereinafter, EAACONE), Carlos Rath, "Descrição da região fluvial da Ribeira de Iguape," 1855–56.

8. Interview with Guilherme dos Santos Barboza, São Paulo, August 12, 2015. Subsequently referred to as "Barboza interview 2015."

9. Arquivo do Estado de São Paulo (AESP), Ofício da Câmara de Xiririca (1856) ao Presidente da Província de São Paulo. Ofícios diversos. "Xiririca (ano 1822/1843–1856)," Ordem 1339, Lata 544. Cited in Paes (2014, 39).

10. For more on the Brotherhood of Nossa Senhora do Rosário Preto, see Alexandre Kishimoto et al., *O Reinado da Irmandade de Nossa Senhora do Rosário do Jatobá: Belo Horizonte, MG* (São Paulo: Edições Acervo Cachuera, 2015), 19–21. See also Donald Ramos, "The Quilombo and the Slave System in Eighteenth Century Minas Gerais," in *Freedom by a Thread: The History of Quilombos in Brazil*, eds. João José Reis and Flávio dos Santos Gomes (New York: Diasporic Africa Press, 2016), 147. On the significance of baptism and *compadrio* for slaves and free blacks in colonial and nineteenth-century Brazil, see João José Reis, *Death Is a Festival: Funeral Rites and Rebellion in Nineteenth-Century Brazil* (Chapel Hill: University of North Carolina Press, 2013), 91; and Luis Nicolau Parés, *The Formation of Candomblé: Vodun History and Ritual in Brazil* (Chapel Hill: University of North Carolina Press, 2013), 49–51; and James Sweet, *Recreating Africa: Culture, Kinship, and Religion in the Afro-Portuguese World, 1441–1770* (Chapel Hill: University of North Carolina Press, 2003), 46–47.

11. Cúria Metropolitana, Pasta da Freguesia de Xiririca. Source cited in Paes (2014, 54).

12. Livro de Tombo de Xiririca (1813–98), Paróquia de Iguape (SP). Source cited in Paes (2014, 47).

13. Arquivo do Estado de São Paulo (AESP), Ofícios Diversos Xiririca, Ordem 130, Lata 545. Source cited in Pães (2014).

14. Oral history cited in Vieira, Stucchi, et al. (1998), 12.

15. Ibid.

16. Krug's description of Pedro Cubas is substantiated by the testimony of Sebastião Furquim, a resident of Quilombo Pedro Cubas de Cima. The transcript can be found in Francisco de Arruda Sampaio, and Sueli Ângelo Furlan. *Government Policies, Agriculture, and Deforestation in Brazil: An Introductory Approach through Five Case Studies* (São Paulo: Instituto de Pesquisas Ambientais, 1993), 20–21.

17. EAACONE, "Memorial descritivo do imóvel denominado "Catas Altas," situado no Ribeirão do Pedro Cubas, deste município e comarca, pertencentes aos herdeiros do falecido Gregório Marinho, representados pelo herdeiro José Silvério da Costa," May 1937.

18. EAACONE, "Cartório do Primeiro Ofício e do Registro Geral de Imóveis e Hipotecas," May 19, 1951.

19. EAACONE, "Memorial Descritivo do 11 Perímetro do Município de Xiririca, Distrito de Paz de Itaúna, Comarca de Xiririca, nos termos do Artigo 6 do Decreto 6473 de 30 de maio de 1934," January 18, 1937.

20. On Brazilian property law and the Republican Constitution of 1891, see James Holston, "The Misrule of Law: Land and Usurpation in Brazil," *Comparative Studies in Society and History* 33, no. 4 (October 1991): 695–725.

21. EAACONE, Haroldo de Barros Cardoso, "Por Artigos de Contestação dizem os herdeiros de Gregório Marinho (José Silvério da Costa e outros) Contra a Fazenda do Estado de S. Paulo, por este e na melhor forma de direito o seguinte," June 30, 1938.

22. EAACONE, "Carta do Estado de São Procuradoria de Terras ao Secretária da Justiça e Negócios do Interior," January 24, 1940. Translation by the author.

23. For more on state-issued identification cards in Brazil, see Brodwyn Fischer, *A Poverty of Rights: Citizenship and Inequality in Twentieth-Century Rio de Janeiro* (Stanford: Stanford University Press, 2008), 120–25; and Peter Houtzager and Marcus Kurtz, "The Institutional Roots of Popular Mobilization: State Transformation and Rural Politics in Brazil and Chile, 1960–1995," *Society for Comparative Study of Society and History* 42, no. 2 (2000): 394–424.

24. For more about external (and internal) accusations of remanescentes de quilombos as "racial frauds," see Jan Hoffman French, *Legalizing Identities: Becoming Black or Indian in Brazil's Northeast* (Chapel Hill: University of North Carolina Press, 2009), 106–13; see also Elizabeth Farfán-Santos, *Black Bodies: The Politics of Quilombolismo in Contemporary Brazil* (Austin: University of Texas Press, 2016), 112–32.

25. EAACONE, Haroldo de Barros Cardoso, "Razões finais dos réus José Silvério da Costa e Outros Herdeiros de Gregório Marinho," May 6, 1940.

26. Ibid.

27. EAACONE, Haroldo de Barros Cardoso, "Razões dos Apelados José Silvério da Costa e Outros Herdeiros de Gregório Marinho," November 12, 1941.

28. Holston (1991, 695) examined how parties involved in land conflicts in Brazil used the law's complications to their advantage, particularly competing legislation that simultaneously legalized and later criminalized the practice of *posse*, or squatting. He argued that attorneys on both sides "expertly manipulated the judicial bureaucracy so that charge and countercharge circulated through the court [system] for many years until an informal settlement regarding ownership could be reached," 703.

29. Rappaport examined how Cumbal Indians in the southern highlands of Colombia couched their claims to ancestral lands with appeals to genealogical memory and references to their descent from the original Indigenous founders of their communities. See Joanne Rappaport, *Cumbe Reborn: An Andean Ethnography of History* (Chicago: University of Chicago Press, 1994).

30. EAACONE, "Cartório do Primeiro Ofício e do Registro Geral de Imóveis e Hipotecas," May 30, 1963.

31. Interview with Aurico Dias, Quilombo São Pedro, March 12, 2015.

32. Interview with Maria Sueli Berlanga, Eldorado, August 17, 2015.

33. Instituto Socioambiental (ISA), Video Testimony, "Sementes de Quilombos," August 2016, www.youtube.com/watch?v=J6nMulSoBvw&t=705s.

34. Interview with Sr. Michael Mary Nolan, São Paulo, August 24, 2015.
35. Those six other communities were Trombetas (Pará), Pacoval (Pará), Agua Fria (Pará), Mocambo (Sergipe), Rio das Rãs (Bahia), and Kalungas (Goiás).
36. "Certidões expedidas às comunidades remanescentes de quilombos (CRQs) atualizada até a portaria no. 104/2016, publicada no DOU de 20/05/2016," accessed February 15, 2017, www.palmares.gov.br/wp-content/uploads/2016/06/COMUNIDADES-CERTIFICADAS.pdf.

Secondary Source Bibliography

Adams, Cristina, Lucia Chamlian Munari, et al. "Diversifying Incomes and Losing Landscape Complexity in Quilombola: Shifting Cultivation Communities of the Atlantic Rainforest (Brazil)." *Human Ecology*, vol. 41 (September 2001): 119–37.
Alberto, Paulina. *Terms of Inclusion: Black Intellectuals in Twentieth-Century Brazil*. Chapel Hill: University of North Carolina Press, 2011.
Andrade, Anna Maria, and Nilto Tatto. *Inventário cultural de quilombos do Vale do Ribeira*. São Paulo: Instituto Socioambiental, 2013.
Andrade, Tânia, et al., eds. *Negros do Ribeira: Reconhecimento étnico e conquista do território*. São Paulo: ITESP, 2000.
Andrews, George Reid. *Blacks and Whites in São Paulo, Brazil, 1888–1988*. Madison: University of Wisconsin Press, 1991.
Arruda, Rinaldo Sergio Vieira. "Relatório técnico-científico sobre os remanescentes da Comunidade de Pedro Cubas de Cima, Município de Eldorado, SP." São Paulo: ITESP, 2003.
Arruti, José Mauricio. *Mocambo: Antropologia e história do processo de formação quilombola*. São Paulo: Edusc, 2006.
Arruti, José Mauricio. "Relatório técnico científico sobre os remanescentes da Comunidade de Quilombo de Cangume, Município de Itáoca, SP." São Paulo: ITESP, 2003.
Barboza, Guilherme dos Santos. "Relatório técnico-científico sobre as organizações descendentes de quilombos de Ivaporunduva, Praia Grande, e Pilões: Vale do Ribeira, São Paulo." São Paulo: CABEPEC, 1993.
Bim, Ocimar José Baptista. "Mosaico de Jacupiranga: Vale do Ribeira, São Paulo: Conservação, conflitos, e soluções socioambientais." MA thesis, Universidade de São Paulo, 2012.
Burdick, John. *Blessed Anastácia: Women, Race, and Popular Christianity in Brazil*. New York: Routledge Press, 1998.
Butler, Kim. *Freedoms Given, Freedoms Won: Afro-Brazilians in Post-Abolition São Paulo and Salvador*. New Brunswick: Rutgers University Press, 1998.
Carneiro, Edison. *O quilombo dos Palmares*. Rio de Janeiro: Civilização Brasileira, 1966.
Carril, Lourdes de Fátima. "Terras de negros no Vale do Ribeira: Territorialidade e resistência." MA thesis, Universidade de São Paulo, 1995.
Casa Paróquia de Eldorado, São Paulo. *Livro de Tombo de Xiririca (1813–1898)*. Paróquia Eldorado, SP.
Centro de Cultura Negra do Maranhão e Sociedade Maranhense de Direitos Humanos. *Terras de preto no Maranhão: Quebrando o mito do isolamento*. São Luiz: SMDDH/CCN-MA, 40–81, 2002.
Chagas, Miriam de Fátima. "A política do reconhecimento dos 'Remanescentes das Comunidades dos Quilombos.'" *Horizontes Antropológicos* 7 (2001): 209–35.

Chalhoub, Sidney. "The Precariousness of Freedom in a Slave Society (Brazil in the Nineteenth Century)." *IRSH*, no. 56 (2011): 405–439.

Chalhoub, Sidney. *Visões da liberdade: Uma história das últimas décadas da escravidão na corte*. São Paulo: Companhia das Letras, 1990.

Comissão Pró-Índio de São Paulo. Terras quilombolas. "Terras tituladas." Accessed February 13, 2017. www.cpisp.org.br/terras/asp/terras_tabela.aspx.

da Costa, Emilia Viotti. *The Brazilian Empire: Myths and Histories*. Chapel Hill and London: University of North Carolina Press, 2000.

da Fonseca, Gustavo. "The Vanishing Brazilian Atlantic Forest." *Biological Conservation*, no. 34 (1985) 17–34.

de Almeida, Alfredo Wagner Berno. *Quilombos e as novas etnias*. Manaus: UEA Edições, 2011.

de Carvalho, Maria Celina Pereira. "Os bairros de São Pedro e Galvão/Vale do Ribeira: Território e parentesco." In Ministério do Desenvolvimento Agrário do Brasil (MDA), *Prêmio territórios quilombolas*. Brasília: MDA, 2007: 195–98.

de Castro, Hebe Maria Mattos. *Das cores do silêncio: Os significados da liberdade no Sudeste escravista, Brasil século XIX*. Rio de Janeiro: Arquivo Nacional, 1995.

de la Fuente, Alejandro. "Slave Law and Claims-Making in Cuba: The Tannenbaum Debate Revisited." *Law and History Review* 22, no. 2 (Summer 2004): 339–69.

de la Torre, Oscar. "'The Land Is Ours and We Are Free to Do All That We Want': Quilombos and Black Rural Protest in Amazonia, Brazil, 1917–1929." *Latin Americanist* 56, no. 4 (December 2012): 33–56.

Dean, Warren. *With Broadax and Firebrand: The Destruction of the Brazilian Atlantic Forest*. Berkeley and Los Angeles: University of California Press, 1995.

"Discriminação de Terras do 11 Perímetro da Comarca de Xiririca." *Diário Oficial do Estado de São Paulo* (August 1942): 48.

do Nascimento, Abadias. *O Quilombismo: Documentos de uma militância pan-africanista*. Petrópolis: Editora Vozes, 1980.

dos Santos, Kátia M. Pacheco, and Nilto Tatto. *Agenda socioambiental de comunidades quilombolas do Vale do Ribeira*. São Paulo: Instituto Socioambiental, 2008.

dos Santos, Patricia Scalli. "Relatório Técnico-Científico Sobre os Remanescentes da Comunidade de Quilombo de Praia Grande/Iporanga-SP." São Paulo: ITESP, 2002.

Equipe de Articulação e Assesoria às Comunidades Negras do Vale do Ribeira (Advisory Team for Black Communities of the Ribeira Valley, EAACONE). Various materials.

Farfán-Santos, Elizabeth. *Black Bodies: The Politics of Quilombolismo in Contemporary Brazil*. Austin: University of Texas Press, 2016.

Fischer, Brodwyn. *A Poverty of Rights: Citizenship and Inequality in Twentieth-Century Rio de Janeiro*. Stanford: Stanford University Press, 2008.

Fraga, Walter. *Crossroads of Freedom: Slaves and Freed People in Bahia, Brazil, 1870–1910*. Durham: Duke University Press, 2016.

Freitas, Décio. *República de Palmares: Pesquisa e comentários em documentos históricos do século XVII*. Maceió: EDUFAL, 2004.

French, Jan Hoffman. *Legalizing Identities: Becoming Black or Indian in Brazil's Northeast*. Chapel Hill: University of North Carolina Press, 2009.

Funes, Eurípides. "I Was Born in the Forest; I've Never Had an Owner." In *Freedom by a Thread: The History of Quilombos in Brazil*. Edited by João José Reis and Flávio dos Santos Gomes, 416–20. New York: Diasporic Africa Press, 2016.

Garfield, Seth. *Indigenous Struggle at the Heart of Brazil: State Policy, Frontier Expansion, and the Xavante Indians, 1937–1988*. Durham: Duke University Press, 2001.

Gomes, Flávio dos Santos. "Quilombos of Rio de Janeiro in the Nineteenth Century." In *Freedom by a Thread: The History of Quilombos in Brazil*. Edited by João José Reis and Flávio dos Santos Gomes, 222–45. New York: Diasporic Africa Press, 2016.

Gomes, Flávio dos Santos. *Mocambos e quilombos: Uma história do campesinato negro no Brazil*. São Paulo: Claroenigma.

Governo do Estado de São Paulo. Decreto-Lei 6473/1938. Articles 2 and 20, 2015.

Governo do Estado de São Paulo. *Desenvolvimento integrado do Vale do Ribeira*. São Paulo: Governo do Estado de São Paulo, 1968.

Grinberg, Keila. *O fiador dos brasileiros: Cidadania, escravidão, e direito civil no tempo de Antonio Pereira Rebouças*. Rio de Janeiro: Civilização Brasileira, 2002.

Guimarães, Carlos Magno. "Mining, Quilombos, and Palmares: Minas Gerais in the Eighteenth Century." In *Freedom by a Thread: The History of Quilombos in Brazil*. Edited by João José Reis and Flávio dos Santos Gomes. New York: Diasporic Africa Press, 2016.

Hanchard, Michael. *Orpheus and Power: The Movimento Negro of Rio de Janeiro and São Paulo, Brazil, 1945–1988*. Princeton: Princeton University Press, 1998.

Higgins, Kathleen. *Licentious Liberty in a Brazilian Gold-Mining Region: Slavery, Gender, and Social Control in Eighteenth-Century Sabará, Minas Gerais*. University Park: Penn State University Press, 1999.

Holston, James. "The Misrule of Law: Land and Usurpation in Brazil." *Comparative Studies in Society and History* 33, no 4 (October 1991): 695–725.

Houtzager, Peter, and Marcus Kurtz. "The Institutional Roots of Popular Mobilization: State Transformation and Rural Politics in Brazil and Chile, 1960–1995." *Society for Comparative Study of Society and History* 42, no. 2 (2000): 394–424.

Karasch, Mary. "The Quilombos of Gold in the Captaincy of Goiás." In *Freedom by a Thread: The History of Quilombos in Brazil*. Edited by João José Reis and Flávio dos Santos Gomes. New York: Diasporic Africa Press, 2016.

Kent, R. K. "Palmares: An African State in Brazil." *Journal of African Studies* 6, no. 2 (1965): 161–75.

Kishimoto, Alexandre, et al. *O Reinado da Irmandade de Nossa Senhora do Rosário do Jatobá: Belo Horizonte, MG*. São Paulo: Edições Acervo Cachuera, 2015.

Krug, Edmundo. "Xiririca, Ivaporunduva, e Yporanga." *Revista do Instituto Histórico e Geográfico de São Paulo*, vol. XVII (1912).

Luz, Viviane Marinho. *O quilombo Ivaporunduva e o enunciado das gerações*. São Carlos: Pedro & João Editores, 2013.

Mintz, Sidney. "A Note on the Definitions of Peasantries." *Journal of Peasant Studies* 1, no. 1 (1973): 91–106.

Moura, Clóvis. *Rebeliões da senzala: Quilombos, insurreições, guerrilhas*. Rio de Janeiro: Conquista, 1972.

O'Dwyer, Eliane Cantarino. *Quilombos: Identidade étnica e territorialidade*. Rio de Janeiro: Editora FGV, 2002.

Oliveira, A. N., Jr., Déborah Stucchi, et al. "Comunidades negras de Ivaporunduva, São Pedro, Pedro Cubas, Sapatu, Nhunguara, André Lopes, Maria Rosa, e Pilões." In *Negros do Ribeira: Reconhecimento étnico e conquista do território*. Edited by Tânia Andrade et. al. São Paulo: ITESP, 2000.

Paes, Gabriela Segarra Martins. "Ventura e desventura no Rio Ribeira de Iguape." MA thesis, Universidade de São Paulo, 2014.
"Para quem nasceu la, quilombo é termo de antropólogo: Entrevista com Guilherme dos Santos Barboza." *O Jornal de São Paulo*, September 9, 1993.
Parés, Luis Nicolau. *The Formation of Candomblé : Vodun History and Ritual in Brazil*. Chapel Hill: University of North Carolina Press, 2013.
Pinto, Maria Aparecida Mendes. *MOAB: A saga de um povo*. Eldorado: MOAB/EAACONE, 2014.
Price, Richard. *First-Time: The Historical Vision of an African American People*. Chicago: University of Chicago Press, 2002.
Price, Richard. "Scrapping Maroon History: Brazil's Promise, Suriname's Shame." *New West Indian Guide*, no. 72 (1998): 3–4.
Queiróz, Renato da Silva. *Caipiras negros no Vale do Ribeira: Um estudo antropológico econômica*. São Paulo: EduSP, 1983.
Ramos, Donald. "The Quilombo and the Slave System in Eighteenth Century Minas Gerais." In *Freedom by a Thread: The History of Quilombos in Brazil*. Edited by João José Reis and Flávio dos Santos Gomes. New York: Diasporic Africa Press, 2016.
Rappaport, Joanne. *Cumbe Reborn: An Andean Ethnography of History*. Chicago: University of Chicago Press, 1994.
Rath, Carlos. *Fragmentos geológicos e geográficos para a parte physica da estatística das províncias de S. Paulo e Paraná*. São Paulo: Imparcial, 1856.
Reis, João José. *Death Is a Festival: Funeral Rites and Rebellion in Nineteenth-Century Brazil*. Chapel Hill: University of North Carolina Press, 2013.
Reis, João José, and Flávio dos Santos Gomes, eds. *Freedom by a Thread: The History of Quilombos in Brazil*. New York: Diasporic Africa Press, 2016.
Resende, Roberto Ulisses. *As regras do jogo: Legislação florestal e desenvolvimento sustentável no Vale do Ribeira*. São Paulo: FAPESP, 2002.
Ribeiro, Milton, J. P. Metzger, et al. "The Brazilian Rainforest: How Much Is Left, and How Is the Remaining Forest Distributed? Implications for Conservation." *Biological Conservation*, no. 142 (2009): 1141–53.
"Rio Ribeira (PR/SP)." Projeto Brasil das Águas. Accessed February 13, 2017. brasildasaguas.com.br/projetos/sete-rios-2006-2007/ribeira/.
Rodrigues, Nina. *Os Africanos no Brasil*. São Paulo: Companhia Editora Nacional, 1933.
Sampaio, Francisco de Arruda, and Sueli Ângelo Furlan. 1993. *Government Policies, Agriculture, and Deforestation in Brazil: An Introductory Approach through Five Case Studies*. São Paulo: Instituto de Pesquisas Ambientais, 1993.
Sansone, Livio. *Blackness without Ethnicity: Constructing Race in Brazil*. New York: Palgrave MacMillan, 2003.
Schwartz, Stuart. *Slaves, Peasants, and Rebels: Reconsidering Brazilian Slavery*. Urbana and Chicago: University of Illinois Press, 1992.
Scott, James. *Seeing Like a State: How Certain Schemes to Improve the Human Condition Have Failed*. New Haven: Yale University Press, 1998.
Scott, Rebecca. "Exploring the Meaning of Freedom: Post-Emancipation Societies in Comparative Perspective." *Hispanic American Historical Review*, no. 68 (1988): 407–28.
Sweet, James. *Recreating Africa: Culture, Kinship, and Religion in the Afro-Portuguese World, 1441–1770*. Chapel Hill: University of North Carolina Press, 2003.

Twine, France Winddance. *Racism in a Racial Democracy*. New Brunswick: Rutgers University Press, 1998.
Valentin, Agnaldo. "Uma civilização do arroz: Agricultura, comercio, subsistência no Vale do Ribeira, 1800–1888." PhD dissertation, Universidade de São Paulo, 2012.
Vieira, Isabel G. Cristina, Déborah Stucchi, et al. "Relatório técnico-científico sobre os remanescentes da Comunidade de Ivaporunduva, Município de Eldorado, SP." São Paulo: ITESP, 1998.

Chapter Four

The Bermuda Assemblage: Toward a Posthuman Globalization

Steve Mentz

The global island-hopping expansion that accelerated out of Western Europe from the medieval period through the seventeenth century needs to be reimagined in posthuman terms. Taking as my subject the peculiar case of Bermuda, perhaps the most isolated of English-settled Atlantic islands in the early modern period, this rearticulation of the Age of Discovery deemphasizes the power of human discoverers in order to emphasize the nonhuman oceanic networks that structured European entry into non-European waters. Bermuda's story humbles human narratives of colonial expansion. Familiar figures such as Spanish, French, and English sailors, colonists, pirates, poets, and ideological champions of transatlantic settlement recede to the background, with nonhuman actants such as rock and coral peeking out above the surf.[1] The resulting "Bermuda assemblage" retells the story of English colonization as the product of multiple alliances between human and nonhuman forces. Posthuman globalization reframes the major narratives of the early history of European expansion.

The narrative of Bermuda's settlement follows well-known generic patterns, and in fact the ancient masterplot of shipwreck, disorientation, and deliverance could be considered a co-author of this history.[2] In its dominant literary form, the Virgilian epic of shipwreck imperialism brings the Trojan refugee Aeneas from North African surf to the founding of Rome; this narrative template provided the accepted script for Europeans entering the New

World. This empire-founding story hardly resembles the freedom-seeking marronage that this volume brings to light. But, as Joseph Kelly notes in the introduction, shipwreck on Bermuda provides a "hinge" between old stories about the heroic founding of Anglophone settlements in the Americas and the radical freedom-seeking of enslaved and indentured people in the New World. My posthuman shipwreck narrative does not directly take up the fates of transported Africans, Native Americans, or low-status European servants. But, in breaking open the old story of survival and colonial conquest, I hope to generate space for new histories of freedom, movement, and circulation. Rejecting the familiar fictional trajectory of the *translatio imperii*, my analysis will unpack the narrative influences of non-narrating bodies. Giving priority to a series of objects that comprise the Bermuda assemblage instead of more familiar Eurocentric factors reveals the confined structures through which sailors brought European culture across the vast global ocean. The Bermuda colony was first occupied mostly by the English men and women transported by the Virginia Company, as well as subsequently by transported Africans, Native Americans, and others. But its history is not only a human history.

My posthuman portrait of Bermuda focuses on thirteen agents assembled in roughly chronological order that together estrange traditional human histories of colonial settlement. These items also serve to reframe island encounters as ecological harbingers. As has been shown by Grove (1995), the most clearly visible examples of environmental devastation in the early historical record appear in island stories, starting in the Canaries and Cape Verde Islands and eventually traveling across the Atlantic, Indian, and Pacific basins. The late medieval narrative *Le Canarien* makes a romance epic out of the settlement of the Canaries by Norman colonists and provides a chivalric template that would inform the expansionary zeal which undergirds the settlement of Bermuda (see Wallace 2004). As Sobecki (2015) has demonstrated, voyage narratives were in no way new to post-1492 Europe. Columbus, Vasco da Gama, and other voyagers acted out established medieval scripts for maritime expansion. The imperialist project, however, changed oceanic space by subjecting islands to political control in a European manner. In the influential formulation of the Fiji-born anthropologist and theorist Epeli Hau'ofa, the pre-contact geography of "our sea of islands" placed human activity in an oceanic context that resisted the "imaginary lines across the sea" that European explorers drew as part of their colonial project (Hau'ofa 2008, 31). The work of medieval and early modern historical and cultural scholarship in relation to oceanic expansion, however, has largely focused on human factors. My reading of Bermuda in its early colonial history aims to emphasize the shaping force of nonhumans in early globalization. In reinterpreting Bermuda, I argue for a posthuman turn in premodern global and maritime studies.

Dehumanizing the colonial experience trims the sails of both old-fashioned triumphalist narratives and more recent anti-imperialist critiques. It also asks for a historical view that obviates the supposed divide between the medieval and early modern periods. The human and nonhuman networks through which the ecologies of the Americas, Europe, and Africa reintegrated themselves over the course of the late medieval and early modern periods—an event that the ecologist Crosby has called "one of the most important aspects of the history of life on this planet since the retreat of the continental glaciers"—create a lens through which the ocean-story of cultural disorientation can be re-seen (2003, 3). The stories of maroons seeking freedom and pirates preying on European shipping rise into view in this newly plural history. The consequences of what I have elsewhere called "wet globalization" (Mentz 2015, 1–24) include unthinkable human suffering, in particular among Native American and transplanted African populations. My hope in this chapter's exploration of nonhuman agency is to unpack the alien pressure of the term "wet." European, African, and American mariners encountered the alien environment of the oceanic world through an unsettling mixture of profound familiarity and fundamental incompatibility. Nearly all human cultures are maritime cultures, though the so-called "oceanic turn" in European history shows itself most clearly in Atlantic-facing communities, as Cunliffe (2001) has demonstrated. But no humans can live long on the sea, and all maritime cultures evince a healthy fear of the ocean.

In what follows, the story of the English settlement on Bermuda reorients itself around thirteen human and nonhuman actants. Some of these forces are material and others ideological, some local and others global, but all exert a shaping pressure on the second-oldest of England's American colonies. The nonhuman additions to the story, I hope, will provide material turnings through which we can reimagine old and new narratives of maritime and colonial history. The progressive encounter of European cultures with the world ocean and its islands emerges as the central collective narrative of premodern history.

1. The Gulf Stream

The single most important geophysical feature affecting Bermuda's history is not part of the island chain at all, but instead the Gulf Stream ocean current that runs just north of them. This "narrow, fast, and deep" current comprises part of the western boundary of the North Atlantic Gyre, whose clockwise-rotating system of prevailing winds and ocean currents fundamentally shaped traffic between Europe, Africa, and the Americas in the Age of Sail (Ulanski 2008). In addition to being a significant contributor to the relatively mild climate of northern Europe, the Gulf Stream and the other currents in the Gyre structured the standard routes of the Spanish *flota* to and from the New World in the sixteenth century and beyond.[3] As Quinn (1988) has noted, the return route from the Americas for most Europe-bound ships in the sixteenth century followed the Gulf Stream north out of the Caribbean before heading east with the current somewhere just past Bermuda. Ships heading north along the North American coast would often encounter headwinds, and if they turned east too soon during hurricane season, Bermuda's reefs lurked. Quinn notes that during the sixteenth century, wrecks on the island are "estimated cautiously as over thirty before 1600" (1988, 3). The location of this island in relation to the North Atlantic Gyre brought it ships and shipwrecks. The English settlers who unexpectedly arrived on Bermuda in 1609 did not directly ride this current to the island, since they were sailing west from England bound for Jamestown when they wrecked, but the island's interaction with the larger Atlantic system was controlled by the Gyre and the Gulf Stream.

2. Hogs

During the first century of Atlantic exploration and settlement by Europeans, between the initial sighting of Bermuda by a Spanish ship captained by Juan Bermudez in 1503 and permanent English settlement of the island after 1612, a population of feral hogs appears to have grown up on the island. These hogs, I submit, were key actors in making Bermuda habitable for English settlement. Stranding hogs on islands on which ships might subsequently become shipwrecked was standard practice for Spanish sailors in the sixteenth-century Atlantic world. The hog populations were designed to provide food for potential future castaways. It is not clear when hogs were landed on Bermuda; the Spanish historian Gonzalo Ferdinandez d'Oviedo y Valdez noted in 1515 that he wanted to land on the islands "to leave in the island certaine hogs for increase" but was prevented by "contrarie winds" (quoted in Wilkerson 1933, 23). Feral hogs were powerful ecological invaders, whose rapid population growth provided food for later European castaways while terraforming fragile island ecosystems. Even before the first permanent English settlement started in 1612, European contact had already released nonhuman agents that were changing Bermuda.

3. "No island is an island": Peter Martyr's 1511 Map

The first published image of Bermuda in Europe appears in a map of the Caribbean, published by Peter Martyr and printed in Seville in 1511. "La Bermuda" appears in a corner of the map, far from larger islands such as Hispaniola and Cuba, and even more distant from the American mainland. Perhaps coincidentally, the orientation of the map forces readers who are looking at the names of better-known islands to encounter the words "La Bermuda" upside down. The marginal place of this island in the Caribbean-centered arc of European colonial interest seems visually clear in this map. One reason the English could plant a colony on Bermuda as late as 1612 is that no previous European power had bothered to do so, though some evidence of a failed Spanish settlement in the mid-sixteenth century has been found. In the apt phrase of historian Jarvis (2010, 1), Bermuda surveyed the North Atlantic like the view from the "deck of a ship." It was the most oceanic and least connected of the Atlantic islands colonized by early modern Europeans (see Mentz 2015, 51–74). From this vantage point, oceanic circulation would become the central feature of Bermuda's place in European transatlantic colonization.

Bermuda's marginal history suggests a possible inversion of John Donne's famous phrase that "no man is an island." Bermuda is maximally island-like, distant from other settlements, and, by the mid-seventeenth century, relatively poor, despite a brief tobacco boom in the 1620s. Even so, Bermuda was never as isolated as Donne's famous sermon implies that islands are. The poet's well-known phrase—"every man is a piece of the continent, a part of the main"—describes human coexistence as a landed, continental phenomenon, in which each individual's participation in a divine whole obviates separation. But the sailor in the poet—Donne sailed on two voyages with Drake against the Spanish between Europe and the Azores—perhaps recognized an oceanic countermeaning in which even isolated islands such as Bermuda are not really islands in the sense of being alone in the ocean. As Hau'ofa's notion of "our sea of islands" implies, oceanic islands should be considered as connected spaces, especially in pre-contact societies. (Bermuda, however, unlike the Pacific islands about which Hau'ofa writes, appears to have been uninhabited before the arrival of Europeans.) The massive nonhuman system of currents and winds, populated in the sixteenth century by sailing ships, structured a network of connections inside which the human and nonhumans populations of Europe, Africa, and the Americas interacted.

4. Utopia

One of the most influential islands in early modern European politics and culture never existed. Thomas More coined the word *Utopia* to describe an imaginary island in 1516, invoking a Greek etymology of impossibility—*ou + topia* = "no place"—that also puns on a different a Greek compound signifying desire, *eu + topia* = "happy or fortunate place" (More 2002, xi). As Gillis (2004) observes in his study *Islands of the Mind*, the settlement of Atlantic islands entailed imaginative as well as geophysical labors. Island settlements were imagined as utopian experiments, in particular after More's fiction provided a blueprint. Islomania—the obsessive love of islands—was a premodern as well as Romantic phenomenon (see Gillis 2004 and Durrell 1960). The association of islands with wondrous and idealized spaces was not new to the sixteenth century; Pinet (2011) has explored the medieval turn to islands as sites of cultural fantasy, from the North Sea locations of Irish monasteries to the circulation of *isolarii* or island-books to, eventually, Sancho Panza's "island" government in the second part of *Don Quixote*. Expansion into the Atlantic rim, like expansion in the island chains of the Indian and Pacific basins, led to historical experiences that would shape and be shaped by powerful utopian fictions of insularity.

5. An Atlantic Hurricane: July 1609

Hurricanes are American storms. They very rarely reach even the Irish and British island outposts off the European continent (see Mentz 2015, 166–71). Created inside the North Atlantic Gyre, these storms usually form off the west coast of Africa. They gain force as they circulate westward into the warm waters of the Caribbean before either turning north toward the Gulf of Mexico or northeast up the North American coastline. Eventually the storms turn out to sea, where they usually weaken before they can circulate all the way back east to the Azores, the British Isles, or the European continent. As Hulme (1986, 93) has observed, these storms represented a radically new weather pattern for European explorers in the early modern period; the integration of the native Caribbean word "hurricane" into Spanish, French, and English epitomizes the arrival of New Word meanings into Old World systems.

The storm that shaped Bermuda's colonial history struck in July 1609. It wrecked the *Sea-Venture*, flagship of a Virginia Company fleet bound from Plymouth to Jamestown. While other vessels in the fleet continued on to

Virginia, the *Sea-Venture* was driven onto the reefs surrounding Bermuda. All 150 passengers survived the wreck, including John Rolfe and his pregnant wife, who would give birth to a daughter, named Bermuda, during the castaways' nine-month sojourn on the island. These castaways represented the first semi-permanent English settlers on the island. They were followed by a permanent colony in 1612. The history of early modern Bermuda, Virginia, and the English presence in the Atlantic owes much to the meteorological happenstance of this storm.

6. Coral

Coral stopped the *Sea-Venture*'s transatlantic voyage. Coral reefs, now bleaching in the global ocean's warming temperatures, thrive mainly in tropical waters. Bermuda's reefs are northern outliers that grow in waters warmed by the Gulf Stream. Early modern European sailors would have encountered coral primarily in the Caribbean or in Southeast Asia, though reefs also exist in mid-Atlantic islands such as the Azores and the Canaries. Coral surrounds Bermuda like a hidden mouth, the teeth of which scraped the bottoms of dozens of European ships during the sixteenth century and against which the *Sea-Venture* came to rest. An imagined coral-free history of Bermuda would lack many of the features that shaped the colony's history: no shipwrecks, no Spanish hogs, perhaps no castaways to prime the island for English settlement.

7. The Starving Time

The survivors of the *Sea-Venture* wreck spent the fall of 1609 and winter of 1610 on the island, eating hogs stranded by Spanish privateers and assorted fruits and seafood available for harvest. During that winter, the English colony at Jamestown, toward which the *Sea-Venture* had been bound, starved. Though Virginia was the place the fleet wished to reach, Bermuda proved an easier place to thrive. The historian Virginia Bernhard (2012), in her parallel study of the Virginia and Bermuda settlements, emphasizes the lack of competing native populations and mild climate of the island as contributing to the easier time the first settlers had on the island as compared to the mainland. Through the mid-1620s, Bermuda's good fortune continued, starting with an ambergris windfall and the colony's early tobacco crop's well-timed arrival on a hungry English market.[4] As Jarvis notes, "Bermuda's healthy environment and lack of a native population were perhaps most critical to its success," though he also notes the arrival even before 1619 of slave labor, probably including African veterans of the Spanish tobacco trade on the Angolan coast (Jarvis 2010, 29–33). Visions of the paradisiacal "Summer Isles," the name under which the fledgling Bermuda colony promoted itself to potential settlers in the early seventeenth century, tended to exaggerate the pleasant conditions on the island.

8. Devils

When the English first arrived in Bermuda, the storm-tossed island was thought to be the home of devils. Even Shakespeare, who adapted descriptions of the storm that wrecked the *Sea-Venture* in *The Tempest* (1611), seems to have thought so. From the decks of a burning ship in the play's second scene, Prince Ferdinand cries, "Hell is empty and all the devils are here" (Shakespeare 2011, 186). Even though the playwright's magic isle positions itself somewhat askew of geographic Bermuda, the long-circulated notion that this stormy place constituted an "Isle of Devils" appears in his play and in numerous early accounts of the island, including the first edition of Sylvester Jourdain's *A Discovery of the Bermudas, otherwise called the Ile of Devils* (London, 1610). In the aftermath of the Virginia Company propaganda promoting the English settlement of Bermuda, Jourdain's history would be retitled when it was republished in 1613, without the author's name, as *A Plain Description of the Bermudas, now called the Summer Isles* (Wright, 2013). The shift from devils to summer defines Bermuda's changing meanings in early seventeenth-century England. The crucial letter, both in Jourdain's first title and in Shakespeare's line, is the "s" in "devils"; the overflowing plurality of stormy devils threatens both Shakespeare's prince and English mariners alike. The purpose of the Somers Isles Company's propaganda was to expel the devils from these islands and make them safe for English colonization. They did so for a while, at least in print.

9. The *Deliverance* and the *Patience*

These two vessels sailed from Bermuda to Virginia in May 1610, carrying nearly all of the survivors of the *Sea-Venture* wreck. (The only exceptions were three castaways, who I discuss in relation to ambergris in the next entry.) In the ten months after the July 1609 wreck, two smaller ships were built out of Bermuda cedar and salvaged rigging from the wreck. Their seaworthiness testifies to the technical skills of the mariners and artisans who were sailing for Virginia with the Company fleet. It would become a point of Virginia Company propaganda that the castaways from Bermuda saved Jamestown; Richard Rich's twenty-two-stanza verse pamphlet *Newes from Virginia* trumpeted the arrival of the castaways' two ships to the mainland as "*The Lost Flock Triumphant*" (Rich 1610). While the starving mainland colony was arguably saved also by the near-simultaneous arrival of supplies from England, the colonists who were shipwrecked on Bermuda certainly owed their escape from isolation to these two boats. The boats' physical make-up combined local and salvaged elements; castaway William Strachey described the *Deliverance*, the first-built of the two: "The most part of her timber was cedar," but "her beams were all oak of our ruined ship" (quoted in Woodward 2009, 93). The ships that carried the castaways to Virginia brought together Old World technology to create an Old-New hybrid structure.

10. Ambergris

It may be an exaggeration to say that the English settlement on Bermuda thrived in its early years because of ambergris, a byproduct of the digestion of sperm whales, but the statement is not entirely false. This rare waxy byproduct, generally found on beaches, was highly valued for its use in manufacturing perfume. In July 1612, after the Virginia Company had expanded its charter to include Bermuda, the first group of settlers arrived on the island under the command of Governor Richard Moore. As had been the case in the settlement of Jamestown, the Company's ships, including the *Plough*, arrived with unclear plans to support the colonists arriving from England and grand illusions about the wealth of the New World. The fifty to sixty settlers who made landfall on Bermuda in 1612 included "diverse gentlemen and men of fashion," as well as a variety of artisans with more practical skills (Jarvis 2010, 17–19). On the island, they encountered three veterans of the 1609 *Sea-Venture* wreck, the so-called "Three Kings of Bermuda," who had mutinied against the rule of Sir Thomas Gates and been marooned there when Gates's party sailed for Jamestown on the *Deliverance* and *Patience* in 1610. These three mutineers, in addition to raising crops, harvesting shellfish, and hunting the feral hogs that had been left on the island by Spanish ships, had discovered a massive lump of ambergris, worth as much as £12,000. This windfall became the property of the cash-starved

Virginia Company, the Bermuda chapters of which would later separate into the Somers Isles Company, though at least one of the three marooned sailors received land on Bermuda in compensation.

The so-called "ambergris affair" motivated some complex infighting among Governor Moore, Captain Robert Davis of the *Plough*, and members of Moore's Council, including Edwin Kendell, a cousin of Sir Edwin Sandys and prominent sharer in the Virginia Company. Of the three men who had remained on Bermuda from 1609 and who had discovered the ambergris, Edward Chard appears to have been, in Moore's words, "the most masterful spirit" and the primary negotiator with the Company (Wilkinson 1933, 68). The wealth that the ambergris provided when sold in London supported the Bermuda colony in its vulnerable early days. Moore himself considered that the ambergris windfall was "the only loadstone to draw from England still more supplies" to support the colony (Wilkinson 1933, 71–73). In the medium term, Bermuda would survive and prosper because of its mild climate, plentiful seafood, and also because it was the first English colony to produce commercial tobacco in 1614 (Jarvis 2010, 18). (The source of the tobacco remains unclear, as I discuss below, but it is likely to be the same Spanish plants or seeds with which John Rolfe was then experimenting in Virginia.) Moore kept careful control of the ambergris, which he sent back to England piece by piece, husbanding the fledgling settlement. It was the ambergris itself, discovered by three marooned sailors on the island between 1610 and 1612, that enabled Bermuda to thrive.

11. *Quo fata ferunt*

The motto of the Somers Isles Company transformed a humanist reading of Virgil into a colonialist program. The motto adapts *Aeneid* 5.709, in which Aeneas is advised to voyage, "where the fates draw us in their ebb and flow" ("quo fata trahunt retrahuntque sequamur") (Virgil 1999: 520). This Latin tag imagined the founding of the Bermuda colony as part of a providential humanist narrative that transformed wandering exile into settlement and empire. This classical "westing" model was substantially Christianized from the Middle Ages to the early modern period. In Renaissance emblem culture especially, it epitomized the central purpose of the relentless expansionary narrative of progress and divine favor. This Eurocentric vision of imperial expansion has contributed to the relative lack of focus on freedom-seeking maroon societies in the New World, which this volume aims to correct.

12. Richard Norwood's 1616 Map

My posthuman history has attempted to avoid placing humans at the center of Bermuda's story, but in this case I cannot avoid using Richard Norwood's name in connection with his 1616 map of the island, which he made after conducting a survey in 1615–16. As D. K. Smith has observed, Norwood's map, which parcels out the island into geometrically regular sections, each with an English name attached to it, serves as a striking visual "act of settlement" that would make this exotic island English (Smith 2008, 157–88). The project of cartographic settlement that Smith describes would extend to literary and cultural domestication of Bermuda by English poets such as Edmund Waller and Andrew Marvell in the seventeenth century. But Norwood's map also points to the continuing need for technical skills, tools, and practices to make sense of this oceanic island. Norwood, whose other books included *A Seaman's Practice* (1637) and *Trigonometrie, or the Doctrine of Triangles* (1631), was an author and mathematical teacher who also served as schoolmaster on Bermuda from 1638–49 and again from 1658–61 (Bender 2004). His technical expertise, both mathematical and nautical, provided tools for the young colony to make use of its oceanic position. After ambergris and tobacco were exhausted, Bermuda would turn to maritime trade. Figures like Norwood would be essential to the colony's future.

13. Tobacco

It is not clear exactly where the first tobacco grown in Bermuda came from. It seems likely that the ultimate source of the seeds was Spanish and the most likely transmitter was John Rolfe, who spent ten months on Bermuda with the *Sea-Venture*'s castaways in 1609–10. Rolfe would go on to cultivate tobacco in Virginia. In the early years of the Bermuda colony, from 1612 through the mid-1620s, tobacco replaced the ambergris windfall as a source of cash for the settlement. Fortuitous market timing and a few good harvests in the early 1620s supported a brief boom in Somers Isles Company finances. Tobacco was not a long-term source of economic support for the colony; the market turned down in the 1630s, in part because of increased competition from Virginia, and Bermuda tobacco proved to be of inferior quality to that from the mainland. In some ways, tobacco worked like a slow-motion repetition of the ambergris find: the crop propped the settlement up for several years but failed to provide long-term footing. The island's ability to produce a tobacco crop before 1620 also strongly implies the presence of Africans with experience in the Angolan tobacco trade, which suggests that Bermuda, like Virginia, played an early part in integrating the British Atlantic into the African slave trade. Over time the relatively poor soil of the island and its distance from the mainland shifted the economic basis of the settlement away from slave agriculture toward maritime trade. As Jarvis notes, "the colony came to resemble Massachusetts more than Virginia" by the late seventeenth century (Jarvis 2010, 49). This isolated outpost in the middle of the Atlantic remains a British holding today, and it still leverages its geographic position and mild climate, though now more for tourism and banking than tobacco, ambergris, and trade.

Three Conclusions

The selection of thirteen nonhuman and human actants in the early modern history of Bermuda has been on some level arbitrary. The list could proliferate, perhaps infinitely. As a large-ish but not unimaginable prime number with a poetic pedigree (see Stevens 1972, 20–22), the number thirteen signals my argument that a posthuman history must embrace multiplicity, even at the risk of making our historical narratives messy. It is possible to gather the thirteen actants I have discussed into groups. One set emerges through the collaboration of nonhuman resources with skilled human labor: ships, maps, tobacco. Another emphasizes human imaginative invention: *Utopia*, devils, a Virgilian motto. Still others are essentially geographic facts: coral, the Gulf Stream. A last group emerges through the considerable power of random chance: a particular hurricane at a particular time and place. Most histories of premodern colonialism include some or indeed most of these elements as background to the more familiar stories of human actors, whether triumphant colonists or black-hearted imperialists, suffering slaves, or heroic maroons. In bringing the background forward and asking human actors to retire into the shadows, a posthuman ecological history of maritime expansion enables new narratives and new understandings. In brief, I will sketch three possible conclusions that can emerge from this kind of posthuman analysis.

Anti-ideological Globalization

A posthuman reading of early modern transatlantic expansion supports neither the European triumphalism that once dominated the field nor the anti-imperialist critique that epitomizes contemporary attitudes toward colonialism. Retelling this story to emphasize nonhuman actants reduces the centrality of both heroes and villains. Turning away from familiar melodramatic stories of exploration and tragic tales of destruction entails some loss of emotional force. It is hard to feel as deeply about ocean currents as we do about Sir Francis Drake, Native Americans being slaughtered, or Africans enslaved. But the pay-off for refusing familiar stories is being able to reframe the ideological debates that such stories raise. After decades or indeed centuries of debate about the legacies of early globalization, a new perspective can be useful. Geography may not quite be destiny, but in today's era of environmental uncertainty, a history that embraces nonhuman ecological systems seems essential. Limiting the ideological force of historical narratives provides space for nonhuman elements to shape our understanding of historical change.

Humans as Objects and Histories of Slavery

The largest risk of a posthuman approach is that it may muffle our moral perspective on the past. In the case of the greatest crime of early modern history, the Atlantic slave trade, emphasizing the nonhuman factors in Bermuda's history might enable a partial reimagining of tragic facts. Bermuda was home to some of the earliest transported African slaves of any English colony. The shifting presence of slave labor and the mixing of populations on the isolated island contribute to Bermuda being a particularly instructive case to evaluate the role of slavery in New World societies. To be thoroughly posthuman requires that we consider African slaves and the tobacco plants they cultivated as equal agents of historical change. This perspective jars our moral senses, but it may also enable a new line of response to American slaveholding societies. While the slaveholders' basic assumption was that only some humans were objects, and the abolitionists' response that no humans could possibly be objects, a theoretical commitment to treating all humans and nonhumans as objects and subjects might reopen the slave economy's representation of human-nonhuman relations. Marxist historians argue that slave labor represents the secret desire of capitalism, but a posthuman ecological understanding of slavery might extend the object-nature of slave laborer into a general theory of the agency of objects. If all objects are ontologically equal, from hurricanes to each shareholder of the Virginia Company to each transported African slave to the Gulf Stream, the slave trade may take its place inside a complex human and nonhuman network of forces and actants. Slavery remains Atlantic modernity's original sin, but slavery also challenges the boundaries of human and nonhuman identities.

Dynamism and Change in Global Systems

Nonhuman actants lack coherent biographies, motivations, and other elements that make narratives matter to human readers. It is hard to write the history of coral or hurricanes without either turning it into a story about how these objects interact with humans, as in Daniel Defoe's history of the Great Storm of 1703, or anthropomorphizing them, as in the subtitle of Iain McCalman's recent study *The Reef: A Passionate History* (see Defoe 1704; McCalman 2015). Nonhuman histories, however, enable us to reconsider the role of change in global history, including the random changes that contribute to a hurricane forming on one day rather than another. Winds, storms, and ocean currents tend to follow predictable patterns, and given the structure of the North Atlantic system, it was likely that shipwreck would precede settlement on Bermuda as transatlantic traffic increased during the early modern period. That this settlement was English, rather than Spanish or French, however, owes itself to a series of coincidences and in particular to one mid-summer storm in 1609. It is not often a part of human nature, and even less often a part of colonial propaganda, to treat such occurrences as arbitrary. But random forces and nonhuman actants control more of our history than we like to admit.

Notes

1. I adapt the term "actant" from Latour 2005, 54.
2. For a broader study, see Mentz 2015.
3. On the controversial question of the Gulf Stream's warming of Europe, see Ulanski, 31–32.
4. The expansion of tobacco production during the late 1620s in Virginia led that market to bust by 1630, after which Bermuda never quite lived up to its early promise.

Secondary Source Bibliography

Bendall, Sarah. "Norwood, Richard (1590–1675)." *Oxford Dictionary of National Biography*, Oxford University Press, 2004. http://www.oxforddnb.com/view/article/20365.
Bernhard, Virginia. *A Tale of Two Colonies: What Really Happened in Virginia and Bermuda*. Columbia: University of Missouri Press, 2012.
Crosby, Alfred. *The Columbian Exchange: Biological and Cultural Consequences of 1492*. 30th anniversary ed. New York: Praeger, 2003.
Cunliffe, Barry. *Facing the Ocean: The Atlantic and Its Peoples, 8000 BC–AD 1500*. Oxford, UK: Oxford University Press, 2001.
Defoe, Daniel. *The Storm*. London, 1704.
Durrell, Lawrence. *Reflections of a Marine Venus*. New York: Penguin, 1960.

Gillis, John. *Islands of the Mind: How the Human Imagination Created the Atlantic World.* New York: Palgrave Macmillan, 2004.
Grove, Richard. *Green Imperialism: Colonial Expansion, Tropical Island Edens, and the Origins of Environmentalism.* Cambridge, UK: Cambridge University Press, 1995.
Hau'ofa, Epeli. "Our Sea of Islands." In *We Are the Ocean: Selected Works*, 27–40. Honolulu: University of Hawaii Press, 2008.
Hulme, Peter. *Colonial Encounters: Europe and the Native Caribbean, 1492-1787.* New York: Methuen, 1986.
Jarvis, Michael. *In the Eye of All Trade: Bermuda, Bermudians, and the Maritime Atlantic World, 1680--1783.* Chapel Hill: University of North Carolina Press, 2010.
Jourdain, Silvester. *A Discovery of the Bermudas.* London, 1610.
Latour, Bruno. *Reassembling the Social: An Introduction to Actor-Network Theory.* Oxford, UK: Oxford University Press, 2005.
McCalman, Iain. *The Reef: A Passionate History.* New York: Farrar, Straus and Giroux, 2015.
Mentz, Steven. *Shipwreck Modernity: Ecologies of Globalization, 1550-1719.* Minneapolis: University of Minnesota Press, 2015.
More, Thomas. *Utopia.* Edited by G. M. Logan and R. M. Adams. Cambridge, UK: Cambridge University Press, 2002.
Pinet, Simone. *Archipelagoes: Insular Fictions from Chivalric Romance to the Novel.* Minneapolis: University of Minnesota Press, 2011.
Quinn, David. *Bermuda in the Age of Exploration and Early Settlement.* Williamsburg, VA: Omohundro Institute of Early American History and Culture Colloquia, 1988.
Rich, Lord Robert. *Newes from Virginia.* London: Da Capo Press, 1610.
Shakespeare, William. *The Tempest.* Edited by V. M. Vaughan and A. Vaughan. London: Arden, 2011.
Sobecki, Sebastian. "New World Discovery." In *Oxford Handbooks Online: Literature, Literary Studies, 1500-1700.* Groningen: University of Groningen, 2015.
Smith, Donald. *The Cartographic Imagination in Early Modern England.* Aldershot, UK: Ashgate, 2008.
Stevens, Wallace. "Thirteen Ways of Looking at a Blackbird." In *The Palm at the End of the Mind: Selected Poems and a Play.* Edited by H. Stevens, 20–22. New York: Vintage, 1972.
Ulanski, Stan. *The Gulf Stream: Tiny Plankton, Giant Bluefish, and the Amazing Story of the Powerful River in the Atlantic.* Chapel Hill: University of North Carolina Press, 2008.
Virgil. *Eclogues, Georgics, Aeneid I-VI.* Edited by H. R. Fairclough; translated by G. P. Goold. Cambridge, MA: Loeb-Harvard University Press, 1999.
Wallace, David. *Premodern Places, Calais to Surinam, Chaucer to Aphra Behn.* London: Wiley-Blackwell, 2004.
Wilkinson, Henry. *The Adventurers of Bermuda.* Oxford, UK: Oxford University Press, 1933.
Woodward, Hobson. *A Brave Vessel: The True Tale of the Castaways Who Rescued Jamestown and Inspired Shakespeare's "The Tempest."* New York: Viking, 2009.
Wright, Louis, ed. *A Voyage to Virginia in 1609: Strachey's "True Reportory" and Jourdain's Discovery of the Bermudas.* 2nd ed. Charlottesville: University of Virginia Press, 2013.

Chapter Five

Bookends of History: Maroonage in *The Female American* and *Die Wand*

Peter Sands

Introduction

In 1767, Unca Eliza Winkfield, the purported author of *The Female American*, published a tale of maroonage, racial mixing, and feminine power near the very beginning of the literary history of the Americas; it is one of the first novels about the New World claimed to have been written by a woman born in the Americas. Its actual author remains unknown. At the other end of history, Marlen Haushofer, an Austrian writer and housewife, published *Die Wand* (*The Wall*) in 1963, a tale of the last woman—the last person—on Earth, marooned outside of history in the Swiss Alps. The two texts bookend one of the narrative arcs of Euro-American history—the first, a tale of English and Native American mixing, predicting development of a New World combining the two cultures (with the English decidedly dominating); the last, a Cold War fantasy of silent, total apocalypse told as an ecofeminist utopian elegy for the human race that was and could have been. The two maroonage narratives are figural explorations of global, transatlantic society and history through the lens of utopia—the imagined alternative to already existing society. Together, their takes on the robinsonade, the genre that begins with Defoe's *Robinson Crusoe* (1719), prophesy and mourn the long, slow centuries of cultural clashes, masculinism, and Christian dominionist ideologies across the globe, as well as show a significant contrast between the roles and self-perception of strong women characters in fiction at either end of the historical spectrum they occupy. In doing so, they employ opposite tropes: at the beginning of the arc, the female protagonist is young, plucky, defiant, mixed-race, and never truly alone in spite of being orphaned and marooned. She is looking backward at the events of her life, but also looking forward at the inevitable subjugation and conversion of the Native American, a process not least indicated by her own mixed blood and complete assimilation. At the end of history, as depicted by Haushofer, the protagonist is middle-aged, determined, and resolutely without human company. The first marooned woman colonizes and denudes the degraded descendants of an ancient civilization of the Americas; the second forms an affective, nonhuman family that models the what-could-have-been.

The two novels have little in common formally—Winkfield's is a rough example of the very early history of the American novel with little literary aesthetic value (McDowell 309), while Haushofer's is a remarkable narrative exploration of depression and despair—but, taken together, they present a prescient view of the modern era and an elegiac backward glance at what a world constructed around an ecofeminist politics of affective community might have wrought. Winkfield's text is a fiction of the anthropocene in that it depicts a rapaciousness toward the material riches of the Earth and even a willingness to shape and destroy natural and man-made landscapes in the service of capital; Haushofer's is also a fiction of the anthropocene in its meditation on the end of history as wrought by human intervention in nature. Here, however, my main concern, is how the two use the concepts of maroonage and utopia (including dystopia, and, in Haushofer's case, critical dystopia, or a dystopia which critiques the concept of dystopia and leaves room at the end for hope), sketching some of the relationships between a Cold War, European, ecofeminist narrative and common tropes of maroonage, and the Adamic/Edenic myth through the particular contrast with an earlier female robinsonade that has quite a different affect and politics. In the first section, I will present a reading of *The Female American* and a brief discussion of its critical reception, locating the text in the literary history of the Americas and as a robinsonade. In the next, I will do the same for *The Wall*, locating the text in its Cold War time period and as a critical dystopia. In the final section, I will attempt to bring the two back together to complete my own conceit of bookends of history.

I. *The Female American*: Prefiguration of Colonial Reality

The Female American tells the story of Unca Eliza Winkfield ("Eliza" hereafter), a Native American "princess" whose father is one of the Virginia colonists of 1607. Her father is captured by local Indians but rescued by an Indian maiden who has fallen in love with him. The novel is a version of the John Smith/Pocahontas tale as well as a sort of female-empowerment version of the robinsonade in which the heroine demonstrates time and again her ability to function as a woman in a male-dominated world. Her mother is murdered by her jealous aunt; she and her father decamp from Virginia to England; they return to Virginia, where her father also dies; she is marooned by an unscrupulous ship captain on a remote island in the Atlantic; she discovers the remnants of a once-great civilization on the island; gains dominion over that civilization's degenerated descendants from a nearby island; is reunited with and married to her cousin; they plunder the island of all its riches and make it their home, with the express purpose of proselytizing the Native American population into Christianity and subordination by white Europeans. Winkfield uses the conceits of maroonage/marronage, island societies, and racialism to outline a prophetic prehistory of the European encounter with and dominance of the Americas, with its attendant global effects.

The reality of colonial America is dominance of the Native New World by Europeans, throughout North and South America. This reality is on full display in *The Female American*, which enjoyed a brief notoriety on publication before largely slipping into obscurity (Burnham and Freitas, "Introduction" 9–13). The novel can be situated in the history of female robinsonades (Blackwell; McDowell; Zuck). The editors of the recent Broadview edition refer to it as "a crucial addition to literary histories of the Anglo-American novel and as a text characterized by a complex intertextuality layered with political and social critiques" (11). They further state that "*The Female American* revises the narratives of capitalist accumulation, colonial conquest, and political imperialism that have been associated with [*Robinson Crusoe*]. Winkfield's story engages instead in fantasies of a feminist utopianism and cross-racial community, both of which are enabled, however, by a specifically religious form of imperialism" (12). They find that "the heroine of *The Female American* . . . represents a radical alternative to dominant novelistic representations of women and to the lives of their readers" (13–14). Winkfield's maroonage is typical of the genre, in that it showcases "resistance to an unwanted marriage," and in which the heroines "typically find themselves living in a utopic environment and practicing sometimes radical forms of independence and power" (19). Winkfield "critiques the helplessness of women within a coercive marriage market [and offers] an alternative fantasy to typical female roles within dominant culture" (19).

In the novel, Eliza recounts both the history of her English colonialist family and of her Native American "princess" mother. Her European history begins with her grandfather settling a Virginia colony in 1607 under a 1584 patent issued by James I; in this section, the novel remains solidly in the ambit of actual historical fact, a convention designed to alleviate the otherwise scandalous independence and willfulness of its single, female narrator. Eliza's father is taken prisoner by Indigenes and recalls that his clergyman brother had warned him that "we have no right to invade the country of another, and I fear invaders will always meet a curse" (47) as a consequence of their presumption. He is eventually rescued by an Indian "princess," marries her, and produces Unca Eliza, the literal product of the New World and the Old. When later marooned, Eliza imagines first a society of one, with a religious mentor, then a society of converted Indians at the service of herself and other Christian Europeans, from which she creates through self-serving deception a plan to convert the Indians to her version of Christianity—explicitly anti-Catholic and post-Reformation—in which she, as few women of her time were, is treated as the living messenger of God to the people. She first creates a solo utopia in her maroonage by exploiting the resources of the island where she is abandoned, then imposes Christianity on the Indians to form a hierarchical utopian society with her hybrid self at its apex. That self is dominated by her European heritage, as the novel argues that the New World can be a transformative and good place, but also that it needs the guiding and shaping hand of the European—dominance, violence, religion—to bring it into the fold.

Winkfield's text contains many of the elements of the coming colonial disaster: Europeans "find" a new land, establish colonies, deal in bad faith with the unscrupulous natives, and forge a new society that combines the old world and its customs with the new—mostly, though, they usurp, dominate, and shape the new land and its peoples with an unfailing sense of their right to do so, and care not for the human cost of their assumption of cultural, moral, and racial authority and superiority. The Indians are presumed to be cannibals and sun-worshippers and driven by base needs and desires they cannot control. Winkfield's father, naked and imprisoned, is apparently so beautiful that not one but two Indian maidens fall immediately in love with him; the one becomes his wife and mother of his child, the other rises to power as the Indian queen and uses her position to kill her sister and attempt to force the Englishman to love her and rule over the Indian country. Winkfield herself is an amalgamation of Indian coloring, English dress, English customs, and Indian skills.

Although the novel is a robinsonade, the editors of the excellent Broadview edition read Winkfield as unlike Defoe, because her novel is best read not "as either a capitalist lesson or a spiritual autobiography [than as a] fantasy of female power exercised within and by means of a Christian colonialist utopia" (21). They see the text as not being about "venture capitalism," although Winkfield's wealth before and after being on the island is derived from exactly that, but as the tale of "an apostolic woman who practices missionary zeal and religious colonialism to make of a New World island a cross-racial Christian utopia that remains deliberately isolated from Europe" (23). They do at least acknowledge that "this text articulates its own forms of imperialist violence" through Winkfield's use of slaves and exploitation of the Indians (23). But, ultimately, they conclude that "the utopian feminist elements of *The Female American* are compromised not just by its Christian imperialism but by its conclusion with a traditional marriage plot that threatens to erase the fantasy of unrestricted female freedom in which the novel otherwise indulges" (24). I generally disagree: the novel is an extraordinary document on several levels, but especially as an example of a female narrator deliberately and willingly reifying a masculinist, penetrative, and dominating Europeanness in a New World where she has, for a moment at least, the possibility of common cause and peaceful coexistence without masculinism and violence. In that sense, the text is at least in part utopian: it presents an alternative to already existing society in Europe and an alternative to violent subjugation of the New World. But its end is the same: the assimilation and conversion and disappearance of native bodies before the European thirst for riches.

A Closer Reading

Insofar as *The Female American* is mostly unfamiliar outside of transatlantic literary studies or studies of the early American novel, let me offer a summative reading with particular attention to the conversion elements of the text. It begins with a narrative comment on the burdens of history, as Eliza looks back on the events that have led her to write her life story: "finding remembrance of it burdensome to my memory, I thought I might, in some degree, exonerate myself, by digesting the most material events in the form of an history" (45). This need for exoneration disappears quickly and morphs into an unabashed justification of her colonial project by the end (162). The narrator is keenly aware of her status as a woman, and draws on that to emphasize the unusualness of her tale: "the lives of women being commonly domestick, the occurrences of them are generally pretty nearly of the same kind; whilst those of men, frequently more vagrant, subject them often to experience greater vicissitudes, many times wonderful and strange" (45). Women's lives are not as interesting because they do not travel as much and do not have as many adventures. Her tale is guaranteed to provide "rational entertainment, and mental improvement" (45). Moreover, by claiming descent from an actual founder of the Jamestown colony (Edward Maria Wingfield), and otherwise connecting her narrative to real-world events (the massacre in 1622 of colonists by local Indians), she connects the novel to the real, which, in hindsight proves prophetic of the future history of the Americas.

Such prophecy appears in the text proper, with Eliza's uncle arguing to her father that colonizing "the country of another" always leads to a "curse" (47). This prophecy comes true quite quickly in the captivity of Eliza's father. While he is captive a "king" of the Indians makes a speech noting the common humanity of the Indians and the Englishmen. He says that the English were sent by an "evil being who made you" to "kill us," even though the Indians would gladly have shared their land and food had they simply been asked; the consequence is that their gods demand the English must die (48). Eliza's father is saved by Unca, a daughter of the king.

As her narrative progresses, Winkfield makes the almost pro forma accusation of cannibalism against the Indians (47–48). Similarly, she presents stock images of the different complexions of English and Indians, as well as the power of romantic love to overcome the natural "disgust" her father initially felt toward her mother's darker skin—"his black deliverer" (49). The love between the "princess" Unca and Winkfield again emphasizes a common humanity. But the possibility of peaceful coexistence is disturbed by Winkfield's insistence upon both an Indian and Christian marriage, refusing the union until Unca converts to Christianity (51). With perhaps unwitting irony, Eliza says that her father also is converted to a Native American sensibility, for he "almost forgot his former situation, and [had] begun to look upon the country he was in as his own" (51).

A love triangle develops as another daughter of the king confesses that she too loves Winkfield, is rejected, and takes him captive. She forces him to drink a poison, saying that he cannot live if he will not marry her. Unca saves him with her native lore and understanding of herbal poisons and cures. The text fully embraces the European narrative of American Indians being closer to the state of nature, as well as undercuts the feminist narrative of independence noted by many readers with a clichéd love triangle predicated on unstable female emotions. The romance narrative—triangle, poisoning, rescue—concludes with the couple returning to the English colony for a Church of England wedding, completing the bi-directional conversion of Winkfield into an Indian and Unca into an Englishwoman (55). Back among the English, Winkfield conceals the vast wealth of his bride's dowry from his fellows because the colonists are less honorable and more devoted to worldly goods than the Indians (55). In this same sequence, the text reveals that the early colony uses slaves.

In due course, Eliza's mother is murdered by agents of her sister (56), she and her father return to England "to give me a better education" (57), and she is welcomed into the family of her clergyman uncle, whose own living is provided for by William's New World riches. She is celebrated for her exotic coloring and dress (58), and shows outwardly the mixing of her Old and New World identities. She lives in England until she is eighteen, rebuffing suitors, including her cousin John Winkfield, and receiving the same education as her male relatives. She erects a monument to the memory of her mother—triangular, with "an inscription in the Indian language, containing a short account of her life and death" on one side, which is repeated on the others in Latin and English. "On the top is an urn, on which an Indian leans, and looks on it in a mournful posture," which prefigures the historical fate of the Indian in America (59). Eventually, however, she wanted to join her father, so "I, with my four slaves" set sail (59). John Winkfield accompanies her, although she makes plain that she will set barriers before his suit by insisting on his mastery of Indian archery and language (60). The Eliza who returns to Virginia is a deeply religious Christian, owing to her clergyman uncle. Her education "converted the heart," and is "not only the greatest comfort to me, but of the highest use; as will appear hereafter," alluding to her use of religion to control and convert the Indians in her exile, permitting them to become in essence Europeans and lose their Indianness (60).

The maroonage narrative proper begins when, at the age of twenty-four, Eliza determines to return to England with a fortune of ten thousand pounds in addition to the income and wealth she will enjoy from the plantation; she arranges with a captain to take her, in exchange for which she will gift him the ship they are to sail on when they arrive safely. She leaves with two female and six male slaves, "who begged to attend me; though I had offered them their liberty, if they chose to stay behind" (62). The captain maroons her when she refuses his demand that she marry his son (64).

On the island, she finds "the ruins of a building" which turns out to be a hermit's lair converted from part of a temple and burial complex left by an ancient civilization (66). The resident hermit has been there for a biblical forty years, and has left her a kind of survival guide in the form of a journal that reveals there are no dangerous animals and no "savages, except once a year" (67). The guide she supplements with bibliomancy. In this, as discussed below, she is similar to Haushofer's heroine, who has a farmer's diary to help her with some of the basics of husbandry. But, unlike Haushofer's heroine, concerned for the lives of the deer and trout she unwillingly kills, Eliza finds it relatively easy to first learn to kill a goat with her knife and learn to skin and roast it (72). She becomes a veritable one-woman harvester of all the fauna on the island—an unintended figure of the coming slaughter and denuding of the New World's animals for the sustenance of hungry Europeans. In this sense, the island becomes a kind of proto-feminist utopia of self-reliance, as Eliza is freed from patriarchal hierarchies and the threats that that these hierarchies might cause, principally through the marriage-related curtailing of her independence and agency.

The temple complex, part of a group of temples or palaces, is large (81). The many other similar ruins are evidence of an ancient, sun-worshipping civilization from which the Indians who occasionally visit are descended in a degraded state; it includes a giant idol under which she finds the apartments or living quarters of the priests who had lived there a thousand years or more (85–86). Elsewhere, she discovers rooms of gold and other treasures (87). Most of the treasure is richly worked into religious vestments for the priests of the temple—a fantasy of New World wealth. Exploring further, she goes into the idol itself, at the top of which she is inside the head and can look out at the island through "mouth, eyes, nose, and ears of it; so that I could distinctly see all over the island before me, of which the height at which I was at gave me a great command," directly alluding to Defoe (88). Sound magnification created by the idol testifies to the advanced state of the ancient civilization and the degraded state of the current Indians. In short, the island is both the record of a lost civilization from which the locals descend and a vast treasury of already mined and worked commodity metals and stones that Eliza will plunder in secret, first to bribe the natives into worshipful obedience and later to fund her New World evangelical crusade.

Alerted by the diary to the imminent annual arrival of the Indians, Eliza decides to convert them (91). She plans to deceive them into thinking she is a messenger from God (92), reasoning that "an attempt to teach the knowledge of the true God to those who know him not, was laudable, and might not warrant a providential sanction" for blasphemy. Echoing Columbus's famous assertion that the Indians he encountered could be easily Christianized and dominated (see Berkhofer, 5–12), she writes that the "Indians . . . are generally of a docile disposition" (92). If she can get them to trust her, they will do so gladly and accept her because of her racial similarity. Indeed, she fantasizes about her command and control: "This moment I imagined hundreds of Indians prostrate before me with reverence and attention, whilst like a law-giver, I uttered precepts, and, like an orator, inculcated them with a voice magnified almost to the loudness of thunder. At another time my soul shrunk within me at the imagined noise of their dreadful yell; whilst my imagination painted to me an enraged multitude tearing down, in their fury, branches of trees with which to surround the statue, and to burn me in it" (94). This passage contradicts both her claim to believe that the Indians are all peaceful and docile, and that she has the conviction of her faith.

Eliza, hiding in the idol and speaking through its voice-amplifying head, converts the Indians through a kind of Socratic dialogue in which the high priest questions and is answered by her in ways that lead toward a monotheistic religious framework intended to show the Indians the folly of their sun-worship and the necessity of acknowledging a higher God who cannot be seen but must be believed in and followed through acts of faith. She Christianizes the natives by deceiving them into thinking that the idol is responding to them and instructing them in a higher and more pure religion. Even as she manipulates and cows the Indians into worshipful acceptance of her spiritual teachings, she says to herself, "I know not whether the casuists may justify this artifice from sin; but to me it appeared expedient," because she used their "fears" to bring them to Christian beliefs (103). Deceit is the foundation of her religious conversion exercise; this continues until she is able to reveal herself and live among the Indians as their Christianizing savior-figure. The novel reveals complicity in colonial destruction in other ways as well. For instance, Eliza reports on the natural world she finds on the island such as a remarkable animal, *pace* Mandeville, that is weirdly built to the size of a dog but with disproportionately long legs and slow locomotion (109). She observes the animal sleeping in a meadow. While sleeping it is covered by field-mice that nibble at its weird fur, which traps them, and the animal eats three hundred of them. This occasions a musing on the workings of divine providence: "the divine being has been pleased to permit animals to support themselves by devouring one another. I say permit; for I cannot think that it was the original design of the Almighty, that animals should at all destroy one another. I suppose it rather to be one of the unhappy consequences of the general corruption of nature" (111)—a justification of colonial exploitation particularly poignant for coming on the heels of her deceitful conversion of the Indians to her religion. Her conjecture on this cycle of life as indicating a natural order in which predator can "secure his prey" (111–12) cannot be read otherwise than as justification of her own colonial enslavement of the Indians. The island which she has lived on alone in a kind of safe, female utopia now becomes a source of wealth and power over the Indians whose ancestors previously occupied it.

While Eliza clearly performs the same masculinist, penetrative, and dominating colonization as male Europeans, her Protestantism does come with a feminine twist in which she determines that she must combat traditional patriarchal knowledge and means of transmission, particularly "from *father to son*, received with reverence, and, no doubt, maintained with obstinacy" (118, emphasis added). Eliza tells them that they will be delivered by the presence among them of a female teacher to whom they "must be sure to show the greatest respect . . . do every thing that she shall command you, never ask who she is, from whence she comes, or when, or whether she will leave you" or otherwise interfere with her comings and goings (119). Ensconced thus among the Indians, her teachings include translating hymns, the Bible, and the Book of Common Prayer into "the Indian language." For two years, she lives among them, periodically returning to the island of her maroonage to retrieve some rings to give to the Indians, waiting several days after her return so that they don't suspect where she is getting them—deliberately deceiving them to keep the treasure for herself and her manipulations, even though the treasures belong to their ancestors (128). She acknowledges, too, that she relies upon the native belief in her divinity: "However, I did not think it my duty, any more than my interest, to undeceive them, as this opinion secured to me that respect and authority which were necessary for me to preserve, in order to carry on the great work among them, in which I was engaged" (127).

In her third year among the Indians, she is rescued by her Winkfield cousin (129). Her cousin presses his suit for marriage; is rejected on the grounds that he would not be happy among the Indians and that she has no need for a husband. But she begins to accept him when he refers to the islands and Indians as "a glorious harvest" and says that he will learn the language of the Indians and live among them (143). The ship and crew maroon the two of them now, leaving his belongings, as well as livestock and arms for his colonial project, and a letter telling him the captain will return to look for him in one year (145–46). The two are married in a double ceremony, Indian and Christian, like Eliza's father had with her mother (148–49). They reify European gender distinctions as they teach the Indians, "he the boys and I the girls," creating "the appearance of a christian country" in which the "natural simplicity and purity of the Indian manners greatly accelerated this work" (149).

By novel's end, the captain who marooned Eliza has been punished, her father's New World riches have devolved to her uncle—which means the riches inherited from Unca's princess mother have now been "transported to the Old World and into patriarchal hands" (editorial note, 161, n1). She and her husband, along with one of the ship captains, are actively Christianizing the Indians (161–62), completing the collapse of her proto-feminist island utopia into a simple colonial conversion project. Her husband returns to England to settle his affairs, including giving half their fortune to his sisters before returning. Eliza describes this final act thus: "But we first determined to go upon *my island*, to collect all the gold treasure there, to blow up the subterraneous passage, and the statue, that the Indians might never be tempted to their former idolatry. When all this was done, and the golden treasure put on board, the captain and my husband set out upon their voyage" (162, emphasis added). Moreover, "we did not suffer the sailors to come any farther upon the island, than just to land the goods, that no discovery of our habitation might be made. As we never intended to have any more to do with Europe, captain Shore and my husband ordered a person who came for that purpose, to return to Europe with the ship, by whom, for my father and mother's satisfaction, I sent over these adventures" (162). The novel ends with her plundering the island of all wealth and the Indians in its vicinity wholly unawares.

Critical reception of *The Female American* has rightly emphasized its place in the history of the American novel, without being able to determine whether it was actually female-written or by a colonial, and of eighteenth-century transatlantic literature (Burnham and Freitas, 9–18; Joseph); as an example of female self-fashioning in explicit contrast to its source material, including Defoe (Burnham and Freitas, 18–25; Joseph; MacNeil; McDowell; Zuck); a critique of colonialism (Joseph); and as a colonialist fantasy of subordinating and Christianizing Native Americans (Zuck, 188). The importance of its purported authorship by a woman and its presenting a strong, independent, marooned woman able to function in male spheres on her own terms is universally acknowledged. A particularly strong statement of the positive reading the text supports is that the novel "presents an alternative to empire building, catalyzed by the female gender, which provides a pathway for European involvement in the Americas while leaving existing American civilizations fundamentally intact" (MacNeil, 118). But this emphasizes Eliza's nonviolence while ignoring the fact that she forms a New World society that largely erases her own Native American heritage, plunders the wealth of the land, discards local religion and replaces it with a highly gendered Christianity, and ultimately also rejects her own independence and solitude for marriage to a man she professedly does not love (146). A close reading of the text does not justify weighting its proto-feminism and nonviolence more than its ultimate acceptance of European dominance and exploitation of the New World, a history it predicts and which comes to a fruition in the post-apocalyptic world of Haushofer's *The Wall*.

II. Alone in the Alm at the End of the World: Haushofer's Robinsonade as Critical Dystopia

In Marlen Haushofer's 1962 novel, *The Wall* (*Die Wand*), a postmenopausal woman finds herself marooned by an invisible, impenetrable wall in the Austrian Alps, where she acquires a small menagerie of animals and, after three years, writes a "report" ("Bericht") of her experience. The novel, relatively unknown in English, enjoyed a brief revival late in the twentieth century as an ecofeminist manifesto, and is probably best known as the source for Julian Pölsler's 2012 film of the same name, a largely faithful reproduction of the text.

The Wall recounts the narrator's life as a marooned person who gradually comes to believe that she is the last person left alive. After a violent encounter with a man spanning three paragraphs and not quite one page in the 244 pages of the novel, it is all but certain that she is fully and truly marooned: literally, by the wall, but also outside of history itself, apart from all males, human and nonhuman, in her little *Gemeinschaft*, away from all human community, eyewitness to, and recorder of, the end.

The novel has none of the robinsonade's adventure-story elements: no savages chase her, nor pirates, nor even beasts of the field. While not an American text at all, its trope of a New Eve in a New Garden resonates with tales of maroonage in the Americas, is part of an historical grouping of female robinsonades in German literature, and can generally be situated in the history of maroonage literature in both European and American traditions (Manuel and Manuel, 433–34; Fisher "The Robinsonade"). As such, Haushofer's reworking of New World tropes provides a lens through which readers can understand their power to shape European understanding and representation of the "American" context of female maroonage. She does not build fantastic shelters or invent new ways of doing things. She does not find herself with a potential mate or companion other than a faithful hunting dog. She is past the age of fertility and cannot continue the species. Her narrative moves slowly and at the level of the quotidian: what she ate, what she grew, how she learned, her bouts of depression, her moments of insight and revelation. Several have noted the mystical or semi-mystical dimensions of the novel that arise from the narrator's austere living conditions and introspection (Kecht 16; Caviola, 103, 104, 105, 110). She meditates on a few memories of her time before the wall appeared, but in large part documents the daily and seasonal labor of transforming her little spot in the Alps into a home for herself and her animals. As bleak as the narrative is as she awaits her own end and that of the human race, the novel maintains an aspect of the critical dystopia, leaving open the door for hope and resolution of the conditions which have led to the dystopia.

There are multiple avenues of investigation into *The Wall*: as an ecofeminist manifesto arguing for a fundamentally different way of being in the world, one which responds to the predominantly masculinist ways of being that lead to the presumed worldwide disaster; as a form of the post-apocalyptic novel of the anthropocene; and as a critical dystopia proffering a possible way out of the apparently inevitable self-destruction of the human race through its persistent drives toward violence and domination. The unnamed narrator models an alternative to narratives of dominance and anthropocentrism; its Cold War setting indicts both the colonialism and violence of states and the paternalism and violence of male-dominated culture.

Although it quickly becomes apparent that everyone outside the wall is dead, the narrator first assumes that it is just Austrians, or perhaps Europeans, who have died. She can see small farmholds on the other side of the wall, with people in arrested poses: taking a morning or evening outdoor bath or sitting on a porch, but never moving, day after day. She can see evidence of wildlife inside but not outside the wall. She thinks that perhaps there has been a military attack and that soon invaders will arrive.

Eventually, she realizes that there are no contrails in the sky, no smoke on the horizon, and no radio signals. No one is left. No rescuers are coming. The implication of her encounter with the murderous madman, given her limited exploration of the mountain, is that there could be others marooned with her, but that is unlikely. The man's brief, silent appearance requires us to read him figurally: as the brief reintroduction of violent masculinism to reinforce the otherwise ecofeminist text. The narrative presents a totality: a woman reduced to bare life and with the reasonable belief that when she dies, the human species dies with her. But where, say, novelists such as Paul Auster and Cormac McCarthy relentlessly refuse even the possibility of hope in their post-apocalyptic visions,[1] Haushofer presents a critical dystopian argument for an ecofeminist change in the present.

In her food-gathering, she has a choice between hunting and farming. She chooses farming, and comments more than once about the undesirability of killing animals—how it makes her feel bad to even take trout from the stream outside her cabin—in direct contrast with *The Female American*, in which Eliza hunts fish and fowl with abandon, choosing to take prey by subterfuge and with a knife rather than even a bow and arrow. Haushofer's narrator carries a rifle sometimes, and butchers the odd deer, but knows that she cannot eat all the meat on her own. She finds the taking of deer an unpleasant task whose valuable protein does not outweigh her revulsion, and stops hunting other than to feed Luchs, the dog.

Thus, she becomes a farmer. Each time she takes in another animal, first a domestic cat and then kittens, a dairy cow and then its calf, she adds to her menagerie and her companionship, and also takes on responsibility for another life. As she says nearly three years into her confinement, "[t]he wall forced me to make an entirely new life, but the things that really move me are still the same as before: birth, death, the seasons, growth and decay" (129–30). Without her, the dog would not have the necessary tasks that have defined its life as a hunting companion until now. A dog under such conditions is lonely, depressed, unhappy, unfulfilled. Her companionship is a kindness to the animal, one which he repays by being steadfast, protecting her, and giving her companionship. The feminist ecotopia as written by Haushofer does not depend on the primitivism and hierarchicalism of Crusoe and Friday or on gendered relationships at all (including inverted gender roles as in Winkfield).

The same holds true for the other animals, whose relationships with the narrator present possible alternative forms of community founded on an affinity between human and nonhuman others.[2] The domesticated cat shelters with the narrator. Theirs is a more distant symbiosis, allowing the cat to nurture and separate from her own young. The feral cat which has impregnated the narrator's cat does not come in from the wild, preferring the wild to the tame, illustrating a range of possible human-nonhuman Other interaction. Bella the cow, and her bull calf, are also in need of the narrator. Without her, Bella would not be milked, a condition which is very painful and can lead to infection and death in dairy cattle. Without her, a difficult birth would result in the death of both the mother and the calf. With her, there is the possibility that she can mate the two, ignoring the human proscription against incest. If she does so, Bella will continue to produce milk and allow her to live a few more years.

The narrator gets something from nurturing: nutrition, companionship, a sense of purpose, and a sense of validation for being a caretaker. She is reduced to bare life, but it is a life stripped of the anxieties and pressures of modern, urban, commercialized living, a life in which simplicity and difficulty are strengthening elements that provide a necessary challenge to the human body and mind. She supplements this with writing and memory, and has a nearly complete life. But because it is only nearly complete—no human companionship, no sexual relationship, no possibility of species continuance—it is a flawed pocket utopia or critical dystopia.

The novel's dystopianism is self-evident: destruction of the species, going from the presence of all backward to the presence solely of the mother, barren and alone, a chiastic inversion of evolution—from slow, biological reproduction and evolution to sudden, non-biological death. The society in which she lived has somehow destroyed itself, inexplicably leaving a single person behind to carry the weight of all those deaths and memories, to have the responsibility to remember and to carry on or to be the agent of species death: if she kills herself, she kills the species. Indeed, at one point, she borders on anti-utopian sentiment, wondering if she would have been happy raising her children in the forest where she now lives, but concluding that "it wouldn't have been paradise. I don't believe that paradise has ever existed. A paradise could exist only outside nature, and I can't imagine that kind of paradise. It bores me even to think about it: I have no desire for it" (65), calling to mind Levitas's definition of utopia as "education of desire" (*Concept*, 6 and passim), as well as embracing a non-hierarchical primitivism without giving it primacy over other modes.

Haushofer's novel presents a counter-narrative of feminist ecotopia inside its dystopian setting. Inside the wall is a totalized dystopia inhabited by a lone, postmenopausal woman who chooses to struggle on each day, documenting in a diary that she believes no one will ever read her efforts to grow food and care for animals. But there is also a model of what Rita Felski calls "a distinctive new narrative structure for women, tracing a process of *separation* as the essential precondition for any path to self-knowledge" (124). There is in the novel a "female community," which "open[s] up a space for nonexploitative relationships grounded in common goals and interests" (139). One could hardly find a better description of *Die Wand* than that it is "grounded in a moral and aesthetic revulsion against the very nature of contemporary social reality, which is perceived as alienating and debased" (142). But, instead of presenting an inevitable decline and fall, she models through her actions and words a way of being in the world that nurtures and cares for it, that emphasizes co-participation in processes of life that include the plant and animal worlds, and that accepts the struggle for existence as a shared enterprise across all species, rather than placing the human at its center to dominate and exploit. As Felski writes, "Unlike the bourgeois public sphere . . . the feminist public sphere does not claim a representative universality but rather offers a critique of cultural values from the standpoint of women as a marginalized group within society. In this sense it constitutes a *partial* or counter public sphere [and] its arguments are also directed outward toward a dissemination of feminist ideas and values throughout society as a whole" (167, emphasis original). The human—literate, able to modify the natural world to create and maintain shelter, heat, and food through the seasons—still is the dominant creature. But Haushofer's narrator adopts an attitude of responsibility as the natural consequence of that dominance. Because the animals can depend on her, she cares for and shares the world with them, rather than, for instance, breeding and eating them. Ultimately, she is not anti-utopian. There is neither possibility of change or improvement nor possibility of restarting the human species. There is no possibility of community in a society of one. The only other human being she meets is irrational, violent, and then dead: the poison of maleness. How, then, is there an element of utopian hope? If, as Sherry B. Ortner says in reference to the cultural devaluation of women for an association with nature and subjectivity versus a masculine association with rationality and dominance or separation from nature, "a different cultural view can only grow out of a different social actuality; a different social actuality can only grow out of a different cultural view" (87), then Haushofer very specifically models an alternative. Her narrator chooses to remember, to memorialize, to nurture, to care for the Earth, to take as little life as she can, and to not just trust in the intervention of men or even the appearance of other women. She accepts her fate, but does not deny its burden or its unfairness. She lives in an alternative social organization that is characteristic of utopia. Rather than making and using weapons, she makes and uses tools. Rather than eating animals, she co-exists with them. Rather than penetrating, climbing, or burrowing under the wall, she practices a kind of serene acceptance of it, and of what it means for her eventual demise. She tries not to impose her own sense that she has suffered an injustice onto the animals and Earth, but instead acts as a mother, adopting these creatures and moving forward as much as she can. She embraces the organic inevitability of her own end, but does not hasten it. She does not cover herself with guilt or the burden of continuing. She simply does, choosing to be Demeter rather than the Furies.

Utopia, Dystopia, Robinsonade, Gynotopia

Haushofer's novel is read by some as an ecofeminist utopia for its depiction of a world devoid of men; by the end of the novel, even the male animals who make up part of the narrator's nonhuman family are all dead, but her intimate relationship with nature, including nonhumans, remains secure. She feeds a white crow that is being ostracized by other birds, and anticipates the birth of a new calf. She muses about possibly digging under the wall again.

Others read it as a dystopia, for its lack of human community, and for the apparent end of the species in the mysterious event and wall. Many characterize it as a kind of robinsonade, while others point out that the novel does not have one of the three essential elements of the genre—a still-continuing outside world against which to measure the alternative form of social organization; another human companion (Crusoe's Friday), creating a minimum human community; and the possibility of rescue (Knapp, 304). The encounter with a lone man toward the end of the novel might imply such a continuation, but not definitively. In any case, most acknowledge Haushofer's novel as a form of the robinsonade that both makes use of the conventions of the genre (maroonage and survival activities) and works against them through radical refiguring.

As for its utopianism, while lay usages since More's 1516 *Utopia* have reduced utopias to idealized societies or perfect places, the reality of the genre has been that the ideal city is only a tiny portion of the varieties of human expression. Generally conceived, utopias are imagined alternatives to already existing societies. Their obverse, the dystopia, is a representation of already existing societies reaching a logical expression of their worst elements and structural weaknesses. Haushofer's novel is generally accepted as a form of ecofeminist utopia, in that it depicts a society organized along one form of feminist principles (Caviola, 101–102, 105). Not all ecofeminist utopias are single-gendered, but those which are, such as Haushofer's, are gynotopias, or utopian spaces occupied only by women. The gynotopia is explicitly separatist. It functions as a critique of male-dominated society by depicting the possible ways in which women would organize a society without the corrupting influence of men. Usually that society takes some form of enlargement of the separate spheres, such that they are all occupied by women. Typically, gynotopias argue for more egalitarian and rational ways of organizing society that depend as little as possible on hierarchies and oppression, and minimize violence—state-sanctioned or personal—as much as possible. In Haushofer's case, her formation of a sole-gendered nonhuman community along with her dog, cats, and cattle explicitly presents an alternative to already existing society and must be considered as utopian in that sense—for the potential community of human and nonhuman beings is precisely the point of the novel.

Haushofer's distinguishing difference is that rather than imagining a true social organization dominated by women or filled only by women, she imagines an anti-society, a world in which only one person remains, a woman, who is radically ambivalent about both the absence of men and other women. She considers whether her lot would be improved by the presence of a man, such as the huntsman who managed Luchs the dog, but decides that the improvement would be offset by the likelihood that he would be stronger and dominate her, returning her to the oppression that the event released her from. She contemplates whether having another woman as a companion would also be an improvement, and decides she might be happier in the presence of an older, intelligent woman, but rejects that possibility too, in part because she would then be dominant but also because that person would probably die before her, leaving her to be lonelier and sad about the loss to boot.

Instead, she forms a completely alternative society in concert with nonhuman others and the Earth. Her gynotopia almost completely concentrates on aspects of the feminine in Haushofer's fairly strict demarcation of men's and women's spheres: motherhood or maternality; nurturing; growing; healing; caring; compassion. By the end of the novel, not only has the only male human survivor she encounters died at the narrator's hands, but all the male animals she is caring for have also died: Luchs, Tiger the cat, Bull the steer. The man dies in an act of necessary violence. He appears toward the end of the novel, disheveled, wordless, violent. He kills Bull with an axe, then Luchs, who is trying to protect his family, including the narrator. She shoots the man with her rifle. She buries Luchs; she shoves the man's corpse off a cliff. The entire encounter, implying that she might not be the lone survivor, is wordless and occupies little more than one page of the more than 200 in the novel. It is the final repudiation of all maleness by the narrator. Some commentators have found the scene gratuitous, and have pointed out its reification of the rigidly defined men's and women's spheres of the novel as a particular problem both of aesthetics and political philosophy, but in the allegorical world of the gynotopia, the man's presence, violence, and death are perfectly consistent and necessary to make the final turn toward the nonhuman sensible and coherent.

Conclusion: Maroonage, Tragedy, Eulogy

It is certainly not the case that a novel of 1767 is the beginning of colonial literature or the history of the Americas. But as one of the first novels purportedly by an American—an American *woman*—*The Female American* certainly is a figural beginning point, a bookend of modern history in at least the limited sense I use the term here. Winkfield's plucky half-Indian heroine makes the most of her maroonage by conquering and evangelizing the Indians living on a neighboring island. Her utopia is a European fantasy in which the English portion of her heritage dominates the Indian; she uses deceit and chicanery to gull the Indians into accepting her as God's spokeswoman; she proselytizes and eventually, upon rescue, marries her cousin and chooses to stay permanently in the New World to minister to the Indians, who are fallen representatives of an ancient race. It is thus easy enough to read in Winkfield's text an originary myth about the settling of the Americas by Europeans, a beginning to the narrative history of the New World. And while Haushofer's setting is not the Americas, its deployment of New World tropes—particularly those of the robinsonade (see Blackwell "An Island of Her Own")—specifically shows what a feminist, non-hierarchical, non-colonial robinsonade or maroonage narrative might look like. But where Unca Winkfield happily slaughters goats and makes use of the buildings and cave dwellings left by others without much thought, Haushofer's nameless woman eschews flesh after her first few experiences hunting deer or fishing for trout, refuses to over-exploit the land, and ultimately demonstrates the possibility of affective community between human and nonhuman others in concord with the natural world.

Eliza and the unnamed narrator of *The Wall* have some things in common. For instance, Eliza ruminates on her fate and goes into a severe fever; the altered state of consciousness marks a rupture between her previous life and her new one. The fever "attended with a delirium" causes her to lose her senses: "I raved, I cried, I laughed by turns" as she first contemplates the privation that she believes will come with winter and a diminution of her available animal proteins, then falls into illness (74). Eventually, weak with hunger and thirst and having exhausted her store of fresh water, she crawls to a nearby river, where she drinks some water and then manages to suckle herself from "a she-goat asleep, very near me," a violation "she happily permitted" (75). After thanking God for deliverance again, and weakly returning to her home base, she drinks some of the "wine" and some of the "root bread" she has made in a weird kind of communion ceremony. She recovers over a week of drinking wine and goat-milk and eating small bits of roots, thanking God all the while. Finally determining to embark on a course of daily meditation and inner investigation as recommended by her clergyman uncle, she becomes a sort of religious, ascetic hermit herself (76–77). Haushofer's narrator has frequent periods of intense reflection and almost metaphysical or gnostic transport in the forest and the *alm*, and she also at first uses animals for food. But there the similarities end. At the beginning of the narrative arc, Eliza assumes dominion over all creatures before her, eating animals and deceiving Indians, manipulating suitors, removing the island's wealth and putting it toward her private interest, particularly the interest in subjugating native peoples and converting them to Protestant Christianity. In direct contrast to Winkfield's quite conventional colonialism at one end of history, Haushofer's narrator, appearing at the imagined end of the world spawned by such rapacious colonial ventures, models for the reader an affective politics and way of being in the world that demands recognition of nonhuman actors as equivalent contributors to the common good, and an ethic of stewardship designed to sustain life without damaging the lives of others, including the Earth itself.

Notes

1. Auster's *The Country of Last Things*, Ballard's *High Rise*, Kunstler's *World Made by Hand*, and McCarthy's *The Road* present more traditional post-apocalyptic/maroonage narratives, with Ballard and Kunstler nodding, at least, toward feminist alternatives to mainstream society, and Auster and McCarthy presenting the other, more common extreme of unmoored masculinity.

2. See Donovan, "Sympathy and Interspecies Care," for a discussion of how a serious philosophy of sympathetic understanding between human and nonhuman others might provide a useful corrective to anthropocentric modes of being. See also Paul Alberts, "Responsibility Towards Life in the Early Anthropocene," *Angelaki* 16, no. 4 (2011); Georgette Burns, "Anthropomorphism and Animals in the Anthropocene," in *Engaging With Animals: Interpretations of a Shared Existence*, eds. Georgette Leah Burns and Mandy Patterson (Sydney: Sydney University Press, 2014); Sherry B. Ortner, "Is Female to Male as Nature is to Culture?" in *Woman, Culture, and Society*, eds. Michelle Zimbalist Rosaldo and Louise Lamphere (Stanford: Stanford University Press, 1974); Val Plumwood, *Feminism and the Mastery of Nature* (New York: Routledge, 1993); Gerda Roelvink, "Rethinking Species-Being in the Anthropocene," *Rethinking Marxism* 25, no. 1 (2013).

Secondary Source Bibliography

Alberts, Paul. "Responsibility Towards Life in the Early Anthropocene." *Angelaki* 16, no. 4 (2011): 5–17.

Auster, Paul. *In the Country of Last Things*. New York: Viking Press, 1987.

Ballard, J. G. *High-Rise*. London: Jonathon Cape, 1975.

Berkhofer, Robert F., Jr. *The White Man's Indian: Images of the American Indian from Columbus to the Present*. 2011.

Blackwell, Jeannine. "An Island of Her Own: Heroines of the German Robinsonades from 1720 to 1800." *The German Quarterly*, vol. 58.1, 1985, pp. 5–26.

Burnham, Michelle, and Freitas, James. "Introduction." *The Female American*, edited by Michelle Burnham & James Freitas, 2 ed. Broadview Press, 2014, pp. 932.

Burns, Georgette. "Anthropomorphism and Animals in the Anthropocene." In *Engaging With Animals: Interpretations of a Shared Existence*. Edited by Georgette Leah Burns and Mandy Patterson. Sydney: Sydney University Press, 2014.

Caviola, Hugo. "Behind the Transparent Wall: Marlen Haushofer's Novel *Die Wand*." *Modern Austrian Literature*, vol. 24.1, 1991, pp. 100–12.

Donovan, Josephine. "Sympathy and Interspecies Care: Toward a Unified Theory of Eco- and Animal Liberation." In *Critical Theory and Animal Liberation*, 277–95. Plymouth, UK: Rowman and Littlefield Publishers, 2011.

Fisher, Carl. "The Robinsonade: An Intercultural History of an Idea." *Approaches to Teaching Defoes Robinson Crusoe*, edited by Maximilian E. Novak & Carl Fisher, Modern Language Association, 2005, pp. 12939.

Joseph, Betty. "Re(playing) Crusoe/Pocahontas: circum-Atlantic Stagings in *The Female American*." *Criticism*, vol. 42, no. 3, 2000, pp. 317–35.

Kecht, Maria-Regina. "The Language of the Female Self Beyond the Boundaries of Discourse: Marlen Haushofer's Re-Creation of the Female Archetype." *Österreich in amerikanischer Sicht, American Council for the Study of Austrian Literature*, vol. 7, 1992, pp. 10–18.

Kunstler, James Howard. *World Made by Hand*. New York: Grove Press, 2009.

Levitas, Ruth. *The Concept of Utopia*. Syracuse University Press, 1990.

MacNeil, Denise Mary. "Empire and the Pan-Atlantic Self in *The Female American; or, the Adventures of Unca Eliza Winkfield*." *Women's Narratives of the Early Americas and the Formation of Empire*, edited by Mary McAleer Balkun & Susan Clair Imbarrato, Palgrave Macmillan, 2016, pp. 10922.

McCarthy, Cormac. *The Road*. New York: Alfred A. Knopf, 2006.

McDowell, Tremaine. "An American Robinson Crusoe." *American Literature*, vol. 1, no. 3, 1929, pp. 307–9.

Ortner, Sherry B. "Is Female to Male as Nature is to Culture?" In *Woman, Culture, and Society*. Edited by Michelle Zimbalist Rosaldo and Louise Lamphere. Stanford: Stanford University Press, 1974.

Plumwood, Val. *Feminism and the Mastery of Nature*. New York: Routledge, 1993.

Roelvink, Gerda. "Rethinking Species-Being in the Anthropocene." *Rethinking Marxism* 25, no. 1 (2013): 52–69.

Zuck, Rochelle Raineri. "New World Roots: Translatlantic Fictions, Creole Marriages, and Women's Cultivation of Empire in the Americas." *Women's Narratives of the Early Americas and the Formation of Empire*, edited by Mary McAleer Balkun & Susan Clair Imbarrato, Palgrave Macmillan, 2016, pp. 18798.

Chapter Six

Castaways, Re-Captive Slaves, and Resistance: Testing the Boundaries of Freedom in the Work of Yvette Christiansë

Simon Lewis

> Freeing yourself was one thing; claiming ownership of that freed self was another.
> —Toni Morrison, *Beloved*

Located 1,210 miles from the West African coast and 2,500 miles from Brazil, just 15 degrees south of the equator, the island of St. Helena might fairly be described as being the middle of nowhere. In "The Name of the Island," the opening poem in Yvette Christiansë's debut collection of poetry *Castaway*, it is described as "wrapped in its own ocean and a fog / that whispers and sings to itself" (1). Throughout *Castaway*, as well as in her subsequent collection *Imprendehora*, St. Helena's oceanic, fogbound locality floats somewhere between the real material island's physical coordinates and its existence in the memory and genetic heritage of Christiansë's grandmother and her descendants. St. Helena occupies a similarly fluid location in relation to the history of slavery and emancipation, troubling the distinction between marronage and maroonage. Following Great Britain's ban on the international slave trade in 1807, the island was used—intermittently—as a kind of proto-refugee camp-cum-detention center for so-called "re-captive" slaves, that is, African men, women, and children who had been captured and sold into slavery but whose trans-shipment to the New World was interrupted by the Royal Navy. Between 1808 and 1863, more than 17,000 supposedly liberated Africans disembarked on Saint Helena (Pearson, 201, da Silva et al., 45). Ostensibly free, these Africans could be held as "prize Negroes" and "distributed" to Sierra Leone or the Cape or indentured in the British Caribbean. As long as slavery was still legal—especially in the Cape, where white settlers formed a narrow majority of the population—their freedom was highly compromised, and even after slavery had been abolished in the Cape and the British Caribbean, their onward journeys from Saint Helena were often barely voluntary (Saunders; da Silva et al.; Pearson, 201–241). In Sierra Leone, some joined other returnee communities established in Freetown from the end of the American Revolutionary War on. Here the Krio-speaking community existed in uneasy relations with the Indigenous Temne, Mende, Bumon, Suso, etc. (Clifford; Fyfe, 31–238; Harris, 9–32). In the Cape, "prize Negroes" and "re-captives" gradually blended into a similarly mixed population group that came to be known as "Coloured" (Saunders; Worden et al., 108–109), the racial classification ascribed to Christiansë on her birth in South Africa in 1954. This community remained nominally free and distinct in Cape and subsequent South African political dispensations, although it was progressively disenfranchised and racially oppressed through the apartheid era.

St. Helena's "misty" location—geographically and in relation to questions of freedom, slavery, imprisonment, exile, etc.—not only troubles the binary of slave and free, maroon (deliberate) and castaway (accidental), but even beyond that, exposes the "mistiness" of race categorization. Both in her two collections of poetry and in her novel *Unconfessed*, focusing on the experience of a former slave imprisoned on Robben Island, Yvette Christiansë probes the boundaries of freedom and slavery, imprisonment and resistance through her poetic representations of a diverse group of characters we might see as at various points on the maroon-castaway spectrum. Close analysis of her work illustrates the point made by Neil Roberts in *Freedom as Marronage* that "slavery and freedom are intertwined and interdependent terms" (4). Indeed, the liminality of Christiansë's various island castaways and captives demands that we follow Roberts's lead in trying to "deepen our understanding of freedom not only by situating slavery as freedom's opposite condition, but also by investigating the significance of the equally important liminal and transitional social space *between* slavery and freedom" (4; original emphasis).

"Voicing the Silenced"

Throughout her career so far, Christiansë has set her literary skills to reconstructing some of the innumerable lost stories of the nameless dead of the middle passage, of chattel slavery, and indentured servitude. Both in her poetry (*Castaway* 1999; *Imprendehora* 2009) and in her fiction (*Unconfessed* 2006), Christiansë has mined the laconic registers of the colonial archives[1] to reconstruct the lives of people rendered, if at all, as mere numbers and names in ships' logs, court records, or colonial administrators' diaries. In creating compelling voices for these previously un-storied diasporan lives that link eighteenth-century Atlantic sites in west Africa, Madagascar and Mozambique, Robben Island and St. Helena, to Brazil, the Caribbean, and North America, via European centers of power in London, Lisbon, and elsewhere, her work crafts new "registers" of language for her freed and enslaved characters: Sila van den Kaap, the tragic infanticide; Fernão Lopez, the tongueless castaway; Sister Thomas, the fanatic convert; and her own grandmother, lost in the mental mist of Alzheimer's disease.

Christiansë's first volume of poetry, *Castaway* (1999), is her most directly autobiographical work, playing intriguingly with the poet's own personal history and the history of St. Helena, and using that interplay to show how her own multiply displaced past and diasporan ancestry embodies some of the unspoken histories of the slave trade and its contemporary consequences. Given her own southern hemisphere trajectory (born in South Africa with a maternal grandmother from St. Helena; brought up in South Africa; educated in South Africa, Swaziland, and Australia), Christiansë's work avoids the usual routes of the North Atlantic's "triangular" trade. Instead, in South African poet-critic Gabeba Baderoon's phrase, she focuses on "The African Oceans." In a provocatively titled essay "The African Oceans: Tracing the Sea as Memory of Slavery in South African Literature and Culture," Baderoon draws attention to the erasure of "Africa" as descriptor in the geographic registers we know as atlases. Baderoon begins her essay where two African oceans—the South Atlantic and the Indian—are said to meet, off Cape Town, South Africa. Referring to colonial-era representations of the city that look back from Signal Hill towards the spectacular crags of Table Mountain, Baderoon points out that these picturesque versions of the city, a city "founded on slave labor . . . rendered that labor invisible" (90). Similarly, the stories of voyages "around the Cape" most prominently played up in local memory and history are those of the Portuguese "explorers" Bartholomew Dias, Vasco Da Gama, or of the subsequent European settlers, whether Dutch, French Huguenot, or British, ignoring the fact that a significant number of enslaved Asians and East Africans were shipped westward to and beyond the Cape. Christiansë's work forces attention on these latter voyages, on the slave labor on which Cape Town was founded, and on the in-between racial category of Cape Coloured that was created in these processes.

That category of "Coloured" is distinct from other designations based on continental (European, African, Asian, American) or national (South African, British, Dutch) designations; in its failure to specify the *particular* color a "Coloured" person exhibits, it is distinct even from supposedly racial categories based on putatively discrete colors (black, white, brown, yellow, red). As such, this category that is not quite a category seems ideally associated with ideas of the black Atlantic and Paul Gilroy's preference of ships and shuttles as metaphors for identity over the false solidity of national metonyms, or of Walcott's and other Caribbean writers' notions of the sea as emblem of the perpetual flux of history rather than linearity. For Baderoon, with a nod to C. L. R. James, it is the sea—those two African oceans that come together at Cape Point—that registers what she calls South Africa's alternative slave-made modernity.

Yvette Christiansë's attempts to register the fact of slavery and the slave trade in South Africa go back to a recognition of her grandmother's slave ancestry. The last section of Christiansë's *Castaway*, headed "St. Helena—Time Line," begins with a series of apparently historical entries, complete with source citations and footnotes, detailing the known history of St. Helena. The reliability of the "information" in the timeline is almost immediately undercut, however, as the second entry, gives the date as "1502?"—conspicuously qualified by the question mark. Subsequent entries, citing various travelers' impressions of the island as well as diaries and memoirs of the retinue surrounding the exiled Napoleon, further indicate lack of objectivity. After two and a half pages of such macro-historical information, the timeline shifts to the genealogical as Christiansë begins to establish her St. Helenian ancestry. This portion of the timeline opens with reference to the registration of the birth of Christiansë's grandmother in Jamestown, St. Helena, in 1898, before tracing the intellectual and physical wanderings of the Christiansë family and of the political circumstances that made them as they were. The generic indeterminacy of the timeline—is it a mere chronology, is it an extended biographical note, is it a poem?—appropriately matches the various indeterminacies of the lives it (and the collection as a whole) contains, crucially concerning birth and race. The timeline records the following less-than-authoritative information about Christiansë's grandmother, for instance: "*1898?* 7 April. Margaret Delphine Ritch born at Jamestown, St.

Helena. / Her father *is said* to have been a first *or* second generation freed slave." As the timeline continues, the indeterminacies abound: "*Nothing is known* of her mother except that she too was born on St. Helena"; she may have had one brother, "*perhaps* two," and she died "*sometime* before 1910' (*Castaway*, 115, emphasis added).² A photograph of a man in the regalia of the Ancient Order of Foresters may be of her father or her brother. The question mark following the date of birth, the vagueness of the passive-voice constructions, the "perhaps" and the "sometime," and the uncertainty about the father *or* brother all indicate that Christiansë does not want readers to treat this timeline as an accurate or definitive text. Its essential vagueness is in fact an important part of the full volume's kind of performative argument against the desire to know, name, and control—represented, for instance, by the island's governor's insistence on referring to his prisoner Napoleon as general rather than emperor and as Buonoparte rather than Bonaparte—and in favor of the radical resistance manifested by the ability to tell one's own story regardless of the official registers.

This implicit, performative argument runs throughout the timeline. Indeed, the official record of Margaret Delphine's life becomes even more clouded as the chronology continues. When she marries, for instance, in 1920, "The marriage certificate, whose same hand signs their names for them, signs her as being born in the Cape. She objects, but the document is official. It stands." The pun on "sign" here is telling: the official (presumably white, presumably male) signs his name to attest to his identity and hence validate/authorize the (inaccurate) document—a document that not only signals and legally creates Margaret's newly married status in line with her wishes, but that also, counter both to her wishes and to actual fact, assigns her a (false) place of birth. Christiansë's re-recording of this official document allows it to "stand" again—as an allegory of the material control that writing exercised in colonial and apartheid South Africa—but ironically: to undercut the "official" and once more register an alternative subaltern voice. The family memory, however hazy and factually inaccurate, insists on its own validity by refusing the naming power of legal authority. As Christiansë puts it, "Nicknames, family names and official names mark the boundaries between the official documentation, that included those raced categories of apartheid, and the private lives in which such categories fail to account for anything but the narrowest designation of a person" (personal email correspondence).

As the timeline proceeds, it again indicates how nation-states do things with words, referring to the Group Areas Act which determines where Yvette's parents live and hence where she is to be born, and to the Bantu Education Act, which the timeline describes as being designed "to 'teach non-whites' how to 'best serve their betters'" (116). The timeline thus links the grand political narrative of apartheid South Africa with the intimate experience of the people whose lives are registered and supposedly controlled within and by it.

The struggle between the official discourse and individual autonomy continues to be reflected in the timeline's recording of Yvette's own birth, childhood, and schooling. The entry for 1954 records not only that Yvette is born on August 4 in the same year that Verwoerd "has written the Bantu Education Act," but that her "birth certificate reads '12th December.' Family secrets." Five years later, in 1959, "Yvette is sent to the white, Catholic, Belgravia Convent near Jeppe with a faked birth certificate and a lecture from Finnie [Yvette's grandmother Margaret] not to confuse it with who she really is: A Doornfontein girl, a Coloured girl. Yvette goes to school with two faces" (116). We might see Christiansë's terse chronology, drawing attention again and again to the powerful but slippery and just-barely subvertable connections among written registers, and the conditions of one's material and psychological experience of the world, as typically postmodern. Sure enough, the final line of "St. Helena—A Time Line" concludes the collection as a whole in auto-referential fashion by recording the following for 1993: "Finnie bumps against the back of Yvette's head. Yvette begins writing: 'My grandmother's island is wrapped . . . '" (117). The book's last line therefore returns us to its beginning, the opening line of the first poem "The Name of the Island," but through a strikingly physical metaphor for memory in Finnie's "bumping" against Yvette's head. In this manner, Christiansë characteristically manages to balance postmodern indeterminacy with physical reality. There are real consequences, felt in the body, to the fallacious but powerful naming practices of imperialist, colonialist, and racist authorities. Thus does Christiansë assert self-naming and the ability to tell one's own story as a theoretical mode of resistance while not diminishing the actual power of states to physically punish and to physically confine those whom they designate as unfree. This balance between an assertion of almost inviolable individual freedom as a mental condition, and the acknowledgment of imperialist, colonialist, and racist political structures to deny or limit physical freedom, runs throughout Christiansë's work.

In Christiansë's second poetry collection, *Imprendehora*, this balance comes across particularly strongly along with the sense that freedom—whether granted by controlling authorities or claimed by those formerly enslaved or imprisoned—is never quite achieved but is a work constantly in progress and against the odds. Whereas *Castaway* tends to focus on individuals exiled on St. Helena, *Imprendehora* comes closer to addressing the communal experience of re-captive slaves and their descendants; consequently, it raises intriguing questions about the nature of freedom claimed (through running away, rebellion, etc.) and freedom given (through legislation by former slave-owners). As mentioned earlier, more than 17,000 men, women, and children were held on St. Helena between 1808 and 1863; those who were resettled in Sierra Leone and in the Cape Colony became part of the ethnically mixed Krio and Coloured populations, respectively. In the same way their ethnic identity represents a kind of in-between status, their status as "re-captives" is similarly in-between, in that "liminal and transitional social space *between* slavery and freedom" that Roberts discerns as important to an analysis of marronage. If maroon communities are created by former slaves "cultivating freedom on their own terms within a demarcated social space that allows for the enactment of subversive speech acts, gestures, and social practices antithetical to the ideals of enslaving agents" (Roberts, 5), can we consider St. Helena's re-captives maroons—either during their sojourn on St. Helena or in their subsequent situations in Sierra Leone or the Cape? On the one hand, the answer is clearly no—their freedom was not cultivated on their own terms, after all, and they were still, especially in the Cape, especially before 1834, constrained by laws drafted by colonial powers.[3] However, Christiansë's work suggests that despite those constraints, the recaptives did resist the terms of their freedom and at least some of them did actively subvert their captor-liberators' ideals even though such resistance might involve self-harm. Indeed, more overtly than in *Castaway*, in *Imprendehora* Christiansë depicts her castaways as potential maroons who physically or mentally resist the terms of their freedom.

The collection takes its title from the name of a Portuguese slave ship captured by the British in 1819—after the ban on the international trade, but before the UK ended slavery in the Caribbean and in the Cape. Although the volume is grounded in archival research, as with *Castaway*, Christiansë takes deliberate poetic license with the historical sources. For instance, even the volume's title comes from a misspelling or variant spelling of *Empreendedora*, the name of a Portuguese ship captured in 1846 by the British anti-slaver HMS *Alert* and taken to St. Helena for "adjudication." *Voyages: The Trans-Atlantic Slave Trade Database* indicates that this vessel was captured before any slaves embarked, which presumably accounts for its being let go after a few months (*Voyage*, 3566). What seems to be the same vessel is recorded leaving Rio later that same year, was intercepted once more, but this time was "condemned" at St. Helena (*Voyage*, 3635). While the ship may have been taken out of the trade, its captain, one Matías José de Carvalho, remained in the business, skippering another *Empreendedora* (*Voyage*, 3825), also captured by the Royal Navy and subsequently condemned at St. Helena in July 1849. In the meantime, a larger *Empreendedora* apparently delivered 350 out of 389 captives from Benguela to Sao Sebastiao in 1842 (*Voyage*, 2239–40),[4] but was subsequently captured by the British in 1847. It disembarked 483 out of an initial group of 608 captives in Freetown, Sierra Leone.

None of this information is explicitly cited in *Imprendehora* either in the poems or in any explanatory apparatus. Christianse's collection is emphatically not a work of history, however archivally it may be rooted. Indeed, in its obliqueness, like *Castaway* it effectively provides an implicit argument against the informational aspect of historical narrative and the potentially reductive narrowing and limiting of experience and empathy that such narratives can bring about.[5] Not seeking to denote and define, or control and confine, the book weaves its separate poems together using repeated images and phrases through which the "meaning" of the poems accretes over the course of the entire collection. In addition, individual poems are gathered into sections. There is one major division into two strikingly unequal sections, "Atlantic" and "Indian," representing Baderoon's twin African Oceans, and responding to the fact that many of the re-captive slaves harbored on St. Helena had come originally from Mozambique, Madagascar, or the smaller Indian Ocean islands. The first section is further subdivided into three parts: "Scraps," "Winds," and "Rust." The poems in "Scraps" mainly use a first-person plural and express a collective response to the experience of being held as re-captives on St. Helena (although the island is named only in epigraphs citing St. Helena sources from 1846 and 1851); "Winds" comprises six poems in the voice of a furiously devout and mystical convert known only as Sister Thomas; the final section, "Rust," gives us twenty-one poems from the perspective of Fernão Lopez, introduced in *Castaway* as the island's "first exile" and cited as a possible model for Defoe's Robinson Crusoe. Lopez, who had sided with local Muslims in Goa in 1512, was confined to St. Helena between 1516 and his presumed death in 1545. As punishment for his traitorous behavior, he had had his right hand, the thumb of his left hand, ears, and nose cut off. In addition, he endured having his hair and beard shaved with clam shells (*Castaway*, 13). On top of all this, Christianse imagines him tongueless, too, leaving him both mute and unable to taste.

In giving each of these groups and individuals a voice, Christianse explores the limits of what it means to be free or not free, all prefaced by a poem that floats outside the collection's structure as a kind of foreword or extended epigraph. The poem itself has its own epigraph, an item from the *St. Helena Gazette* from March 7, 1846, recording the suicide of "a Liberated African woman, who had, the night previous, hung herself to the tree in Rupert's

Valley" (9). The poem's title "Felony" picks up on the jury's verdict of "Felo-de-se" recorded in the epigraph; what the authorities see as a crime (felony) may be a final assertion of autonomy (felo-de-se). In Roberts's terms, this "Liberated" woman has performed the ultimate act of subversion, "antithetical to the ideals" of the authorities, by taking her own life. The poem uses many of the images (night, moon, island, stone, spider, light, dark) that recur throughout the collection, and opens with an uncontextualized exclamation of "Imprendehora!" suggesting that the woman (along with the "we" of the entire "Scraps" subsection) is a re-captive taken from one of the Portuguese slavers active at the time. The exclamation is also an implicit rejection of the "enterprise" of slave-trading, invoking, as Christiansë says, "the awful history that unfolded from Columbus's 'enterprise' to the Indies."[6]

The notion hinted at in "Felony," that freedom might ultimately reside in the ability to take or at least risk one's own life, is reinforced in the first poem formally included in "Scraps." Ironically titled "Abundance," the poem, in form almost like a children's rhyme or counting song, is set in bitter counterpoint with another epigraph, this time from an 1851 edition of the *St. Helena Register*, recording the presumed death by drowning of "seven slaves" who, "in a fit of despair ... seized a boat ... and put off to sea" (15). "Caught," the third poem of "Scraps," presents the speakers being told to "be grateful, give up rage, give thanks"—presumably for their having been "liberated"—but recording that "thanks come hard" and asserting that "those who arrive and die chant/ not joy but our strongest refusal." Those who survive are said to "fall into such names"—presumably their designation by the British as "liberated Africans"—as they "learn this world's lessons" (17). In "We Are Not Sure," the message is plainer and more explicit:

> They call our days liberation,
> our feet know otherwise
> this ground hurts. (25)

The recaptives may not here be actively subverting their captor/liberators' values or explicitly countering their language, but the "knowledge" of their feet suggests that they retain an understanding of what true freedom would mean if they had the power to cultivate it on their own terms.

Here, Christiansë seems to follow the line pursued by historians critical of the self-serving nature of British emancipation procedures and the self-congratulatory narratives thereof. Writing about representations of emancipation from an art historical perspective, for instance, Marcus Wood in *The Horrible Gift of Freedom*, argues that European representations of emancipation in writing and in visual art "constitute an extended archive of liberation fantasy" (2). These fantasies, Wood writes,

> [r]epresent liberation or emancipation as an enforced donation from the empowered possessors of freedom to the unfree and disempowered slave. From the viewpoint of the giver the slave has no choice about the terms of this gift, about when, where, or how it is imposed, or about whether to accept it or not. (2)

Discussing this notion in relation to the revolutionary rhetoric of Frantz Fanon, Wood argues that "what Fanon exposes is the inability of white European and American cultures to understand that freedom, in a terribly real sense, was never something they had the power to give the slave populations they had created" (29). The actual history of the various groups of re-captive slaves shipped from St. Helena indicate that, in addition to any philosophical qualification on their notional freedom, even their material conditions were extremely constrained and they had very little choice or agency in determining their onward "distribution." Hence Christianse's representation of the suicide in "Felony," the effective suicide of the seven escapees in "Abundance," and the supposed ingratitude of the speakers in "Caught."

The absence of autonomy of the re-captive slaves is perhaps most clearly indicated in the final section of *Imprendehora*. This section is entitled "Indian," but it also has as a kind of floating subtitle the word "Katembe," referring both to an area just south of modern-day Maputo in Mozambique and to the concept of mercy. The section consists of a single long poem called "Ship's Register." Numbered entries from 343 to 372, presumably from a captured slave ship's register,[7] recording the names of the human cargo—men, women, and children as young as one year old—are set in counterpoint with a voice that speaks in a very different register. The painfully reticent descriptions of the freed captives—"353 Female Tomasine. Age 5. Stature 3-4 / Mother's name Lorratia / Several scars on left side of chest" (85)—are balanced by the poem's guiding voice, a speaker who vigorously resists being reduced to name and number. "They have no idea / who I am, and who I am / is a parcel I keep / right in my throat / like seeds in many layers/ against bad weather" (87), this speaker says, and the poem concludes with a powerful invocation from the speaker to her daughter to sing her own and her family's story: singing the names will allow her to be "reborn / On the edge of their world" and "make a dawn for them / In the reds and yellows / Of remembrance" (93).

The appeal to a resistant remembrance, here by way of hanging on to the ability to name and define one's own people and one's own circumstances, provides a link to the work of Toni Morrison, to whose *Beloved* Christiansë's only novel, *Unconfessed*, has been compared.[8] In the same way that Morrison's novel took an actual account of infanticide to create the character of Sethe, Christiansë researched the actual account of an enslaved woman known as Sila van de Kaap who had killed her own son rather than let him endure a life of enslavement. Unlike Morrison, whose Sethe diverges considerably from the real-life Margaret Garner, Christiansë remains remarkably true to the historical record.[9] Her first-person narration, however, giving consistent voice to Sila as a self-defined human being, is as plainly at odds with her representation in the historical record as the persona's voice in "Ship's Register" is at odds with the actual register's objectifying entries. In this regard, it is fascinating to read Christiansë's own account of her research into the real-life Sila as a supplement or parallel text to her novel, especially in thinking about marronage in Roberts's terms as a "liminal and transitional social space *between* slavery and freedom."

In "'Heartsore': The Melancholy Archive of Cape Colony Slavery," Christiansë gives a detailed account of the real-life Sila, reading the few "fragmented records and palpable silences" in which she appears as an implicit "repudiation of colonialism's will-to-power in knowledge. Sila van de Kaap's story," she writes, reveals "a desire for speech resulting from the inability to be heard from within slavery's discourse" (1). Citing Gayatri Spivak's influential essay "Can the Subaltern Speak?" Christiansë argues that "Sila is structurally muted in that, although we have words from her, the state never granted her full subjectivity, and her utterances remained, for them, utterly illegible" (1). *Unconfessed* seeks to redress that structural muting and denial of subjectivity and render Sila appropriately, humanly legible. Christiansë takes all of the known facts of Sila's life—her capture and enslavement in Mozambique, her supposed manumission on the death of Hendrina Jansen, and her subsequent re-enslavement, trial for child-murder, and incarceration first in Cape Town jail and subsequently on Robben Island—and allows a barely fictionalized but fully imagined Sila to tell her own story.[10]

In Christiansë's rendering Sila is as fierce in her assertion of her own freedom as any maroon. Indeed, it is her insistence on her free status on the farm of Jacobus Stephanus Van der Wat that earns both the envy of the farm's other enslaved laborers and the wrath of Van der Wat himself. In her own head, she insists on thinking of herself as a "maid—she refused to call herself a slave" (21);[11] She views Van der Wat, who serially beats and rapes her, solely as "filth"—"filth was what he was. And filth was what she called him." Despite the law's failure to recognize her status (and hence the free status of her children born after her manumission, including the murdered son Baro), Sila shows herself fully aware of how the law is supposed to operate, and struggles constantly to have others, both her fellow prisoners and the authorities, acknowledge her freedom. Precisely because she is aware of "the thinness of laws and the words that speak them" (69), she actively resists the rhetoric of the minister and minister's wife who wish to baptize her, and seems to embrace with subversive pride the warden's descriptions of her as "impertinent, sullen, disobedient" (84). When her life sentence is commuted to a fourteen-year term, she scornfully rejects the "horrible gift" of the royal "pardon." The deliberate vulgarity of her language here is in itself a kind of enactment of her repudiation of the authorities' values: "I should send a message of my own, tell them, *you bags of piss and wind who blow the stench of your nine days into fourteen years, you know nothing*" (130; italics in original). Unlike her fellow prisoner Mina, who attempts to comply with the authorities in hope of getting more lenient treatment for herself and her daughter, Sila stubbornly refuses to accept the terms applied to her. Such refusal to accept the definer's definitions, of course, has material consequences, and indeed at times the material surroundings and mental pressure on Sila seem almost to derange her. As in the case of the seven re-captives' doomed attempt to escape from St. Helena in "Abundance," there is, nevertheless, still something heroic in it.

At the core of Sila's resistance of course is her rejection of the court's narrative that casts her as child-murderer. In "Heartsore," Christiansë offers a complex and detailed reading of this process based on the court documents. While Sila did have the benefit of legal representation, and while Christiansë describes the appeal of Van Ryneveld, the advocate on her behalf, as presenting "a tableau that clearly attempts to negate and redeem Sila's image as a rebellious monster-slave" (19), Christiansë insistently reminds us that we have only the barest traces of Sila's own words; "she may speak but only as a slave woman is expected to speak, and in a manner that makes her speech evidence of her confinement to that status. In effect, when she is before the courts, Sila can only answer, and what she says is what has already been said, but not by her" (20). In the novel's versions of the court proceedings, filtered through the fictional Sila's consciousness, Christiansë succeeds in affording Sila the subjectivity denied both by her slave status and by her representation in the archive; at the same time, in typically oblique fashion, she reasserts Sila's inability to speak. Sila recalls, for instance, the moment during her trial when she "could not say as they wanted me to say" (232) about her killing of Baro. Where the historical record is silent, Christiansë fills in the "palpable silences" between the lawyer's insistent questions, but Sila's words are all presented under erasure of her "could not say." She could not say, for instance,

> that I had loved him and held him in my lap when he at last cried himself to sleep. I could not say that the hand that stole the knife shook, or that I lifted my dear boy into my lap and held him, and stroked him and known that he was already beyond all of them, even me. . . . No. I could say nothing of the way that love had required that I crush all horror even as I faced it. (232)

As a result of her silence, her act is recorded as a "heinous crime." "Yes. Yes. That is its name in this room," thinks Sila, but she knows they are framing the wrong questions: "They wanted to know about that last moment my boy was of this earth. But not if he suffered" (233). While her refusal to answer is recorded in the court account as "insolence," Christiansë recasts her eloquent but unexpressed thoughts as resistance. Like the castaways and re-captives in her poetry, Christiansë's Sila lays claim to a maroon's right of self-naming and self-definition despite her legal lack of freedom and physical powerlessness.

While it may be a stretch to compare Sila and Christiansë's other island captives with the twentieth century's most famous inhabitants of Robben Island, the refusal of Nelson Mandela and the other political prisoners incarcerated with him on the island to accept the apartheid regime's definitions of them does offer the intriguing possibility of considering Mandela and his co-prisoners as a kind of maroon community. Despite their material conditions, Mandela and his fellow prisoners famously transformed the island into the "University of the ANC." As early as 1964, Ahmed Kathrada wrote in a letter that "when Ma or anyone at home starts worrying about me, they must just imagine that I'm not in jail but at university" (Kathrada 39), and over time it became almost commonplace to consider former prisoners as "graduates of Robben Island" (Sampson).[12] This is not to suggest that conditions on Robben Island were remotely comfortable—far from it—but Mandela himself later described how "the inmates not the authorities, seemed to be running the prison" (Mandela 536). In his famous rejection of an offer of conditional release in 1985 by then state president P. W. Botha, Mandela showed how well he understood the manner in which a conditional offer would have meant not only accepting the specific terms of the release, but also conceding the power to define terms in general. Mandela could not be tempted by the immediate material benefit of release, uncompromisingly writing to Botha that "if I emerged from prison into the same circumstances under which I was arrested, I would be forced to resume the same activities for which I was arrested" (621). The reasons for Mandela's and Sila's imprisonment may not have much in common, but, if we accept Christiansë's rendering of Sila's resistance, both illustrate an indomitableness of spirit that ultimately counteracts and overcomes the physical limitations of unfreedom.

As with the inner freedom of her other castaways, re-captives, and exiles, Christiansë does not romanticize Sila's material conditions. Mandela, as we all know, completed his long walk to freedom in triumphant style; of the real-life Sila, following 1827, when her prison term was shortened, we know absolutely nothing. If she survived the remaining years of her prison term, she would have emerged not just as a free woman, but into a society where slavery was no longer legal. However, as Christiansë states in her nonfiction account, not only does Sila vanish from the record after 1827, but her son Baro is only ever absent; there is not even a record, after all, of him *not* responding to official discourse. Christiansë thus "cautions contemporary historians against appropriating Sila for the cause of resistance and the history of Western subjects-in-the-making.... The certainty of Sila's act may transform her by extending her beyond her delegated position, but the fact that Baro bears the full burden of this violence puts the brakes on any runaway 'triumphalism' of late twentieth-century readerly practice" (21).

The ending of *Unconfessed* accordingly offers an ending even more qualified, aporetic, and self-referential than *Castaway*. Throughout her captivity on Robben Island, like Christiansë's earlier castaways, prisoners, exiles, and re-captive slaves, Sila's ability to voice memories of freedom in the past had been crucial in allowing her to envisage the possibility of freedom in the future. The novel's final page offers a mere two paragraphs in which a variety of different versions of what happened to Sila are proposed, including the possibility that she died while still imprisoned. The last of these severely qualified versions imagines Sila improbably achieving her wish to live out the domestic life she has always dreamed of: "a quiet freedom in the shadow of Signal Hill" (341). This final image of wished-for domestic peace contrasts starkly with the violence and brutality of Sila's lived experience, as fantastic and ridiculous as Baderoon's picturesque colonial images of Cape Town that attempt to erase the materiality of slavery.

In voicing the unvoiced, Christiansë helps us fully to register both the enormity of slavery and the persistent possibility of resisting the status of slave. Whether the voices are characterized by the ethereal beauty of the reds and yellows of remembrance of the speaker of "Ship's Register," by the vulgarity and near-derangement of Sila, the fanaticism of Sister Thomas, the tonguelessness of Fernão Lopez, or the memorial haze of Christiansë's grandmother, they all acknowledge the power of having been named, categorized, and imprisoned/enslaved by external forces. All are thus only liminally free, but all demonstrate the desire to "cultivat[e] freedom on their own terms" that Roberts sees as definitive of marronage. Never fully free but always resisting freedom as a gift on the terms of the giver, Christiansë's castaways and prisoners might be considered to be in a perennially precarious state of ongoing self-freeing, a state indeed of marronage. While Roberts is more interested in discussing maroon *communities* that can create their freedom "within a demarcated social space," Christiansë is more concerned with the individual "enactment of subversive speech acts, gestures, and social practices antithetical to the ideals of slaving agents" (5). In expressing themselves in the language of these slaving agents, they find themselves only partly able to express/free themselves. Cut off from mothers and mother tongues, their texts are conveyed in an English that is, as Marie Nourbese Philip has it, a "foreign anguish." Although Christiansë seems to insist that self-naming can be a liberatory act of mental marronage, the weight of history, the weight of those terse sentences in the ships' registers, is felt as physically as the weight of slave shackles.

Notes

1. In discussing her own practice of archival research, Christiansë draws attention to the different functions of the formal archives maintained by British colonial, apartheid-era South African, and current national South African administrations. Under the current administration, records are no longer expected merely to contain "information" but also to provide evidence of absence and exclusion that may allow researchers to "vindicate their rights" ("Heartsore" 2).

2. In fact, Christiansë's own genealogical research suggests that the family name was probably "Thomas." St. Helena genealogical researcher Chris Hillman was unable to find anyone with the surname "Ritch" (personal email correspondence).

3. Among other factors, the demographic differences between the almost entirely African Freetown, dominated by resettled former slaves from Britain's American colonies and transported Jamaican Maroons, and the white settler-dominated Cape means that the two communities have very little in common beyond absorbing a certain proportion of re-captives.

4. For details of these ships' voyages, see the website *Voyages: The Trans-Atlantic Slave Trade Database* at http://www.slavevoyages.org. Christiansë would probably take wry note of the database's fallibility in this particular case, where the same voyage appears to have been entered twice.

5. Christiansë's "Heartsore" explicitly critiques the "mining" of archives for historical "nuggets of fact" (4), critiquing the way, for instance, the language of the archive can reduce someone like Sila to the status solely of "slave": "the single noun 'slave' exists before and after all (slave) names" (22).

6. Personal email correspondence, August 29, 2017.

7. Although Christiansë does not indicate the source of the ship's register, Shaun de Waal's review of *Imprendehora* for the *Mail and Guardian* identifies it as coming from "the

Columbine, a British ship policing the Mozambique Channel in the years after the official end of slavery." While the names and details are presumably drawn directly from this archival source, Christiansë appears to want to avoid having her work read *as* history, or as a supplement to history.

8. The Barnes and Noble site advertising *Unconfessed* gives prominence to extracts from reviews in *Kirkus Reviews* and the *Library Journal* (https://www.barnesandnoble.com/w/unconfessed-yvette-Christianse/1103165522), while Tavis Smiley referred to the comparison as part of his introduction during his interview with Christiansë on his television show on February 15, 2007 (https://www.ket.org/episode/TASM%20%20001029/).

9. Unlike Sethe, the real-life Margaret Garner was re-enslaved and sold "down the river," dying of typhoid on a Mississippi plantation in 1858, two years after killing her two-year-old daughter. For further details and links, see the "Margaret Garner" page of the Cincinnati Museum Center (http://library.cincymuseum.org/aag/bio/garner.html). For details of the real-life Sila van den Kaap, see Christiansë's "Heartsore."

10. The novel uses actual names of the people who claimed ownership of Sila as well as actual Cape Colony officials and precise dates for key events, including Sila's murder of her son Baro on December 24, 1822.

11. Cf. Christiansë's discussion of the significance of the word *meid* (maid) in the legal hearing of 1827. Sila's attempt "to define the meaning of the word maid as [free] domestic servant, as opposed to the 'very common practice' of referring to a female slave as a junior and unmarried woman" failed to persuade the court ("Heartsore" 19).

12. For a full discussion of the formal and informal curricula of the "university," see Buntman, chapter 4, "Resistance Beyond Survival" (61–80).

Secondary Source Bibliography

Baderoon, Gabeba. "The African Oceans: Tracing the Sea as Memory of Slavery in South African Literature and Culture." *Research in African Literatures* 40.4 (Winter 2009): 89–107.
Buntman, Fran Lisa. *Robben Island and Prisoner Resistance to Apartheid*. Cambridge: Cambridge University Press, 2003.
Christiansë, Yvette. *Castaway*. Durham, NC: Duke University Press, 1999.
Christiansë, Yvette. *Imprendehora*. Los Angeles: Kwela Books, 2009.
Christiansë, Yvette. *Unconfessed*. New York: Other Press, 2006.
Clifford, Mary Louise. *From Slavery to Freetown: Black Loyalists after the American Revolution*. McFarland, 1999.
Fyfe, Christopher. *A History of Sierra Leone*. Oxford University Press, 1968.
Harris, David. *Sierra Leone*. Oxford University Press, 2014.
Kathrada, Ahmed. *Letters from Robben Island: A Selection of Ahmed Kathrada's Prison Correspondence, 1964–1989*. Michigan State University Press, 1999.
Pearson, Andrew. *Distant Freedom: St. Helena and the Abolition of the Slave Trade, 1840–1872*. Liverpool University Press, 2016.
Roberts, Neil. *Freedom as Marronage*. Chicago: University of Chicago Press, 2015.
Saunders, Christopher. "Liberated Africans in Cape Colony in the First Half of the Nineteenth Century." *The International Journal of African Historical Studies* 18.2 (1985): 223–39.
Worden, Nigel, Elizabeth van Heyningen, and Vivian Bickford-Smith. *Cape Town: The Making of a City*. David Philip, 1998.

Chapter Seven

The Opacity of Home—Being Marooned at the End of the World

Claire P. Curtis

Stop that, Toby, she tells herself. This is how it starts, among the closed circles of the marooned, the shipwrecked, the besieged: jealousy, dissention, a breach in the groupthink walls. Then the entry of the foe, the murderer, the shadow slipping in through the door we forgot to lock because we were distracted by our darker selves: nursing our minor hatreds, indulging our petty resentments, yelling at one another, tossing the crockery.
—Margaret Atwood, *MaddAddam*

There is a natural convergence between utopian texts, post-apocalyptic texts, and maroonage tales. To start with, many utopian texts, both contemporary and classical, begin from a maroonage premise. For example, Charlotte Perkins Gilman's *Herland* recounts a group of women marooned in their home valley after an earthquake closes off the only pass to the outside while all of the able-bodied men are at war. Edward Bellamy's *Looking Backward* has Julian West marooned through his 120-year sleep to awaken in a Boston radically different from the one in which he fell asleep. Thomas More's eponymous *Utopia* describes an origin story based upon a group of Romans and Egyptians who were shipwrecked on Utopia 1,200 years prior to the arrival of Raphael Hythloday. So a compelling argument can be made that utopias are often constructed in relation to the experience of being marooned. While not classic maroonage tales, these utopian accounts do use the maroonage experience to create or encounter new and better societies. The classic visitor who narrates a utopian text is marooned in the utopian space (as compared to the dystopian text where the protagonist is usually a resident of the dystopian space).

Post-apocalyptic texts also begin with being marooned. What is an account of the end of the world but an account of the survivors marooned from all that they once knew into a world of zombies, rising seas, or plague wastelands? Margaret Atwood's MaddAddam trilogy and Kim Stanley Robinson's *2312* are both post-apocalyptic critical utopian texts that use marooonage as heuristic about the idea of home and as an occasion for self-understanding. Constructed specifically on an apocalyptic premise, each novel considers the utopian enclave, the limits of home as safe space, and the problematic idea of rescue. These are "critical utopian" accounts[1]—not the classic blueprint utopia that narrates the lived details of a radically better world as, for example, in the three examples of utopia cited initially, nor the Enlightenment-style post-apocalyptic tale that uses the purported end as a backdrop for the heroics of world building. Instead, these are accounts that wrestle with the idea of a space or society being radically better while still infused with hope. And the hope is connected to this wrestling with the idea of being better. "A central concern of the critical utopia is the awareness of the limitations of the utopian tradition, that these texts reject utopia as blueprint while preserving it as dream.... Finally the novels focus on the continuing presence of difference and imperfection within the utopian society itself" (Moylan, 10). The idea of home is part of both the utopian and the particularly critical utopian nature of these novels. And maroonage is a useful method for highlighting how we should learn to think about home.

If a utopian enclave is one "in which new wish images of the social can be elaborated and experimented on" (Jameson *Archaeologies*, 16)—or, put another way, if describing a utopian enclave is "to create a space in which the reader is both brought to experience an alternative and called to judgment on it" (Levitas, 56)—then how might the maroonage premise impact these "wish images" or these alternatives? Maroonage can be examined as precisely the way into the critical utopian imagining of the utopian space: a space that is not ideal or perfect—one that is not a creation of a new home toward which we should all strive. Instead, the maroonage premise allows the reader a method by which the questioning of the utopian space as potential home and a questioning of the idea of home. What does home mean? Is home the thing from which we are marooned? And, if it is, then is the goal rescue or return?

This chapter looks towards the post-apocalyptic as a new site for the maroonage premise of utopian space. On the one hand, the chapter is built on a claim that is only defended briefly: that post-apocalyptic novels are the new site of utopian imaginings—of creating Jameson's "wish image." On the other hand, we explore the ways in which the idea of maroonage helps to clarify the particular content of the post-apocalyptic imagining. One can best understand the way in which maroonage does this clarifying work by focusing on particular instances of being marooned that wrestle with the idea of home.

Being marooned is both an act of resistance and the happenstance of being lost. Those who are lost are marooned from something—from their journey or their home or their expectations—and their purported aim is then to return home. Those who manage to escape, who choose being marooned as an act of freedom understand being marooned differently. Here, maroonage is not something that happens to you, but something out of which you create a new way of living, a new idea of home. The epigraph above from Atwood and a related quotation from Robinson—"I hate this." (Robinson 2312, 171)—highlight these modes of maroonage. In Atwood's epigraph, Toby considers the fact of living after a worldwide pandemic. Her reference to "stop that" highlights the precarious bonds of community among those lost and trying to start over. Yet I argue that Toby is not simply counseling herself to be better at creating a home at the end of the world. Instead, she is able to see the inherent problems in home building. Toby is not seduced by the promise of an empty world in which she can create a "city on a hill." This image of the city as *example*, so central to the Puritan and later Reaganic imagination, is far from Toby's understanding. Neither Atwood nor Robinson are participating in that style of heroics. In the above quotation from Robinson's *2312*, Swan reflects on how she hates being marooned from the home, now destroyed, that she helped to create and loves. Warham responds with the insistent lesson of both of these post-apocalyptic maroonage stories: "and yet, here we are" (Robinson, 171).

This chapter uses that insistent "here we are" to consider the idea of home, the limits of both the safety that home can provide and of rescue. Analyzing each novel in turn, the chapter argues that both novels use maroonage as a method toward capturing the critical utopian "wish image" in the precarious idea of home. Highlighting the repeated use of the language of being marooned in both novels illustrates a different way to read the equally repeated language of home and community building. With the language of maroonage as the lens through which these critical utopian novels are read, we will consider a rethinking of home built on the premise that to be marooned is to be human.

Margaret Atwood: *MaddAddam*

The MaddAddam trilogy is set in an unnamed city in North America beginning in a future unidentified other than by teenagers recounting parental memories. "Remember hamburger chains, always real beef, remember hot dog stands" (Atwood 2003, 63). That timeline seems to put the trilogy in the 2050s, when corporations and corporate enclaves now seem to run everything, climate change has radically altered familiar cities, and New York is now New New York, shifted inland with rotting skyscrapers disrupting the sound of the surf that daily eats away at them, and genetic engineering is producing human-pig splices (called pigoons, which were bred to grow human organs),[2] dog/wolf splices (wolvogs, bred for protection), and a new iteration of humans: the Crakers. The three novels are set in two futures, the one described above and also a post-apocalyptic world after the ravages of a purposefully released viral pandemic (referred to as the waterless flood). The three novels follow a small number of characters through the years preceding and the months following this apocalyptic collapse.

Toby in the Atwood epigraph above uses being marooned to describe, not simply those marooned after the plague ("Beleaguered groups are prone to such festering: such backbiting, such infighting" [90]), but also the community of those in love. To succumb to the jealousy she feels at Zeb's wandering eye is to break the bonds of those marooned. As a woman in love at the end of the world, Toby is both experiencing something wholly familiar, uncertainty about the depth of her love interest's reciprocity, and the challenges of living in this post-apocalyptic world, largely denuded of people, but still including threats. Toby is part of the "closed circle of the marooned" who can be torn apart by their "darker selves." She notes that the younger survivors are both amused and perplexed by the love between Toby and Zeb. "Romance among the chronologically challenged is giggle fodder," she thinks (89). She could take herself down the dark spiral of self-doubt and the momentarily satisfying tearing down of those others that she fears her love may desire. But doing so will create that first "breach" in what she calls the "groupthink walls." Why "groupthink"? In part, this references the prior existing community of the Gardeners. On the other hand, Toby is noting the necessity of a kind of groupthink among the marooned: survival may demand it.

Toby, who does not appear as a named character until the second novel, was previously a leader, a former "Eve" among this group of God's Gardeners, who had lived as a group of vegan, survivalist doomsday preppers in the corporate enclave world prior to the plague. Toby is then both marooned by the waterless flood among God's Gardeners (plus some add-ons) and marooned by her emotions. Loving Zeb and living after the plague both displace her from where she expected to be. In neither case is Toby "at home." She notes earlier, thinking about her love of Zeb, that "she'd longed for this, and denied it was possible. But how easy it is, like coming home must have been once, for those who'd had homes" (49). This final novel of Margaret Atwood's MaddAddam trilogy explicitly offers a critical utopian moment of hope on the idea of home as contrasted with the darker, dystopian imaginings of the two previous novels, which more directly use maroonage as a sign of the failure of the home creating traditions embedded in the heroic maroonage account.

The first novel of the trilogy, *Oryx and Crake* (Atwood 2003), describes Snowman (known as Jimmy in the scenes prior to the apocalypse) as a failed Robinson Crusoe. Imagining himself to be alone after a plague has wiped out the rest of humanity, Snowman lives in a tree to escape the pigoons and wolvogs, eating melted and half-crushed protein bars that he finds in the decaying ex-urbs surrounding the park to which he has withdrawn. Snowman is an incompetent survivor, not resourceful or resilient. He seems unable to muster even the energy to build a reasonable shelter or to find a source of food more reliable than the weekly fish he has convinced the Crakers (the human 2.0 photosynthesizing and plant-eating genetic marvels that he has freed from the lab dome home) to ritually bring him. Snowman experiences no pleasure in being the Last Man Alive. If this first novel is using maroonage as a heuristic the lesson is harsh: don't expect heroics or a new vision of home.

The second novel, *The Year of the Flood* (Atwood 2009), follows roughly the same time span, but instead of Snowman's post-apocalyptic apathy it focuses on a trio of women, all resourceful, who knew each other in their pre-apocalyptic lives (all lived among God's Gardeners) and come back to one another in the post-plague landscape. Toby, of the initial epigraph, is the oldest of the three, and she has been living in the AnooYoo spa, eating vegetables from the garden she has planted. She gets fats and proteins from the leftover spa products and the other materials she had stashed in her "Ararat," as she was instructed by God's Gardeners in preparation for the waterless flood. In both the pre- and post-apocalyptic world, Toby is reliable and resilient. From the perspective of maroonage, she has already experienced being marooned from the relative safety of her early family life after the suspicious deaths of her parents, and then marooned again among God's Gardeners who rescue her from the violence of her boss at Secret Burgers. Among the Gardeners, on the rooftops of a decaying city, Toby learns how to garden and keep bees and eventually becomes an Eve, a member of the governing council. Toby is taught precisely those skills she will need post-apocalypse. These are skills that Jimmy/Snowman never receives in his more pampered, gated, corporate life. And yet possessing those skills is also not the key to rebuilding or to coming home. The second novel ends on a moment of spectacular failure of rescue. Despite all of Toby's skills, this new world is not one in which old skills will guarantee success.

By the third novel, *MaddAddam* (Atwood 2013), the tension between incompetence and competence, between apathy and resilience has been complicated. It is not that Snowman is a failure and that Toby and company are successful maroons. Rather, readers notice that the very experience of starting over means recognizing that there is no rescue. This "wherever you are, there you are" moment clarifies the ideas of both rescue and home. To be marooned is not to be rescued, or at least not to be rescued in order to go home again; to be marooned is to see yourself as you are. Toby's susceptibility to jealousy is not the sign that she has somehow failed the test of the waterless flood. Instead, Toby's description in the initial epigraph highlights precisely what Atwood, and Robinson, are using maroonage to do in these critical utopian post-apocalyptic novels. The acts of maroonage are simply moments in these texts of reminder that being human is to be marooned.

Three particular moments in *MaddAddam* highlight the ways in which the characters in the novels come to this recognition of being marooned as being human. First is the utopian enclave, the wished-for space that the marooned imagine will recreate home. In post-apocalyptic texts, the creation of this space is the most Robinsonade moment of the texts.[3] The nesting or setting up of a home space is often the source of the post-apocalyptic novel's utopian sensibility. *MaddAddam* includes two such spaces: the pre-apocalyptic rooftop enclaves of the God's Gardeners and the post-apocalyptic space for survivors in the cob houses. In both instances, spaces are identified that are able to be protected from external threats and within the spaces the communities nest—creating homes. Both the protective mechanisms and the nesting are sensitive to conditions, so that the God's Gardener's choose the rooftops and top floors of largely abandoned buildings in the pleeblands, presuming (rightly at first) that they will be both ignored and easily ignorable using space no one wants in an area few with wealth and power care about. It is here that they can establish their vegetarian doomsday prepping lifestyle.

After the plague, the few survivors end up in a park pavilion made of corn cob houses from which they can start a garden, utilize the bathroom solar power, and establish a fence line to protect against the pigoons and the escaped painballers. They begin to build new living spaces once their numbers increase, and everyone decorates and tends to wear the differently decorated sheets (as makeshift weather-appropriate attire in the high heat and humidity) that seem to be as ubiquitous as the fast growing kudzu that they are learning to eat. But building these spaces is not itself the act of creating community or even of coming home. "'What to eat, where to shit, how to take shelter, who and what to kill: are these the basics?' thinks Toby. 'Is this what we've come to, or come down to; or else come back to? And who do you love?'" (98). This passage begins with the daily needs—the stuff of the utopian ingenuity of the classic heroic maroonage tale. And yet Toby is not asking these questions to introduce a rich description of the innovations of the cob house space. Instead, she is noting here, first, that the basics are not enough, which is clear once Toby asks "who do you love" at the end of her more prosaic account of enclave creation. Second, embedded in Toby's account here is not simply the plaintive questioning of who to love but also the realistic asking of "who and what to kill." The threats to the utopian enclave of the cob houses will not be the glorious moment of establishing the sanctity of home, but instead a messy reckoning with the limits of building a space that is safe.

This is then the second moment of rethinking home through the act of maroonage: recognizing the limits of safety of the utopian enclave, seeing the necessary precariousness of the home being built. To create a utopian space and imagine that, unlike the original home from which one has been marooned, this new home will be safe is an illusion that *MaddAddam* (and *2312*) confronts. Neither the rooftop enclave, nor the cob houses provide physical or psychic safety. Zeb readily admits "this place is hardly a fortress" (274) as they prepare to fight back against the painballers. Atwood has included in her post-apocalyptic trilogy a threat that is not unlike the seemingly ubiquitous cannibals of other post-apocalyptic novels.[4] The painballers are survivors not simply of the plague, but also of the underground, money-making privatization of punishment that the pre-apocalyptic world embraced. Painball was a televised game in which convicts were offered the opportunity of freedom in the guise of winning a killer-takes-all game for the pleasure of the audience. However, the winners of the games did not acclimate well to living back in society. The violence that the painballers seem to love is a challenge to any safe living (before and after the plague). But defeating the painballers is not a triumphant battle that will highlight the safety of the enclave. It is a messy slog that simply reminds readers that safety is illusory. Even the conclusion of the battle, with a trial over what to do with the injured painballers, signals that glorious victory is less likely than tense deliberation.

Atwood only recounts the story of the battle with Blackbeard telling it to the other Crakers after the fact. The storytelling is then told in the stilted language of a group of humans who do not really see the world the way the reader does (which is a source of humor in the book, but also a tactic of yanking the reader out of her own imagining of what matters in the world). Blackbeard begins: "This is the Story of the Battle. It tells how Zeb and Toby and Snowman-the-Jimmy and the other two-skinned ones and the Pig Ones needed to clear away the bad men, just as Crake cleared away the people in the chaos to make the good and safe place for us to live" (358). He frames the story as precisely an attempt to create a "safe place." And yet as the story goes on, recounting the death of some of the "Pig Ones" (pigoons), of Adam, Zeb's long-lost brother, and of Snowman, the reader sees this as a child's story of trying to make the world right again.

MaddAddam is not a novel that celebrates the creation of a utopian "safe space." Instead, it is a novel that uses the marooned state of its characters to note that such safe spaces are an illusion; they are a child's story. The novel ends ambiguously. On the one hand, the more obvious threat of the painballers is gone (after a trial and a decision to execute them). On the other hand is the more elusive recognition that humans will have to learn to live with and among the Crakers and the pigoons. Recognizing these new inhabitants in their community expands both the meaning of home and the problem of being marooned. Living in this new world will require an expanded understanding of what it is to be human.

Being marooned is now the new normal. And those who have survived realize that there is no rescue. The novel ends with another story inserted into the larger story that has framed the novel—the story that Toby has been telling the Crakers about their own history and the people that they love, as Snowman did in the first novel. Blackbeard, the Craker child that Toby has taught to read and write, inserts the story of Toby's departure and death. "The three beloved Oryx Mothers cried very much when Toby went away. We cried as well, and purred over them, and after a while they felt better. And Ren said, Tomorrow is another day, and we said we did not understand what that meant, and Amanda said, Never mind because it was not important. And Lotis Blue said it was a thing of hope" (390). It is this "thing of hope" that not only signals the novel as a critical utopia, but also clarifies the way in which this community of the marooned will come together.

The tension between building a home and wanting to be safe is made clearer in Kim Stanley Robinson's 2012 novel, *2312*. As with Atwood's novel, Robinson's is not presented as a maroonage tale. But it is a novel that uses multiple instances of being marooned that link the utopian with the post-apocalyptic. If *MaddAddam* focuses on the creation of the utopian enclave as the response to being marooned, then *2312* focuses on instances of being marooned to highlight what it means to recognize a space as utopian, as a kind of home.

Kim Stanley Robinson, *2312*

2312 is a novel that could be read as an extended utopian story of maroonage: 300 years in our future, humans live on Saturn, Mercury, Mars, in asteroids, and on the moons of Jupiter. Those who live off Earth, the spacers, return to Earth every seven years for a bone-building sabbatical that contributes to the longevity of spacers (it is common to live 200 years). Earth is thus home, the place to which we must return. But Earth is also the thing from which we have escaped: it is degraded, overpopulated, and yet it "exerted a fatal attraction" (349).

In the opening epigraph "I hate this" is Swan's declaration about the fact of her being marooned, with Warham, in the tunnels under Mercury after the city Terminator is destroyed. And Warham's phlegmatic response "and yet, here we are" recalls the blunt fact of being marooned. Swan may well hate walking the tunnels under the surface of Mercury aiming for the dark side of the planet after the destruction of Swan's home city, Terminator. Hating the walk, its repetitions, does not change the fact of the walk.

2312 is more overt in its use of maroonage. Rather than the global act of being marooned after an apocalyptic event, as in *MaddAddam*, Robinson includes two particular moments when his two main characters are specifically marooned: the experience of Swan and Warham in the tunnels under Mercury and their later experience after the explosion of the space ship ETH Mobile. The novel ends with the final, more problematic moment of maroonage in the purposeful return of North American mammals to North America. This final moment is not described as a maroonage story, and yet reading it as such again emphasizes that stories of being marooned need not be stories of heroic conquer.

Early in the novel, Swan and Warham leave the city Terminator to attend a concert in a crater concert hall carved into the surface of Mercury. While walking back to the city, both it and the tracks on which it circumnavigates Mercury (to escape the full force of the sun) are destroyed (the novel is also a mystery, the destruction of Terminator is an act of sabotage). Swan and Warham must run in their spacesuits across the landscape to beat the sunrise and find access to the repair tunnels beneath the surface. Once beneath the surface they can either wait for the sun to recede (three months) or they can walk east and emerge after sunset forty-five days later. They are thus marooned from the safety of the city (which has been destroyed) and also, in the case of Swan, marooned from the very existence of her city. They must survive under the tunnels, but that survival is not the exciting and masterful search for supplies or subduing of the local environment. Instead, survival is a slog. And the slog is the point. There is no home to be built under the tunnels. The questions Toby asks—"what to eat, where to shit, how to take shelter" (Atwood 2013, 98)—are answered here. But the answers are not the result of ingenious problem-solving. The tunnels are built as a space of refuge from the surface sun. This is the point of the opening passage: "I hate it here" "And yet here we are" may well be the message of the use of being marooned. Rather than an opportunity for heroic self-determination, maroonage is instead an opportunity to experience the "iterative," the daily, often pointless, routine of human living.

Warham and Swan are marooned from the safety of a domed city on a planet uninhabitable for humans without a spacesuit, space vehicle or the city, Terminator. Swan is specifically marooned from her home. She is a designer of worlds, an artist who not only was raised in Terminator, the city, but who also helped design that city, which is no more. "So much got left behind. A whole world. If a world dies, its people don't matter anymore—so the howl [Swan's] seemed to say" (152). Swan's grief is not for the deaths of the people of Terminator. It is clear that the vast majority of people were able to be evacuated safely.[5] Instead, Swan's howl is about the destruction of her home, the place where her work has the most meaning. "It was ever so much better to be home, getting back into her living and her hands dirty" (388). The "better" here is in contrast with Earth—better to be home, in the rebuilding of her city, than to be on Earth, the problem that she feels obligated to solve.

But if Swan is marooned from her home city and all that city represents to her, she is also marooned as a claustrophobe who hates routine. Just as Toby is marooned as a woman in love, each is marooned as herself and part of being marooned is the experience of living with herself.

"They lived only to hike around Mercury" (162). Day in and out, three hours of walking, a half-hour of rest, three cycles a day, and then sleep in the tunnels only to wake up and walk more the next day. "So, walk for an hour, in a tunnel that changed very little, and only in iterative steps" (164). They whistle symphonies together, tell their life stories, complain, sleep curled next to each other, and eventually Warham will push Swan in a cart because she suffers from radiation poisoning. The walk is tedious, yet comforting. For Warham, comforted by the practice of daily routine, the walk is both an experiment in living and an opportunity to know Swan. "It was the most iterative pseudoiterative he would ever live, thus interesting" (181). For Swan, who is claustrophobic and averse to any routine, the walk is both anxiety-producing and also the instance of her body's breakdown. "This motif, of the unhappy voyage of necessity, it's limited. It's played out. I want a different story" (166). And who does not want a different story?

In some respects, the survival tale, the maroonage tale, the post-apocalyptic story, the utopia—all of these are the "different story" that we seek. In the "different story," we think of ourselves as being in a better space, because that space is whatever we are *not* experiencing right now. But Warham, again, notes that it is in the wanting of the different story that we find the *will* (not the strength, nor the narrative that everything happens for a reason, but simply the will) to be where we are. "Here the pseudoiterative needed to be held to as a comfort. Lick one's wounds. All these things had happened before and would happen again" (196). So, in this first, expanded instance of being marooned, Swan and Warham, who are rescued (or who, more accurately, stumble upon two people in a space rover after Swan insists they go up to the surface to the noon sun), find that their experience of being marooned in the tunnels of Mercury becomes the fact that launched their relationship. "They were being rescued. Swan and Warham stared at each other. 'Oh no!' Swan said faintly—as if they had tripped into an unexpected disaster—as if she were going to miss the second half of their walk. That made him smile" (206). Perhaps we are to understand Swan's perplexing response here as a recognition both that rescue is never simple and that the tunnels provided a space that she will miss. The enclave of the tunnels is not simply a space from which one must be rescued.

Towards the end of the novel, Swan and Warham find themselves marooned again. The spaceship in which they are riding has to intercept another attack (by the same group that had attacked Terminator's track) on the Venusian sunshield. And so they, and the other thousands of passengers on the spaceship ETH Mobile must evacuate,[6] some on rescue ships, and some, like Warham and Swan, in spacesuits. But then the rescue ship coming to get them was hit by debris, and Swan and Warham are flung further into space, with Warham injured by that debris.

Just prior to their evacuation, Swan makes a distinction between the vulnerability of the human body ("your body can break—it will break") and the hoped for invulnerability of home. "You should be able to count on them lasting. Someone should not be able to pop all that, like popping a soap bubble with a pin" (539). This is, in part, a comment on the vulnerability of living in outer space, always dependent on the external. It is, in part, Robinson's reminder to his readers that we are in the only inhabitable planet in our solar system and that a comment by a fictional person living three hundred years in our future could remind us of our living in a place where it may take more than the proverbial pin to pop our world. But this is also a comment on their upcoming evacuation and their being marooned in space, tethered by their suits, this time with Swan caring for Warham.

"Nothing to do but wait. Keep breathing. Wait and see. It had been a luxury in her life always to be able to do something, never to have to wait. Now reality kicked in. Sometimes you had to wait for it" (564). The first moment of Swan and Warham being marooned in the tunnels of Mercury found them walking toward their rescue in order to cut down on the time of their being in the tunnels; this time, they can do nothing. This is not the apathetic doing nothing of Snowman in *Oryx and Crake*, but the end result may well be the same. Being marooned does not have to signal an adventure of "doing" peopled with those savvy and skilled to recreate the necessities of life under dire circumstances. Nor does being marooned mean that rescue, or even survival, is likely. "Swan recalled stories of castaways, adrift unfound, frozen for eons. How many had gone that way in the history of the world? Scores? Hundreds? Thousands?" (563). We expect rescue. And absent rescue, we expect survival (there is no thought that MaryAnn and the Professor and Gilligan will all die, of dehydration, illness, or accident). Major Tom is the exception, not the rule.

Swan and Warham are rescued; they will not be among "the forgotten ones," who have just now been remembered. At this point, being marooned with Warham in space provides an opportunity for Swan and Warham to commit to one another; this maroonage is simply the fictional device for their declaration of love. "He interested her. She was drawn to him as to a work of art or a landscape. He had a sense of his actions that was sure; he drew a clean line. He showed her new things, but also new feelings. Oh to be calm! Oh to pay attention! He amazed her with these qualities" (568). Like Toby, in the opening epigraph, Swan is focusing on the idea of love, on thinking about Warham, and thinking about what it means that Warham loves her at a moment when other novels in similar settings might focus on the doings of survival.

Swan wants to be rescued, and is comforted by the radio contact that assures her that she and Warham are seen and will eventually be picked up, however, rescue seems to mean something different to her now. "Calm down, she thought again. You're marooned in space, they will rescue you eventually. Meanwhile here you are, and Warham is with you, and Pauline [Swan's implanted and potentially conscious AI]. No moment is ever fundamentally different than this one" (571). Swan is always already marooned. She will likely always be the "big bag of problems" that Warham initially notes her to be. And the novel will end happily, with her wedding to Warham.

Both Robinson's sweeping space opera and Atwood's more explicitly post-apocalyptic imagining, then, end with weddings, although Atwood goes on and includes the deaths of Zeb and Toby. Both texts use the experience of being marooned as a way to name the human condition and also to remind readers of the iterative of that experience.

If it all ended there, then the argument that maroonage is used specifically as a method to clarify the critical utopian imagining of a "better space" would be clear. Maroonage highlights that neither being safe nor being rescued is the basis for moving forward. Instead, maroonage highlights the daily struggle of being who and where we are, and the challenges of still needing to imagine worlds where that daily "iterative" is what describes being at home.

However, reading Robinson and Atwood as challenging the heroic maroonage tale is incomplete without a further complicating factor—a factor that seems to thrust Robinson's text back into heroic maroonage narratives. Robinson includes a nonhuman maroonage, which seems to conflict with lessons of the previous examples of recognizing that escape and rescue are illusory and that home is not a place to which one can return. As background, Swan and Warham are brought together initially both to solve the mystery of the destruction of the city Terminator and to puzzle over the problem of Earth. Swan, in particular, is continually perplexed and enraged by what she sees as the apathy of the people of Earth: "It's so hot and dirty, and so damned heavy. Maybe they're simply weighed down by this planet, rather than their history" (353).[7] In order to help Earth along, a group of spacers has been planning to jump-start a revolution by reintroducing to Earth the many mammals now extinct, who have been bred for generations in specially made asteroid aquaria in space. The return of these mammals, the "great thing" that Swan celebrates, is seen in the novel as nothing other than remarkable: " . . . sky all strewn with clear seeds, which from any distance were only visible from their contents. . . . thousands of flying wolves, bears, reindeer, mountain lions" (453). While the people of Earth are both shocked and put a little off-kilter by the mammals' return (which is the goal), Swan and Warham and the others praise the return, and the text resounds with images familiar to a reader (on an Earth where caribou do still migrate) but made novel through Swan's enthusiastic observations. "All God's children are home at last" (455) Swan reports.

But what does this coming home really mean? From what have these mammals been rescued? They have lived for generations within asteroids—not bottled or kept in cages, but simply living their lives in the appropriate setting with ample areas to roam, other animals to hunt, and plants to eat. If we believe that by being removed from their asteroid homes and being dropped back on Earth is a coming home for the caribou, the wolves, and the grizzly, then what does that mean for the human animals? In a novel that is critical about home being what you learn to take with you, why is the return of these mammals so celebratory? Is the caribou more free on Earth as it crosses a river to head north than it was on an asteroid doing exactly the same thing? It seems that readers are being asked to think of the caribou as coming home in a way that we are not to think of humans being able to do the same. And so what does that mean for reading the novel through the lens of maroonage? It seems to me that the very complications Robinson was putting into the text, the very ways in which he is cautioning the reader against the grand narrative, is undermined by this grand narrative of mammalian return.

Atwood seems to give a kind of response to this moment of mammal romanticization. Her third novel, which brings the hapless Snowman together with the resourceful Toby, also reminds the reader that this post-apocalyptic world is peopled not only with human survivors, but with the genetically modified Crakers and the genetically modified pigoons (and wolvogs, rakunks, etc.). While analyzing the different ways in which Atwood and Robinson confront the nonhuman animal (which would have to include an extensive discussion of human diversity in Robinson) is beyond the scope of this chapter, the connection to what I have argued is the heuristic of maroonage is telling. Robinson uses the human accounts of maroonage to challenge the typical Enlightenment-era heroics, heroics often found in similar Enlightenment-style post-apocalyptic accounts.[8] And yet he seems to undermine his own argument with a romantic (and romantically compelling) account of mammalian "return home."

Atwood, on the other hand, notes that both the Crakers and the pigoons are better fit for the post-apocalyptic world in which the survivors all find themselves. Yet part of what the Crakers begin to do in the third novel of the trilogy is tell stories and learn to write their collective history with the human, the pigoon, and the hybrid Craker-human offspring. Here, storytelling (one form of which is the retold maroonage stories told by Toby to the Crakers, especially the story of Zeb) is the means by which the Crakers make meaning of their lives as purposefully created pseudo-humans.

At the moment of realizing that she and Warham would be rescued from their drifting in space, Swan notes that "they were only continuing by way of rescue" (574), and she goes on to think that "our stories go on a while, some genes, some words persist; then we go away. It was a hard thing to remember" (574). That Robinson frames the story of Swan and Warham and their relationship through multiple instances of being marooned reminds the reader of the fact and the problem of rescue (and thus the fact and problem of home). It is perhaps this hard thing that Swan notes above that Atwood is using at the end of her trilogy, a hard thing that she lets the Crakers and pigoons puzzle over, alongside the humans.

Maroonage has provided a way into the "different story" that Swan wanted, if you add to that idea of a "different" story the idea here of storytelling itself—the ways in which Blackbeard furthers the role that Toby played as chronicler of her community. When Toby first starts telling the Crakers the story of their past, she notes, "There's the story, then there's the real story, then there's the story of how the story came to be told. Then there's what you leave out of the story. Which is part of the story too" (Atwood 2013, 56). Maroonage stories are often told as one particular kind of story: the heroic conquering of a wild space in which one finds oneself. But the story of being marooned and the story of marronage are not simply singular stories. In the study of utopia, the story of being marooned has been ignored. These two novels illustrate the ways in which focusing on the different kinds of maroonage stories gives a different angle of analysis on how the "wish image" of utopia can be understood.

Notes

1. Tom Moylan, *Demand the Impossible*, 1986.
2. The prospect of such genetic mixing may have seemed fantastic to a reader in 2003, but in 2017 we know that scientists are working toward the creation of such "chimeras," although the progress is slow (cf. Nicholas Wade, "New Prospects for Growing Human Replacement Organs in Animals," *New York Times*, January 26, 2017.)
3. Post-apocalyptic texts are often traditional survival tales that use the maroonage of the apocalyptic moment to highlight a different message about being human. In these texts, to be human is to be the resilient maker of new worlds even in the face of terrible disaster. Pat Frank's *Alas, Babylon* is a classic example of such a text. But, as I hope the examples offered in this chapter make clear, not all post-apocalyptic texts work this way.
4. Cannibals are used to represent both the depravity of those who "fail" the apocalyptic test and the means by which traditional post-apocalyptic heroes show off their superior strength and will. For example, in Larry Niven and Jerry Pournelle's *Lucifer's Hammer*, the ritual cannibalism of the New Brotherhood Army is the shorthand standard used to illustrate their depravity and thus the narrative "rightness" of their defeat.
5. In *2312*, many of the apocalyptic events include a specific mention of the majority of people surviving. Robinson seems less interested in building the possibility for post-apocalyptic utopia on the deaths of millions. The exception here is on Earth.
6. Again, Robinson here includes a potentially violent mass-casualty moment that instead includes a clear description of the ways in which the ship was equipped to save all

of its passengers. As with the tunnels under Mercury, refuge from disaster is built into, and part of the utopian imagining, of Robinson's universe.

7. Atwood's novels give another potential future for these same apathetic people of Earth.

8. Frank's *Alas, Babylon* is one of the most famous but certainly not the only post-apocalyptic story that is really just a retelling of the Enlightenment dream of bringing rational people together to create something better out of a post-nuclear landscape. Frank's novel emphasizes the heroics of the white, male protagonist who leads others in the town of Fort Repose, Florida, to create a space safe.

Secondary Source Bibliography

Frank, Pat. *Alas, Babylon*. Philadelphia: J. B. Lippincott & Co., 1959.
Jameson, Frederic. *Archaeologies of the Future*. New York: Verso, 2007.
Moyland, Tom. *Demand the Impossible: Science Fiction and the Utopian Imagination*. New York: Peter Lang, 2014.
Niven, Larry, and Jerry Pournelle's. *Lucifer's Hammer*. New York: Del Rey Books, 1977.
Wade, Nicholas. "New Prospects for Growing Human Replacement Organs in Animals." *New York Times*, January 26, 2017.

Chapter Eight

"Lest Darkness Fall": Castaways in Time and Space in Popular Turn-of-the-Century Fiction

Richard Bodek

At one moment in 1939, Martin Padway, a mere graduate student trying to finish his dissertation in archaeology, is driving the Via del Mare. This road, opened by Benito Mussolini in 1928, was designed to glorify Rome, himself, and his regime at the cost of the destruction of two historic squares (Baxa, 87). The next moment, Padway finds himself standing in the Pantheon, looking for the modern Senate House and the Fascist Ministry of Communications—both missing (de Camp 1939, 12). After chatting with others hanging about, others who speak not-quite Italian, Padway realizes he is cast away in sixth-century Italy. In another novel on a different continent, Dana, whose last name is never revealed, also finds herself marooned in the past (Butler)—in her case, in antebellum Maryland, where she is viewed as a slave even as she has to interact with a white ancestor to ensure that another direct ancestor would come to be born. Padway and Dana are neither the only nor even the most famous people marooned in time. That honor belongs to Hank Morgan. If a lightning strike sends Padway hurtling backwards fourteen centuries, and a mysterious call from the past pulls Dana backwards, a blow to the head is all Hank Morgan needs to send him from his job supervising machinists in nineteenth-century Connecticut, to sixth-century England—indeed, to King Arthur's court.

Who are these people? What assumptions do they bring about their respective presents, the pasts in which they find themselves, and, in the case of the men, what an alternative future might look like? How might they "help" their newfound societies develop? What could be built? What could be avoided? Indeed, are time-castaways maroons? If so, what do their maroonages tell us about the cultures that produce them? This article answers that such castaways are unquestionably maroons. By exploring these cases and these questions, we will see how science fiction's maroonage subgenre contributes towards a three-dimensional understanding both of maroonage and, in the case of *Kindred*, marronage. The authors, all social critics, all interested in the social ills of their respective worlds, all writing texts that either expose those ills or expose them and propose improvements, very self-consciously poke and prod at thinly-veiled versions of their reality. All include examples of slavery and its horrors in their meditations on the world, as well as the nightmare to which it had descended even as their central characters, much like the true maroons in the historical and anthropological chapters in this volume, tried to build better, healthier polities than the ones they left.

We will briefly touch upon Mark Twain's imagined Arthurian court, and then explore late antique Rome, as imagined by L. Sprague De Camp, and Octavia Butler's antebellum Maryland. We will see how some nineteenth- and twentieth-century American authors use the idea of the modern American, cast into alternate realities, to diagnose and cure, valorize and validate, understand, or simply rehabilitate their societies—or ultimately fail to make any significant difference.

Mark Twain's *A Connecticut Yankee in King Arthur's Court*

Mark Twain's 1888 novel, *A Connecticut Yankee in King Arthur's Court*, is sometimes analyzed as a tale contrasting the modernizing United States with an ossified Great Britain, and sometimes as Twain's analysis of the difference between the Northern and Southern United States—or the Union and Confederacy—especially of their differing views of honor, the importance of technology, and the dream of industrial progress.[1] One need not, though, take a stand on the question of Twain's geographical preferences and dislikes to quickly come to the conclusion that he used this text to express skepticism about both older, traditional means of social organization and the horrors inherent in modern technology. Indeed, the tale is a meditation on both the sad state of traditional societies and the horrors that modernity can visit on them, even when the modernity comes in the guise of progress and improvement. A quick recap of the issues in *A Connecticut*

Yankee in King Arthur's Court provides the necessary preamble to a detailed discussion of *Lest Darkness Fall* and *Kindred*.[2]

Hank Morgan, Mark Twain's thoroughly modern late nineteenth-century protagonist, is hurled backwards into King Arthur's Britain after having been hit on the head. (The concept of the time machine as developed by H. G. Wells still lay six years in the future.) Attempting to prevent his being burnt at the stake, Morgan calls down a solar eclipse (or rather, he remembers that such an eclipse took place on that day in history and thus invokes it), an event that, in his words, would be, "in a business way ... the making of me" (Twain, 31). In a gesture indicating that Twain himself thought he was telling a maroonage tale, he borrowed this episode from a narrative of Columbus's fourth voyage, when the admiral, shipwrecked and castaway on Jamaica, plays the same trick on that island's Indigenes.[3]

Morgan rises in the kingdom's hierarchy, has a series of adventures—some humorous, some not—and assumes the title "Boss." He restructures the kingdom's economy, technological basis, and religious life. He has his men crisscross the kingdom with telegraph wires that would eventually improve communication (Twain, 52). He sponsors the development of newspapers (Twain, 148–49), which—like the telegraph—are designed to improve the kingdom's population of educated people (Twain, 148). He even works to end the institutions of slavery and the caste system, because he believes that, "in a country where they have ranks and castes, a man isn't ever a man, he is only part of a man, he can't ever get his full growth. You prove your superiority over him in station, or rank, or fortune, and that's the end of it—he knuckles down" (Twain, 110, 172). Fundamental to much of this is his belief that the independent farmers, artisans, and other free men are "all ... that was useful, or worth saving, or really respectworthy; and to subtract them would have been to subtract the Nation and leave behind some dregs, some refuse, in the shape of a king nobility and gentry, idle, unproductive, acquainted mainly with the arts of wasting and destroying" (Twain, 64–65). Indeed, at one point he believes that his very American reforms have been completely successful, and would only continue to improve his world. Even the discovery of America is on his horizon (Twain, 228).

From Morgan's standpoint, much of Britain's backwardness is due to its cultural strangulation by the church, an institution he means to weaken beyond recognition. Morgan feels that by its preaching of humility and obedience among other things, the church acts to keep the population down (Twain, 43). His solution is to break the monopoly of one church and replace it with a religious cafeteria, as he believed that, a man is only at his best, morally, when he is equipped with the religious garment whose color and shape and size most nicely accommodate themselves to the spiritual complexion, angularities, and stature of the individual who wears it; and besides I was afraid of a united Church; it makes a mighty power, the mightiest conceivable, and then when it by and by gets into selfish hands, as it is always bound to do, it means death to human liberty, and paralysis to human thought. (Twain, 50)

Morgan returns to this point many times in his narrative, seeing established churches as a kind of established crime or slave-pen (Twain, 78), as justifiers of the horrors perpetrated by nobles (Twain, 83), as more interested in money than in the well-being of poor children (Twain, 103). Improvement would only come, at least in Morgan's eyes, with better education, which equals freedom (Twain, 78), the abolition of slavery—which he believes in but waffles on (Twain, 111)—and improved technology (Twain, 228).

This last belief, as readers of Twain know, was tinged by heavy irony. It was exactly the technology upon which Morgan pinned so many of his hopes that brought about the death of so many. Modernity, in the form of dynamite, kills such a vast number in the civil war that ends the book that the dead "did not exist as individuals, but merely as homogenous protoplasm, with alloys of iron and buttons" (Twain, 249).

Critics generally agree that the novel is a study in pessimism. Readers—and Morgan—are presented with a world mired in darkness. Morgan brings all of his Yankee ingenuity to bear on it, "inventing" telegraphy, bicycles, and newspapers. He works to reform religion and modernize attitudes of the kingdom's youth, all of which is meant to pull Britain out of the Dark Ages into a modern, progressive condition. Ultimately, this project not only fails, but also ends in an orgy of death and disaster. Not only do we see the horrifying death of Britain's aristocracy, but also the crumbling of all the changes meant to improve the world. Readers are left to scratch their heads in sorrow at the hopelessness of the human condition, regardless of technical progress.

L. Sprague de Camp's *Lest Darkness Fall*

Lest Darkness Fall is a seemingly more optimistic view of alternative pasts than *Connecticut Yankee*. Originally published in the December 1939 issue of *Unknown* (a fantasy/science fiction pulp magazine of the era), L. Sprague de Camp attempts to think about, and perhaps improve upon, Twain's novel.

A Cal Tech trained aeronautical engineer, de Camp decided in the mid-1930s to make a living writing both science fact and science fiction.[4] He wrote at least 100 books and was one of the major writers of the golden age of science fiction and fantasy, but both de Camp and his work are largely unexplored by scholars outside of the field of science fiction.[5] Although it is probably impossible to retrace the route by which a writer decides to pen a particular work of fiction, the building blocks for *Lest Darkness Fall* were certainly assembled in the 1930s. After taking his masters in engineering from Stevens Tech in 1933, de Camp landed a $75-a-month editorial position with the Inventors Foundation, an organization designed to help young inventors navigate patent law (de Camp 1996, 122–23). Certainly the experience of looking into how technology is developed, and what would or would not work in practice, must have made an impression on de Camp's thought. At the same time, as he himself explained, he decided that, "with the world situation growing more menacing by the day, I wanted to see how the brightest minds had coped with the problems of political economy. So I plowed through Stuart Chase, Friedrich Engels, Nikolai Lenin, Karl Marx, John Stuart Mill, Lewis Mumford, Ortega y Gasset, Vilfredo Pareto, David Ricardo, Bertrand Russell, Adam Smith, Pitrim Sorokin, Oswald Spengler, Lincoln Steffens, John Strachey, Arnold Toynbee, Leon Trotsky, and Thorstein Veblen. I got some ideas about the causes and cures of civilization; but these would be for another book" (de Camp 1996, 129). He both bounced around from editorial job to editorial job and continued to hone his craft as a science fiction writer, although even he admits that much of his work from the mid-to-late 1930s was rather poor and crude (de Camp 1996, 130–37).

From the spring of 1937, de Camp became more tightly connected to other science fiction writers, honing his craft and becoming an ever-more-successful published author (de Camp 1996, 143–50). These forays culminated in the publishing of *Lest Darkness Fall*, in which de Camp consciously refracts Mark Twain's *A Connecticut Yankee in King Arthur's Court* through his reading of Gibbon, Toynbee, and Robert Graves's *Count Belisarius* (de Camp 1996, 151). Of special interest to him, at least in retrospect, was the question of how somebody with a good understanding of technology could translate that knowledge into an era in which many of the basics needed for technological progress did not yet exist: in other words, an encounter between civilization and the "primitive" (de Camp 1996, 151).

Finding himself in Rome on the eve of Count Belisarius's re-capture of the city for the Roman Empire, Martin Padway, a realistically drawn graduate student who suffers both from an unhappy marriage and periodic bouts of depression (de Camp 1939, 27), must use his knowledge of history and the history of technology to thwart the temporary ascension of Byzantium, keep the Goths in power—indeed, expand their power base—and invent enough era-appropriate technology to prevent the thousand-year collapse of Western civilization. In the course of telling this tale, L. Sprague de Camp explores the differences between what he sees as a "real past" (as distinct from Twain's Camelot) and the benefits and problems of the modernity that he inhabited. Through a series of decisions and "inventions," Padway is able to steer European civilization away from the Dark Ages that would otherwise descend upon it.

Padway first finds his assumptions tested when he asks a Roman for the current date, and is told, "twelve eighty-eight *Anno Urbis Conditae*" (de Camp, 1939, 13). Upon asking what the Christian date is, his interlocutor responds, "Well, now—I don't know; five hundred and something. Better ask a priest, stranger" (de Camp 1939,13). With this, Padway's and the reader's expectations are decentered if not shattered. The novelette will present unexpected signposts and opportunities. Not only might the "future" be changed, but the past might not be as one imagines it, either. Padway encounters odd food, no modern utensils, a straw-stuffed mattress for a bed, alkaline soap little better than sandpaper, and a razor seemingly better suited for causing pain than for shaving (de Camp 1939, 17). What he brought with him was very different from what he would want for a time-travel adventure. Rather than the books or modern weapons he might desire, Padway had travelers' checks, a street map, and a passport—all of no value (de Camp 1939, 18). Most importantly, and unsurprisingly in a work of science fiction, he had his wits and the knowledge base of his creator, L. Sprague de Camp.

In his private correspondence, de Camp was quite clear about his objection to, "mixing legends with history. After all, historiography is a science, and it might even be a useful one some day if anybody ever thought to ask historians whether a plan under discussion has ever been tried before, and if so how it worked."[6] It was in *Lest Darkness Fall* that de Camp set out to test just such an idea. What might happen if, rather than slipping into the Dark Ages, Europe were to receive era-appropriate technology in the Sixth Century, C.E., technology that would prevent cultural collapse? Certainly this idea did not arrive out of nowhere. De Camp had a long-standing interest in both history and historical novels—as long as they were true to the period about which he was writing. His works about the ancient world included *An Elephant for Aristotle*, *The Bronze God of Rhodes*, and *The Arrows of Hercules*, as well as a never-written novel about the Punic Wars, meant to be serialized in *Argosy* but forestalled by *Blue Book*'s publication of a similarly themed serial which appeared as he was beginning his research.[7]

Over the course of the novelette, readers see Padway use his knowledge of ancient history both to worm his way towards the center of political power in Italy and to transmit technology to improve the chances of keeping civilization's lights on. These technologies range from Arabic numerals and double-entry bookkeeping (de Camp 1939, 21) to pockets (de Camp 1939, 22). Along the way he introduces distilling (de Camp 1939, 22), methods to improve communication (de Camp 1939, 32), printing (de Camp 1939, 32), the horse collar (de Camp 1939, 35), telescopes (de Camp 1939, 41), and more. Other technologies, such as gunpowder, remain tantalizingly beyond his grasp (de Camp 1939, 135). Padway's own inventor (unlike Mark Twain, creator of Hank Morgan) realizes the difficulties inherent in reverse-engineering technology into the past. Perhaps as a joke at Twain's expense, de Camp's readers are privy to all the difficulties one would meet in bringing the printing press to sixth-century Europe.[8] He or she would have to "invent" type, printer's ink, and paper (de Camp 1939, 32). The technology to develop quality type was missing (de Camp 1939, 33); the ink and paper that Padway could develop resulted in smeared print (de Camp 1939, 33). Although these problems were all eventually smoothed out, they remind the reader of the fundamental problem of ripping technology out of the fabric of time.

Most fundamental though, and this is key to understanding the Maroonage/Robinsonian nature of the tale, is less the question of technology and more the intertwined issues of culture, religion, and politics, issues addressed in Twain's work. Here we see de Camp's commentary on his own interwar world, a world about to experience its own fall into darkness. For example, when faced with the first of the bewildering assortment of Christian doctrines he will encounter, Padway claims to be a Congregationalist, a claim which he follows with what is to become his obligatory following line: "That's the nearest thing we have to Nestorianism in my country" (de Camp 1939, 20). As the omniscient narrator tells readers, "It was not really true, but he guessed an agnostic would hardly be popular in this theology-mad world" (de Camp 1939, 20). Such maneuvering, though, will only get Padway so far.

Finding himself in a tavern conversation with a native Roman, Padway must deal with the man's perceived religious persecution. Padway questions this view, stating: "I thought the Goths let everybody worship as they pleased." The response he gets is telling:

> "That's just it! We Orthodox are forced to stand around and watch Arians and Monophysites and Nestorians and Jews going about their business unmolested, as if they owned the country. If that isn't persecution, I'd like to know what is!"
>
> "You mean that you're persecuted because the heretics and such are not?"

"Certainly, isn't that obvious? We won't stand—What's your religion by the way?"

"Well," said Padway, "I'm a Congregationalist. That's the nearest thing to Orthodoxy that we have." (de Camp, 1939, 24)

The conversation being overheard, and all possible theological positions being represented, the tavern soon breaks out into a melee, with adherents of each Christian strain fighting with the others (de Camp, 1939, 25). From Padway's—and probably de Camp's—point of view, the silliness of such disagreements is endless, and at best a hindrance to the kind of progress that he would like to see take place. Indeed, it seems to be ideal for hastening the fall of darkness that Padway believes is his mission to prevent. The one religious "calamity" that Padway (and perhaps de Camp, in his imagination) seems to be intent on preventing is the rise of Islam. In a letter that Padway sends to Justinian in the novelette's final two pages, he warns of an impending disaster.

> ... in about thirty years there will be born in Arabia a man named Mohammed, who, preaching a heretical religion, will, unless prevented, instigate a great wave of fanatical barbarian conquest, subverting not only the present rule of Persia, but that of your serenity's dominions as well. We therefore urge the desirability of securing control of the Arabian Peninsula forthwith, that this calamity shall be stopped at the source. (de Camp 1939, 161)

Here, both Padway and, presumably, de Camp show themselves to be men of their times, able to laugh off the excesses of Christianity, or at least see them as issues which can be dealt with. Islam, though, struck them as beyond the pale and the herald of disaster.

Also making this piece a work of its times are the frequent allusions to the Fascist Italy in which the story begins. When stepping out onto a curb in front of the Pantheon, Padway had to jump out of the way of a uniformed Fascist on a motorcycle (de Camp 1939, 12). This is a small detail, but a telling one. Making the rude rider a uniformed Fascist is the kind of significant detail that will inform readers of the tale's attempt at verisimilitude and subtly alert them to the writer's political bent. Upon having been transported into the past, Padway needs to take psychological stock of his surroundings. The world of Gothic Italy, at least as seen through Padway's eyes and described by the omniscient narrator, sounds both foreign and yet eerily familiar:

> He was living in the twilight of western classical civilization. The Age of Faith, better known as the Dark Ages, was closing down. Europe would be in darkness, from a scientific and technological aspect, for nearly a thousand years.

> That aspect was, to Padway's naturally prejudiced mind, the most, if not the only, important aspect of a civilization. Of course, the people among whom he was living had no conception of what was happening to them. The process was too slow to observe directly, even over the span of a lifetime. They took their environment for granted, and even bragged about their modernity. (de Camp 1939, 31)

A central character who understands the darkness about him, yet thinks that science and technology would suffice to fight it off, is no poor choice for understanding the Fascist world. Narrow-minded secondary characters who think they are surrounded by the trappings of modernity when an unprejudiced eye recognizes collapse would seem uncomfortably recognizable to the clear-eyed observer of contemporary politics after seventeen years of Fascist power and on the eve of World War II.

Padway needs first to deal with conflicting theories of history. On the one hand, if he chooses to think like a Marxist (a consideration within the story's frame), he will conclude that, "the environment fixes the pattern of a man's accomplishments and throws up the man to fit that pattern" (de Camp 1939, 31). He rejects this to him probably pessimistic conclusion and instead adopts a more "Carlylean" stance. As a man previously living in Fascist Rome, he is rather well-placed to deal with what he finds in the sixth century. Two competing security apparatuses struggle to decide which of them has the authority to arrest and hold him. Either would torture him for information. After some bureaucratic wrangling, Padway finds himself under the control of Count Honorius, the city's governor, who, in his overly aesthetic and easily-bribed way, embodied numerous democratic stereotypes of the typical Fascist upper-level official, vaguely reminiscent of Hermann Goering (de Camp 1939, 38–40).

Later in the story, once he has achieved real political influence and power, Padway faces a king who is much more concerned with self-aggrandizement than with proper governance, mirroring Benito Mussolini's own incompetence (46). Perhaps as one last description/criticism of contemporary Fascism, the narrator describes General Belisarius, the one truly competent military leader whom Padway encounters, as having Slavic cheekbones (de Camp 1939, 68). Although this is a winking nod to Robert Graves's description in his novel—"Only from his cheek-bones, which were somewhat high, would his barbarian descent have been guessed" (Graves, Kindle edition)—contemporary readers would notice that the one competent contemporary is from a "race" generally regarded as inferior by race-conscious Fascists, and certainly by the most infamous of the Fascists, the Nazis.

Padway finds himself flattering a ruler, King Wittigis, who is in search of scientific glory, and sparring with a contemporary Gothic princess who claims that her fellow Goths and the Franks are defending Western civilization "from the real wild men like the Bulgarian Huns and Slavs. I can't think of a time when our Western culture was more secure" (de Camp 1939, 74–75). Padway's pessimistic response befits a twentieth-century mind, as he chooses to focus on Italy's declining population and the volume of shipping. Among his hopes to stop the collapse is the belief that faster methods of communication could help to square that circle (de Camp 1939, 75).

Padway also finds himself increasingly troubled by the Franks. In a rather prescient moment, one in which the world of 1939 speaks directly to and through the tale, Padway sees his Goths in conflict with the Franks, and realizes that appeasement would be a failure: "He knew that that fierce and treacherous tribe would only take each concession as a sign of weakness. The time to stop the Franks was the first time" (de Camp 1939, 86). Fierce, treacherous, no respect for discussion—certainly a well-composed set of attributes in the era of the Third Reich. Although Franks can be bribed, they are a people that "won't stay bought" (de Camp 1939, 138). This echoes Winston Churchill's 1938 comments on the Munich Agreement; indeed, de Camp provides a good, quick description of the Third Reich on the eve of the Second World War.

Other political aspects of this world would strike American readers as familiar. Padway engineers elections that are violent affairs, accompanied by threats, swaggering candidates, ballot box stuffing, and floaters (de Camp 1939 142, 144). In some ways, de Camp's mockery of the American electoral system was rather gentle, referencing barbecues, ward heelers, and fitted with campaign placards like:

VOTE FOR URIAS, THE PEOPLE'S

CHOICE!

Lower Taxes! Bigger public works!

Security for the aged! Efficient

government! (de Camp 1939, 141)

Padway also makes some moves that valorized the American system, or at least that system as practiced by the northern states. Certainly the electoral system as instituted by Padway was superior to anything found in the increasingly Fascist Europe. Indeed, in a Lincolnesque move, Padway issued a proclamation freeing the serfs. This was not only the morally correct thing to do, but also would provide more manpower when "his" Gothic kingdom found itself at war with the Byzantines (148–49). He also instituted a constitution that limited the power of the monarchy and, in a move that his new contemporaries could not grasp, instituted a progressively expanding tax on slaves, designed to make the practice increasingly expensive, ultimately leading to emancipation (de Camp 1939, 159).

It is worth noting, though, that his freeing of the slaves, gradual as it was, had nothing to do with the issue of race. Indeed, racism raises its head in the story in ways disturbing to the twenty-first-century reader. When first introducing the character of Ajax, while processing his first batch of brandy, the narrator claims that all of the observers of the still looked nervous, "and the Negro seemed all teeth and eyeballs" (de Camp 1939, 22). Later, when trying to influence the outcome of a royal election, Padway has Priam, Ajax's eldest son, "a chocolate-colored, frizzy-haired boy of ten," run up to one of the candidates who was speaking from the state and shout, "*Atta! Atta!*" to the amusement of the onlookers. This was certainly a move designed to degrade the man's dignity (de Camp 1939 145–46). Yet the character of Padway is troubled by the boy's servile manner. This is the moment in the tale that decides Padway to work towards slavery's abolition (de Camp 1939, 145).

In short, the novelette works as a kind of wish fulfillment. In an era in which democracy in Europe is failing, and darkness is, unquestionably, falling, L. Sprague de Camp uses the maroonage trope to investigate how good, old-fashioned American know-how could save Europe from itself. Modern technology, in the minds of its bearers unencumbered by either religious dogma or prejudice, could bring the idea of limited government coupled with modernity to a tired continent. It would not be absurd to argue that this kind of thinking would be at play again six years later when much of Europe lay in ruins and thousands of Padways came to Europe to bring it the light of American reason. On the other hand, white America's blindness to its own racism and corrupt electioneering practices would cause it a host of problems in the second half of the twentieth century.

Octavia Butler's *Kindred*

In Octavia Butler's tale of time-maroonage, Dana, a young African American writer, finds herself removed from California in 1976 and sent back to the antebellum Maryland plantation of Rufus Weylin, one of her ancestors. Sometimes she is accompanied by Kevin, her husband, and sometimes not. She has to rescue Rufus from a series of self-inflicted dangers, keeping him alive long enough to repeatedly rape Alice, one of his slaves, until Alice gives birth to Hagar, another of Dana's ancestors. After Hagar's birth, and after killing Rufus, Dana returns to contemporary California, having lost one arm in what was presumably her final time trip.

Over the course of her and her husband's multiple visits to Maryland, the heroine, who is also the narrator, discovers the nuanced horrors of American history and the psychological distortion that the institution of slavery caused to those enmeshed within it. Perhaps the most significant victim of this is Rufus, whose growing cruelty and selfishness seems to be encouraged by the opportunities made available to him by slavery. Dana is subject to repeated maroonage in the past. Before she realizes the full gravity of her situation, she is terrified by the dangers of running away, but ultimately she attempts marronage when she believes that her personal situation could not possibly worsen (Butler 156, 170–74). As she contemplates the nineteenth-century world about her, Dana comes to question a series of assumptions about how one ought to behave if enslaved. Among the most important of these was the question that every maroon faced: whether endurance is less courageous than attempted escape. As a castaway in time, she finds that she initially understood herself to be an observer/outsider more than a full-fledged participant. Although that would change over the course of the novel, it serves to make readers of other castaway novels rethink their perceptions of the works' central characters, especially, as in the case with Twain, when the central character also narrates the tale. It is also a wry commentary on the psychological state of those thrown into situations as opposed to those who have the ability to make important choices about their fate. In this section of our study of time-travel tales, we will look at some isolated moments in *Kindred* to analyze how a close reading of the novel helps us to use the tropes of maroonage and marronage to make sense of our own tangled time.

Upon being sent back in time, Dana finds herself in a world where the rules look superficially similar to those with which she is familiar, but which she quickly comes to understand are far more vicious than she expected. She does, though, come to the realization that, indeed, although her twentieth-century present is less brutal, it is less dissimilar to the past than she would have liked to believe. She refers to her twentieth-century temporary jobs, mostly meaningless, soul-destroying warehouse work (which she describes as "nearly always mindless work, and as far as most employers were concerned, it was done by mindless people. Nonpeople rented for a few hours, a few days, a few weeks") as "working out of a slave market" (Butler 53). In other words, the whippings of slavery might have disappeared, but the contempt for the humanity of the workers has not. Maroonage on a plantation reinforced her understanding of the perceived cheapness of human life. If it manifested itself in the late twentieth century by disdain for workers and their lives, on a plantation their economic worth was fully understood; slaves were, after all, seen as property, even if their potential for agency was grudgingly (and fearfully) acknowledged. Although nowhere is this comparison explicit, the novel forces its readers to think about the differences between subtle dehumanization and overt brutality.

Yet, it was the discrepancies of the plantation world that most fascinated Dana. Rufus's father seems to have no regard for slaves as people. He would sell, rape, and torture them with impunity. Indeed, he sold children to purchase unnecessary goods (Butler 95). Nevertheless, he believed that if one gave one's word to a slave, that word must be honored (Butler 179). In other words, Weylin Sr. believes, wrongly in the context of the novel, that one's decisions are independent of the social system within which one lives, that morality could be a series of personal choices rather than choices largely dictated by social factors.

In a kind of parallel case, Dana also comes to see, if never fully understand, how plantation slaves could at one and the same time both love and hate their masters. This was certainly true in the case of Sarah (the novel's character closest to a stereotypical "Mammy") and her ambivalence towards Rufus, an ambivalence mirrored by Dana. Dana does, though, come to understand how the system encompassed a slow process of dulling all those who were enmeshed in it, not only the slaves, but the masters, too. Indeed, moral dulling was part of this process. Ordinary people, given extraordinary power, could easily do monstrous things without ever reflecting on their own morality (Butler, 100–101, 134). After having lived in the plantation world for a while, even Kevin begins to remind Dana of the Weylins (Butler, 190–94). An especially acute example of this is Dana's thoughts on first seeing Kevin after he has been alone for five years:

> His face was lined and grim where it wasn't hidden by the beard. He looked more than ten years older than when I had last seen him. There was a jagged scar across his forehead—the remnant of what must have been a bad wound. This place, this time, hadn't been any kinder to him than it had been to me. But what had it made of him? What might he be willing to do now that he would not have done before? (Butler 184)

In a brief but crucial moment of enlightenment, Dana comes to understand the quintessential twentieth-century's parallel to the antebellum south, Nazi Germany, commenting that, "the Germans had been trying to do in only a few years what the Americans had worked at for nearly two hundred" (Butler, 117). For example, in a move that paralleled Nazis' general disdain for the morality of Jews, Weylin Sr. professes to believe that African Americans were intellectually inferior to white people. Yet he fully understands the power of knowledge and feared their learning to read. This is compounded by his own semiliterate state (Butler, 97–98). This fear, when read against Dana's contemplation of German treatment of Jews, should make even the most nostalgic reader recoil at the culture of antebellum America. Like the Germans of the twentieth century who, in a kind of false mimesis, wanted to project their own moral failings onto a stereotypically drawn Jewish figure, Weylin externalizes his intellectual shortcomings and projected them onto his slaves even as he himself realized the weakness of this kind of understanding.

Dana herself comments on the ease with which the unacceptable could be accepted and comes to understand the attraction of stereotypical analyses that give one the illusion of understanding without its reality (Butler, 101). Even Alice, in some ways Dana's nineteenth-century counterpart (certainly the ancestor whom she most resembles both physically and psychologically), tells Dana that she would become a kind of Mammy herself, doing the bidding of whites, if she is not careful. Dana hates this observation, as she has one kind of understanding of the figure, an understanding that the reality of plantation life complicated (Butler, 157).

Octavia Butler's novel does two very different kinds of cultural work, and it does them quite well. The first of these is that, in the context of a time travel narrative, she portrays in vivid, painful detail aspects of American history (especially the history of Maryland which has reinvented itself as a mid-Atlantic state rather than a bastion of Southern racial norms) that many readers of popular fiction would like to forget or romanticize. Indeed, at one point Dana picks up a copy of *Gone with the Wind* as a kind of reminder of the danger that such historical claptrap can represent. As she notes, "But its version of darkies in tender loving bondage was more than I could stand" (Butler, 116). In addition, she forces a thought experiment on readers of time-travel science fiction, asking what one's moral requirements are when visiting the past. For example, she questions whether one can be an observer. At one point, Kevin says that he would be interested in traveling west to see the expansion of the US. Dana quickly reminded him that a different but equally horrible episode of American history would await him there, one—when stripped of all romance—that was interwoven with the genocide of native peoples (Butler, 97). Butler also asks whether self-preservation for its own sake is morally sufficient. Ought one endeavor to align oneself with the progressive forces of the past? Would it be justifiable to change history's timeline? All of these are questions, which could easily be transported back to the other narratives, which these science fiction maroonage tales force us to consider.

Conclusion

For Mark Twain, the father of the genre of time travel/maroonage, catastrophe was inevitable. Seemingly, the human condition alone dooms his characters to their fate. It is possible to read L. Sprague de Camp's work as slightly less grim. Perhaps, for de Camp, the nightmare that seemed to be brewing in the interwar world could be averted. In other words, maybe one lone castaway, able to muster science, employ clear-headed agnosticism, and introduce the elements of democracy and a free press could, with luck, prevent a dark age from descending. Even in 1939, such a dream would be hard to maintain, but we need to remember that the horrors of the next half-decade had not yet occurred. Nevertheless, de Camp's tale reads more like wish fulfillment than anything else. In other words, the story represents what ought to be possible given human potential, rather than what is likely, also given human potential.

Octavia Butler's heroine's encounter with the past showed her how much the United States had—and had not—changed between the early nineteenth century and the nation's bicentennial. Butler's Dana managed only to keep her personal present intact. In short, with Octavia Butler, readers interested in stories of maroonage in time return to the grimness of Mark Twain and the possibility that indeed there is no way out.

Notes

1. Mark Twain, *A Connecticut Yankee in King Arthur's Court* (New York: Charles L. Webster and Company, 1889; reprint, New York: W. W. Norton and Company, 1982). Citations refer to the Norton edition, which provides a good sampling of critical commentary on the novel.

2. Some of the issues we will explore in this piece have been touched on in recent criticism. See notably Lydia Cooper, "Human Voices: Language and Conscience in Twain's *A Connecticut Yankee in King Arthur's Court*," *Canadian Review of American Studies/Revue Canadienne D'etudes Américaines* 39, no. 1 (2009): 64–84; and Cushing Strout, "Crisis in Camelot: Mark Twain and the Idea of Progress," *Sewanee Review* 120, no. 2 (Spring 2012): 336–40.

3. See R.H. Major, *Select Letters of Christopher Columbus With other Original Documents relating to his Four Voyages to the New World*, 2nd ed. Burlington, VT: Ashgate, 2010. (I am indebted to Joe Kelly for this reference.)

4. Brief biographical sketches of de Camp can be found in both David Cowart and Thomas L. Wymer, *Twentieth-Century American Science-Fiction Writers: Part 1: A–L* (Detroit: Gale Research Company, 1981), 112–19; and E. F. Bleiler, ed., *Science Fiction Writers: Critical Studies of the Major Authors from the Early Nineteenth Century to the Present Day* (New York: Charles Scribner's Sons, 1982), 179–84. De Camp also wrote an autobiography, *Time & Chance* (Hampton Falls, NH: Donald M. Grant, 1996).

5. David V. Barrett, "L Sprague de Camp," *The Guardian*, November 17, 2000.

6. L. Sprague de Camp to S. C. Goud, April 10, 1939, Ransom Center II, Correspondence and Documents, ca. 1929–87: 3; 1938–39.

7. L. Sprague de Camp to Lewis Terman, December 16, 1939, Ransom Center II, Correspondence and Documents, ca. 1929–87: 3; 1938–39.

8. The story of Mark Twain's investment in an ultimately unprofitable printing technology is told in Paul Collins, "Mark Twain's Big Mistake," *New Scientist*, December 3, 2005, 54, accessed March 3, 2017, http://link.galegroup.com/apps/doc/A140241305/SCIC?u=cofc_main&xid=f27b5e13.

Secondary Source Bibliography

Barrett, David V. "L Sprague De Camp." *The Guardian*, November 17, 2000.
Baxa, Paul, *Roads and Ruins: The Symbolic Landscape of Fascist Rome* (Toronto: University of Toronto Press) 2010.
Bleiler, E. F., ed. *Science Fiction Writers: Critical Studies of the Major Authors from the Early Nineteenth Century to the Present Day*. New York: Charles Scribner's Sons, 1982.
Collins, Paul. "Mark Twain's Big Mistake." *New Scientist*, December 3, 2005, 54. *Science in Context*. Accessed March 3, 2017. http://link.galegroup.com/apps/doc/A140241305/SCIC?u=cofc_main&xid=f27b5e13.
Cooper, Lydia. "Human Voices: Language and Conscience in Twain's *A Connecticut Yankee in King Arthur's Court*." *Canadian Review of American Studies/Revue Canadienne D'etudes Américaines* 39, no. 1 (2009): 64–84.
Cowart, David, and Thomas L. Wymer. *Twentieth-Century American Science-Fiction Writers: Part 1: A-L*. Gale Research Company, Detroit, 1981.
de Camp, L. Sprague. *Time and Chance: An Autobiography*. Hampton Falls, NH: Donald M. Grant, 1996.
Major, R. H. *Select Letters of Christopher Columbus With Other Original Documents relating to his Four Voyages to the New World*. Burlington, VT: Ashgate, 2010.
Strout, Cushing. "Crisis in Camelot: Mark Twain and the Idea of Progress." *Sewanee Review* 120, no. 2 (Spring 2012): 336–40.
Twain, Mark. *A Connecticut Yankee in King Arthur's Court*. New York: Charles L. Webster and Company, 1889.

Chapter Nine

Maroons and the American Epic

Joseph Kelly

Ten years before the *Mayflower* arrived at the coast of Massachusetts, a less-fortunate English ship, the *Sea Venture*, failed to cross the Atlantic. It was the flagship of the so-called "third supply" of Jamestown. Two types of settlers contracted with the Virginia Company. The "better" sort, the gentlemen, invested both money (at £12.5/share) and their bodies, having signed on for a share in the labor. The others had no money. These were laborers, tradesmen, and housewives—those called "the common sort"—who traded their bodies for a share in joint stock company. The commoners would provide the strong backs for the colony. The gentlemen would defend the colony against Indians and the Spanish, and, though this was not adverted to in the recruitment letters, they would police the commoners. Along with these two types of "adventurers," the Virginia Company sent a Second Charter to Jamestown, which gave the new governor, General Thomas Gates, sweeping powers to punish offenses even so slight as whispering complaints about the Company leadership. The commoners did not know it when they signed on for the trip, but the moment they set foot on the *Sea Venture* they delivered themselves into a discipline stricter than the military rule imposed on English soldiers garrisoned in Ireland.

But tyranny came later. On May 15, 1609, when the *Sea Venture* set sail from London at the head of an impressive fleet, crowds along the bank of the Thames cheered. Five hundred settlers, horses, pigs, forges, arms, adzes, and axes crowded into the ships. For weeks they slid across the water on fair winds until in mid-ocean a hurricane swept up from the Caribbean. Some ships were de-masted; all were damaged. Yet each managed to carry its settlers and supplies, sodden and ruined by seawater, into Jamestown. Each, that is, but the *Sea Venture*, the largest of them, which besides the governor carried the admiral, George Somers, and most of the supplies. She had disappeared: lost at sea. All hands drowned was reported to England.

The *Sea Venture* did not sink. Leaking from dozens of places and with water rising below decks, it came aground, miraculously, on a reef in the middle of the Atlantic, part of the vast complex of shallows protecting the archipelago known to sailors as the Devils' Islands. Not a soul died. One hundred-fifty-three people, including sailors and two Powhatan ambassadors to the Court of St. James, splashed through the surf to blink at the tropical sun reflecting off the sand and at the dark jungle of dense vegetation. Among them was one William Strachey, a gentleman-poet who quaffed ale with London's theatricals at places like the Mermaid Tavern. He recorded the remarkable story of the castaways in a narrative he called *A True Reportory of the Wracke and Redemption of Sir Thomas Gates Knight, upon and from the Ilands of Bermudas*.

In its narrowest sense, the purpose of this chapter is to prove that the *True Reportory* belongs at the head of the canon of American literature, just before—if not in the place of—William Bradford's *Of Plymouth Plantation*. It's also an argument for maroonage tales in general. The *True Reportory* is the first significant story about marooned castaways emerging from the English encounter with the Atlantic. (Spain already had produced some narratives, such as those recording Columbus's wreck on Jamaica at the end of his ill-fated fourth voyage to the New World.) Strachey imagined that the experience of these castaways was the stuff of epic. Like Virgil and *The Aeneid*, he believed that he told the story of an empire's birth. Strachey was righter than he knew. While Jamestown might rightly be considered the start of the extensive British overseas empire, Strachey's narrative also heralded the new *homo politicus* who would discover democracy. In a wider sense, then, this chapter asserts that these shipwrecked castaways provide a better myth of the United States' origin than the Puritans who later settled Massachusetts. In fact, though the editors of the literature anthologies have not yet caught on, maroonage tales are the rich clay, the "useful past" from which purveyors of American culture mold their new tales about democracy. Already, maroonage provides the framework we use when we reimagine the meaning of the American polity. In this wider sense, this chapter is meant to reveal this cultural practice.

The Puritan Rise

In the early nineteenth century, most Americans used Jamestown to construct their image of America's difference from old-world nations. Those richly evocative characters, Pocahontas, John Smith, and John Rolfe, were especially useful. Even as Native Americans were driven out of the eastern states, the marriage of Pocahontas and Rolfe symbolized American exceptionalism. Eventually, their union helped romanticize and justify slaveocratic Virginia.[1] But in the mid-nineteenth century, Pilgrims and Puritans emerged as a rival point of origin; the competition between Jamestown and Plymouth symbolized the increasingly divergent ideologies of south and north, slave states and free states. The Massachusetts claim to supremacy was supported by the rediscovery of key Puritan texts. In the 1830s, John Winthrop's sermon "A Model of Christian Charity," delivered two hundred years earlier as the *Arbella* crossed the Atlantic, was first published to wide audiences. If God should deliver the Puritan settlers from storm and spared them from wrecking on the rocks, it would be a sign of divine election. In return, the Puritans would have to make their colony as a city upon a hill, exposed to all eyes, a society so righteous that it would shine as a beacon to the world. William Bradford's *Of Plymouth Plantation* was not published until 1856; it supplied characters with the color and nuance needed to rival Smith and Pocahontas. Two years later, Henry Wadsworth Longfellow's long narrative poem, *The Courtship of Miles Standish*, gave the country a Northern epic of mythic origin. Northern scholars like the young Henry Adams discredited John Smith's *General History of Virginia*, an intellectual exercise he considered "a flank, or rather a rear attack, on the Virginia aristocracy," which was then assaulted at its front by the Army of the Potomac.[2] Abraham Lincoln gave the Pilgrims a push when he nationalized Thanksgiving in the midst of the Civil War. It took several generations, but our Thanksgiving celebrations, replete with mythic images of Indians and Pilgrims sitting down to a cornucopia of plenty, were spread everywhere, even in the South, and were finally ratified by the enthusiastic nationalism surrounding World War I.[3]

Nevertheless, the Puritans had not yet infiltrated the influential, scholarly histories. According to Carl Becker's 1920 text, *Our Great Experiment in Democracy: A History of the United States*, the nation originated through an amalgam of the three main colonial regions—New England, the Middle Colonies, and the South—and their variety of economic and political experiences. Becker's section, "Origins of Democracy in America," does very little storytelling, but the raw material he provides for composing a national origin epic is the story of the French and Indian War, through which the

Americans learned to raise, equip, and finance their own armies. "That complex force which we call American national character," he concludes, was formed by our expansive geography: "the United States has always had, until very recently, more land than it needed." The crucial event creating this uniquely American "condition" occurred in 1783, when the western lands "became the public domain of the federal government" rather than the property of individual states.[4]

The recognized literary canon is, perhaps, more indicative of and productive of national culture than histories. As one literary historian put it, anthologies of literature form the "archival repository of the American spirit," serving as a surrogate Bible, the sacred book of American civics. Just as a canon of sacred texts constitutes the Bible, so the editors of college anthologies collect texts they think embody, preserve, and reproduce the soul of the nation.[5] Fred Lewis Pattee, who edited one of the first anthologies of American literature just after World War I, believed that the cultural role of a literary canon was to form national identity.[6] His version of American cultural origins ignored the Pilgrims. Believing that the "American soul" or the ideology of "Americanism" that should be transmitted to students was the spirit of democracy, he began his anthology with Enlightenment figures Benjamin Franklin and George Washington. In 1919, Edwin Greenlaw, a professor at the University of North Carolina, published another popular textbook, *The Great Tradition: A Book of Selections from English and American Prose and Poetry, Illustrating the National Ideals of Freedom, Faith, and Conduct*. Only a few of more than 600 pages were given to Puritans, who play almost no role in the sections titled "Ideas of the State," "The Rise of Modern Democracy," and "American Ideals." Even the large section called "Puritans and Kings" leaves out Bradford and the Pilgrims, and Puritans are represented almost exclusively by the English epic poet John Milton. In Greenlaw's view, Virginia played a larger role than Massachusetts in the development of the American soul, though both were mere streams of deeper English springs.[7]

This state of affairs dismayed the literary critic Van Wyck Brooks. His impassioned polemic "On Creating a Usable Past" declared that the corpses mummified by the professors like Pattee and Greenlaw were of too wan a complexion to vivify contemporary American life. The living artists of the old-world nations could draw upon myths and legends of their ancient dead. The United States needed patrimony just as rich, and the prose of practical, commercial men like Benjamin Franklin were useless. Lifting the Puritans into place took a lot of work by early twentieth-century intellectuals. Brooks's 1915 treatise *America's Coming of Age* credited the Puritans (for good or ill) with laying down the foundations of American civilization.

His own prodigious output obsessed over the New England writers who were considered the legacy of Plymouth Plantation—Hawthorne, Emerson, Melville—and his career culminated with his two-volume "history of American literature," which he prejudicially named *The Flowering of New England*. In 1936, Malcolm Cowley summed up the state of American letters when he declared in the *New Republic* that Brooks's *The Flowering of New England* "recovers for us a 'useable past.'" Twentieth-century writers finally had a rich loamy soil in which to sink their roots. That soil, according to Cowley, was the "Puritan Legacy." The vacuum Brooks identified in 1915 had been filled with people like Bradford, Winthrop, and Cotton Mather.[8]

New anthologists began reflecting the view of critics like Brooks and Cowley. By the 1930s, the Pilgrims and Puritans had become the foundation of the American literary tradition. Even critics hostile to their creed, like H. L. Mencken and William Carlos Williams, admitted that Puritanism was "the root of any number of American traditions." The first textbook designed exclusively for college courses in American literature was the 1925 *American Poetry and Prose: A Book of Readings, 1607–1916*, and though it did begin with Jamestown, the Puritans thoroughly dominated its opening section. The years between 1919 and 1962 saw what Jane Tomkins calls a "virtual rewriting" of our literary history, so that the anthologies of the 1960s and '70s presented Puritan New England as the unchallenged font of American culture.[9]

In the 1980s and '90s, the canon certainly expanded. Responding to critics working on women and minority writers, editors finally realized that preferences supposedly based on objective aesthetic judgments were actually tainted by ideology. Change came late, but college students studying American literature today read more diverse textbooks than their parents and grandparents did. By 2004, for instance, the ninth edition of the *McMichael Anthology of American Literature* included *The Examination of Anne Hutchinson*, twenty-five pages of Anne Bradstreet's poems, and more than thirty pages of Mary Rowlandson's *Captivity* narrative. The Iroquois League and Christopher Columbus were also represented. However, in that same year, Puritans and Massachusetts still dominated the opening section of the McMichael anthology, "Literature of Early America": twelve of fifteen selections. Half of the twenty pages allowed to John Smith come not from his three years living in Virginia but his three months sailing the coast of New England.

This situation is typical today, forty years after the opening of the American canon. The Pilgrims still hold pride of place. The current *Heath Anthology of American Literature* divides its "Beginnings" into six sections, including Indigenous oral traditions, New Spain (represented by Columbus), New

France, Chesapeake (or Jamestown), and New Holland (or New York). But the New England section is by far the largest, including among other selections Winthrop's sermon and generous portions of William Bradford's *Of Plymouth Plantation*. In the 2012 *Norton Anthology of American Literature*, a portion of John Smith's writing about Jamestown is dwarfed by seven Puritan writers, starting with Bradford and Winthrop and ending with Cotton Mather. Of the 260 pages in this section, all but sixty come from Massachusetts.[10] While the anthologists did add new voices, they never relinquished their reverence for the Puritans. The ninth edition of the *Norton Anthology of American Literature* (2015) includes thirteen seventeenth-century writers: twelve of them were Puritans. The exception is John Smith, and two of his four selections treat New England, not Virginia. The Heath anthology and nearly all of the standard textbooks tell the same story about our origins. They have added the voices of a few "others," but the Puritans are still presented as the progenitors of American literature, culture, and values. Penguin is the worst offender. The 2004 *Penguin Anthology of American Literature* (vol. 1) excludes all mention of Virginia. John Smith gets three pages, but that selection comes from his description of New England. The Penguin classic edition of *Early American Writing*, first published in 1994 but still in print, tells students that William Bradford's

> vivid and moving account of the Pilgrims' arrival in America . . . planted some of the most durable images in terms of which Americans have defined themselves and their cultural project: of America itself as a kind of last chance for mankind; of the American adventure as a voyage into the unknown and the untried; of the American people as a community knit together by suffering and upheld by a sense of hope tempered with an understanding of always threatening defeat; and of the American experience itself as a grappling with adversity and dissension.[11]

Here is everything but divine selection.

God's Chosen People

Divine selection is inherently part of the Exodus myth. What's implicit in the college textbooks is made explicit in popular culture. Take for example the television programs that teach children the myth of origin. NBC broadcast the animated, feature-length film, *Mouse on the Mayflower*, on Thanksgiving Day in 1968, perhaps the most unsettling year of racial activism in the US. Narrated by Tennessee Ernie Ford, this film tells the story of Willum Mouse and his Native American counterpart, a "red" mouse called "Little Big Thunder," who together arrange the racial harmony of the first Thanksgiving. My own generation was indoctrinated by 1975's *Schoolhouse Rock* episode, "No More Kings": an image of the *Mayflower* crossing the Atlantic leads to this iconic scene; a foot stepping ashore onto a rock emblazoned with "1620" as the narrator sings, "They finally knock / On Plymouth Rock/ And someone said, 'We're there! / It might not look like home / But at this point I don't care!'"[12] More charming then either of these and probably more effective in its imaginative work was the 1988 *Peanuts* version of this story, "The Mayflower Voyagers," the first episode in the children's miniseries, *This Is America, Charlie Brown*. Snoopy, Linus, Lucy, and the rest of the gang act out the mythic tale: the flight from England like the Israelites' flight from Egypt; the trial of storms during the Atlantic passage; the Mayflower Compact enshrining government by consent of the governed; disease and near-starvation during the first winter; the generosity of Native Americans; the racial harmony of the Thanksgiving feast; as well as several events described as "miracles," understated but unequivocal suggestions that God bestowed upon the Pilgrims, and by inheritance all Americans, his particular favors. Such pop-culture versions of the myth should not be dismissed: children's stories might wield more power than any other cultural artifact. They pour the cement that sets our deepest ideological foundations. This providential story of America's founding, copied from William Bradford's *Of Plymouth Plantation*, which heavily alludes to the Old Testament's Book of Exodus, lures the child's psyche, implying that this special blessing belongs to all Americans. God's selection binds Americans to each other and distinguishes them from the people of other nations.

Today's most popular, best-selling historian of early America, Nathaniel Philbrick, agrees that the school-textbook Pilgrims sporting "wide-brimmed hats and buckled shoes" have come to "symbolize all that is good about America." He remembers, "like many Americans," growing up and "taking this myth of national origins with a grain of salt." Philbrick wrote *Mayflower* to replace the stereotypes with a complex, historically accurate, three-dimensional portrait of "real-life Indians and English": men and women who were "too smart, too generous, too greedy, too brave—in short, too human—to behave predictably." But in the end, he concludes that "there is a surprising amount of truth" in the old stories. And his later book, *Bunker Hill: A City, a Siege, a Revolution*, treats American history as if it were a Pilgrim's progress. The republican ideals of 1776 Boston are the fulfillment of Winthrop's "The City on the Hill."[13]

What are those things that comprise "all that is good about America"? Philbrick assumes his readers know what they are, and it is likely they do.

They correspond to the virtues Americans assigned to themselves through much of the last century. We might take, for example, the list provided by Henry Luce in a 1941 issue of *Life* magazine, as Americans debated what was their appropriate role in world politics. In essence, the meaning of "America" was up for grabs. Trying to persuade the nation to lead the fight against fascism, Luce famously declared that the twentieth century ought to be the "American" century. "A love of freedom," he wrote, "a feeling for the equality of opportunity, a tradition of self-reliance and independence and also of co-operation." These things, he continued, "are infinitely precious and especially American." In addition, Americans "are the inheritors of all the great principles of Western civilization—above all Justice, the love of Truth, the ideal of Charity." After the war, when atheistic communism became the enemy, Dwight D. Eisenhower cast these ideals in religious terms, calling them "abiding creed of our fathers" and attributing America's leadership role (as Luce did not) to divine election.[14]

Yet when Eisenhower recited this creed in his first inaugural address, he did not invoke the Pilgrims. John Kennedy is the one who really introduced them to the mainstream national political vocabulary. In 1961, Kennedy declared that "in every branch, at every level, national, state and local, [we] must be as a city upon a hill." Modern times, he explained, send Americans "out upon a voyage no less hazardous than that undertaken by the *Arbella* in 1630. We are committing ourselves to tasks of statecraft no less fantastic than that of governing the Massachusetts Bay Colony, beset as it was then by terror without and disorder within." It became the central image of America at the height of the Cold War. Ronald Reagan made the shining city his signature trope, opening and closing his political career by imagining twentieth-century America as the inheritor of Pilgrim ideals. After their first harrowing winter, Reagan repeatedly explained, the "small community of Pilgrims prospered and . . . went on to become a beacon to all the oppressed and poor of the world." Even after the Cold War, Americans still used the image to imagine their identity. In one 4th of July message to the nation, Barack Obama told his listeners that the story of 1776 began with the Pilgrims' difficult winter in 1620. Totalitarian communism might have been defeated, but America was still Winthrop's city on a hill: a "land of liberty and opportunity, a global defender of peace and freedom, a beacon of hope to people everywhere who cherish those ideals." Sacvan Bercovitch, for instance, calls the motif of the city on a hill "key to the social-symbolic game through which the United States has perpetuated itself as America."[15]

Perhaps Bercovitch's statement is too wide. Transmitting freedom and opposing oppression around the globe, the city on a hill created the internationalist view America had of itself after World War II. There are, though, problems at the foundation of this rhetorical formula. Obvious is the historical inaccuracy. This chapter is not the first to point out, for example, that the Pilgrims established a regime even less tolerant of other faiths than the regime it fled, or that New England's Puritans hardly subscribed to the racial harmony symbolized by Thanksgiving dinner. James Loewen's *Lies My Teacher Told Me*, to cite one popular example, devotes a full chapter to "The Truth about the First Thanksgiving," a corrective history that, as an origin story, shames more than inspires. But worse than such ironies is that after Exodus comes Jeremiah. Imagining one's nation as God's chosen people seems to lead, inevitably, not to liberal cosmopolitan ideals but to illiberal, highly nationalist rhetoric of purity. If Bercovitch, a titan of American Studies in the 1980s and '90s, credited Winthrop's sermon on the *Arbella* with initiating the enduring and characteristically American literary template—the covenant with God; faith rewarded by possession of the Promised Land—that sequence is, he pointed out, followed by backsliding and then hortatory visions of rededication to the purity of generations past. Bercovitch called the genre the "American jeremiad." A fine example is the second half of Bradford's *Of Plymouth Plantation*, which carps long and loud against the prosperous second and third generation of Massachusetts' settlers, whose lack of puritanical zeal dulled the righteous city's shine.

In political rhetoric, the jeremiad manifests as nostalgia and racial purity. We might interpret the Republican Party's so-called "Southern Strategy" as one example of how this genre can be exploited. Reagan's "It's Morning in America" envisioned a rebirth, a revival of old values, a return to the days before the Vietnam War, before America was beset by self-doubt and acrimony. Why did Reagan kick off his presidential campaign in Philadelphia, Mississippi, if not to invoke nostalgia for America as it was before the Civil Rights movement unsettled society? So long as Americans think of themselves as the descendants of the Chosen People, some demagogue will promise to make the nation great again, if only it would raise again the citadel's walls to keep out the heathens. The isolationism of America First is the logical end of the Pilgrim myth of origin. The Puritans, after all, did not come to Massachusetts to be transformed. They did not want to mix their culture with the Indigenes in the "middle ground."[16] We tend to forget the Pilgrims did not seek a new life in the wilderness of America to escape religious persecution. They already had found sufficient refuge in Holland. The problem, as William Bradford himself admits, was that Dutch middle-class life was luring the Pilgrims' children away from the rigid faith of their fathers. The Pilgrims suffered the trials of journey and settlement in what they considered a wilderness to better yoke their children to their arcane doctrines. They thought they could protect their families from ideological corruption more efficiently if they removed themselves from contact with other types of people. Isolation and purity provide the spit and polish of Winthrop's hilltop city.

An Unusable Past

The foregoing is admittedly polemical. What makes a myth "appropriate" or "inappropriate" depends upon one's own political ideology, and extreme nationalism will always find a use for the "chosen people" myth. Less susceptible to prejudice should be assessments of how useful a myth has actually been to the producers of culture. If the Pilgrims have provided America with the usable past Van Wyck Brooks so fervently desired, we should see Exodus reflected not only in the political rhetoric of the last sixty years but also in our cultural texts. With its ascendency in the hallways of edification, Exodus should be writ not only in New England's literature but everywhere in American narrative. This does not mean we should find allusions to the Pilgrims or Puritans, but we should find the essence of Exodus, what Paul Innes calls an epic "template," the deep structure of the narrative, even if the surface details change.[17] Stripped down to its essential plot elements, Exodus consists of expulsion, trial and temptation, demonstrations of faith, and reward. The jeremiad adds backsliding, reproach, and rededication to faith. The key element is steadfastness in faith, the refusal to be transformed by the encounter with trials, because Exodus figures change as corruption. If Exodus has proved "usable," we should find contemporary artists erecting their own stories on this scaffold, especially when artists take up the heady cultural work of reimagining for their own generation the meaning of those "American" values touted by the politicians. But Exodus is not ubiquitous in American culture. In fact, it so rarely animates our narratives that it seems that artists have found it almost entirely unusable.

An example from the 1950s is particularly instructive. After World War II, as Americans adjusted to the Cold War, when their erstwhile ally became their existential enemy, they found themselves in possession of powers unprecedented in human history. Media was calling it a "super" bomb. Imitating the mechanisms of the sun, the *New York Times* suggested, this new weapon would be 1,000 times more powerful than the atomic bombs that the United States dropped on Hiroshima and Nagasaki. Suddenly America had the power to destroy all civilization, a dreadful responsibility undreamt by the founding fathers. "These are strange times," the *Times* editorialized, as it voiced the "moral qualms" that would haunt public discourse in the coming years.[18] On Halloween in 1952, the United States exploded the first hydrogen bomb at Eniwetok Island in the Pacific. Such powers demanded a reassessment of national identity. The usual existential questions asked of each generation were asked with greater than usual urgency: *Who are we? What are our values as a people? How is America different from other nations? What is our role in this world?*

Epics are supposed to settle these fundamental questions. Given the ascendency of the Puritans in American histories and the literary canon, artists wanting to create a modern American epic might "use" the Pilgrims. They were the available past, a ready-made myth verified by historians and literary anthologies as the originators of our national values. About a month after Eniwetok and a day after Thanksgiving, on November 28, 1952, Metro Goldwyn Meyer presented to audiences its film epic, *Plymouth Adventure*. Advertisements called it the "Screen Event of the Year." MGM's trailer ballyhooed it as "Most Exciting Sea Adventure Ever Filmed." The Pilgrims were "marked for greatness," audiences were told. "Something new and bright and glorious," the trailer insisted, a *free world*, "has its beginning" in their story of "immortal courage." MGM even tried to put modern science within the scope of their world: the film's opening caption told viewers that the "immortal men and women who undertook the Plymouth Adventure" were the seed of those who "dared to adventure" into the "depths beyond the microscope, into the mysteries behind the stars, into the hidden areas of the mind." Scientific inquiry "into unknown realms" was equivalent to settling in "the wilderness of new continents." The answer to how to cope with the awesome powers science had put into American hands might be found in this story of the nation's first settlers.

The trailer's reference to "[h]idden areas of the mind" alludes to discoveries that unsettled Americans nearly as much as did thermonuclear weapons. Sigmund Freud's theories about primal impulses lurking beneath the consciousness of civilized man, first popularized in America by his lectures at Clark University in 1909, grew in clinical practice and in the popular imagination till they reached their apex in the 1950s. In May 1956, the centenary of the psychiatrist's birth, the *New York Times* hailed Freud, the discoverer of the Unconscious, as "the foremost disturber of human complacency in our time."[19] Like Darwin before him, Freud forced people to re-evaluate what it means to be human. Such re-evaluations were the work of culture's purveyors. Jane Tomkins, for instance, notes how the editors of American literature anthologies responded to the new way of "describing and interpreting human behavior that arose after psychoanalysis took root in the United States." They came up with a new narrative of American literature that gave "the American people a conception of themselves" that was more relevant to the modern world.[20] *Plymouth Adventure* tried to deal with the unconscious by inventing a love triangle between Dorothy Bradford, her husband, and the *Mayflower's* captain, Christopher Jones. The film turns Bradford's real-life accidental drowning into a darkly motivated suicide. But the whole thing seemed contrived.

The studio invested mountains of money and talent into the making of the film. Executives were sure they had a hit. The acting was great: Spencer Tracey, Leo Genn, and Lloyd Bridges starred in key roles. Gene Tierney played Dorothy Bradford. The film won an Oscar for its impressive storm scenes. But few people bought tickets. It never caught fire. "The Most Exciting Sea Adventure Ever Filmed!" proved dull to audiences. Studio execs "quickly dubbed" it "MGM's Thanksgiving turkey."[21] Nor is it remembered today. The story does not resonate. For the purposes of epic, which is much more complex than the slogans of politicians, the Pilgrims are not *usable*. They were out of joint with the modern world.

America needed another myth. It already had one.

Maroonage

The same year *Plymouth Adventure* flopped, writers drafted the screenplay for another MGM film, this one set not in the past but in the future. Like the "Thanksgiving turkey," it attempted to confront the current events that were demanding a reassessment of national identity—the awesome power of the hydrogen bomb and the deep mysteries of the unconscious. The film begins with a starship coming into the orbit of Altaira, where, several years earlier, a party of colonizers went missing. The rescuers discover only two survivors of the shipwreck, a philologist named Morbius and his daughter. Morbius discovered and exploited the remains of an advanced civilization, the Krell, who destroyed themselves by developing—and mishandling—a powerful new technology. They invented machines that created matter from mere thought. But inadvertently, they released "monsters from the id," the unconscious and primeval impulses long-since suppressed and forgotten by the hyper-civilized people. Morbius succumbs to the same hubris, while the starship's crew, who might have stepped off the deck of a ship in a World War II movie, rescue his daughter and manage to escape. The message for audiences was effective: anyone possessed of such awesome power must guard against the instinctual Freudian impulses lurking in all human beings. With the high seriousness of epic, the final sequence of the film interprets Morbius's fall as a cautionary tale. "About a million years from now," the captain tells Morbius's daughter, "the human race will crawl up to where the Krell stood in their great moment of triumph and tragedy.... It will remind us that after all we are not God." *Forbidden Planet* opened in American theaters in 1956. Another H-bomb vaporized Bikini Atoll.

Leslie Nielson delivered those concluding lines, and, while his comic tones in the *Airplane* movies will make them sound campy to today's audiences, no one was snickering in 1956. *Forbidden Planet* successfully reinterpreted national values in the age of nuclear weapons and Freudian psychology. Into the bargain it threw in artificial intelligence in the shape of Robby the Robot, the film's most iconic character who raised the question of what it means to be human in a technological age. The film did moderately well at the box office, earning MGM two or three hundred thousand dollars. But the real success of *Forbidden Planet* must be measured by its influence. Robby the Robot became the template—a ubiquitous motif—in later narratives: Robot in *Lost in Space*, Hal in *2001: A Space Odyssey*, the emotionless Mr. Spock in *Star Trek*, the android Data in *Star Trek: The Next Generation*, the Cylons in *Battlestar Galactica*, Samantha in *Her*, the hosts in *West World*. *Forbidden Planet* gave us a cultural vocabulary by which we might continue working through what it means to be human, what is the proper relation between humanity and the technology we create, how might we bear the responsibility of our superpowers, and what values set us apart from other nations.

Forbidden Planet might be a futuristic science fiction adventure, but it was erected on another epic "template." The film borrowed key elements from William Shakespeare's *The Tempest*, a play about shipwreck in the age of exploration. Morbius is Prospero; his daughter is Miranda; Robby the Robot is the magical spirit, Ariel; and Caliban, Prospero's acknowledged "thing of darkness," symbol of the native peoples that Europeans encountered in the Americas, corresponds to the monster unleashed from Morbius's id. Almost immediately upon the film's release, critics noticed the uncredited debt to Shakespeare's tale. No one then or since recognized that *Forbidden Planet* can trace its pedigree further back, to the first genuine maroonage tale in the English tradition, the text that inspired Shakespeare: William Strachey's *True Reportory*.

Forbidden Planet succeeded where *Plymouth Adventure* failed because Americans find the deep structure of maroonage more compelling than Exodus. As discussed in the introduction, Steven Mentz has uncovered that deep structure: shock, immersion, salvage. As Claire Curtis has demonstrated above, all sorts of popular genres employ this structure. For instance, zombie apocalypses tend to follow the same pattern: the shock of being hurled out of the familiar, known world; immersion, a sort of baptism or transition into the new world; and the work of salvage, in which a new society confronts new challenges using old-world detritus and the resources of the new. The key to this structure is transformation: the encounter with the wilderness transforms the castaway into a new way of being. Change or die. *The Walking Dead*, for example, has proven to be a rich venue for exploring American values during the War on Terror. Other genres use the same deep structure. Many Westerns, for instance, like John Ford's *Stagecoach*, feature several mismatched Easterners cast out of civilization into a forbidding wild west. Their encounter with the frontier is transformative, and Ford's film gives audiences his own rumination about what American values ought to be in 1939. But maroonage structure is not always hidden: Edgar Rice Burroughs's *Tarzan*, the film franchise *Planet of the Apes*, the television series *Lost, Survivor, Naked and Afraid*, etc., all hurl castaways into a wilderness. The examples are almost endless. The "template" that artists tend to choose when they reimagine national ideals and identity is not Exodus: a wandering, righteous, oppressed people looking for a promised land, suffering trials but always maintaining their purity. It is not making a bargain with God: *if you keep our ship from wrecking on the rocks, we will build a righteous city on a hill.* The true template of American epic requires the ship to wreck on the rocks. Castaways are cut off from rescue, marooned in a wilderness, left to their own devices, transformed, and then work out for themselves the forms of a new society. Though I do not have space here to elaborate the connections, my argument coincides with the general contours of Frederick Jackson Turner's "frontier thesis" of American exceptionalism and Richard White's "middle ground": that the encounter with the wilderness transforms the marooned castaway.[22]

There is no guarantee that the society reimagined by many of these texts will coincide with the values of a modern liberal democracy. Though these tales always enact the castaways' transformation, they do not always proffer the egalitarian values we associate with *marronage*. Just as Turner's frontier thesis—in its original form—was highly problematic in its characterization of Native Americans, so do maroonage tales often lend themselves to racism. The master/slave relation embodied in Robinson Crusoe and Friday hardly represents those values touted by Henry Luce and Dwight D. Eisenhower. Half-wild and half-civilized, undeniably transformed by his encounter in the wilderness, Tarzan might be considered Edgar Rice Burroughs's version of the prototypical "American." But that did not prevent the novel, published in

1912, from validating the white supremacist ideology of Jim Crow's America. I am not advocating here that American society should embrace these tales naïvely. I am arguing that we should recognize as a fact of literary history that writers use maroonage to reimagine the meaning of America.

Bermuda's Maroons

This fact, that the structure of the American epic is not Exodus but maroonage, brings us back to where I began, with the *Sea Venture*, that first shipwreck of American history, stuck on a reef on the edge of what the sailors' lore called the devil's islands. The 153 castaways quickly found that the woods weren't haunted. Wherever they turned, they found abundance. Fish, foul, fruit, pigs enough for years of barbecue. They found they were in a paradise that offered "plenty of victuals" for the taking. Hunting and gathering would sustain them for some long time.

On the first day, the two Powhatan Indians bolted into the woods, opting out of whatever camp the English castaways might establish near the beach. They would live off the land. The Indians were a worrisome example. Bermuda had too many victuals too easily gotten, according to Thomas Gates, the old soldier-turned-governor. The first thing he did was recruit out of the ranks of the gentlemen a personal "corps du guard" to guarantee his own authority. He monopolized the salvage from the wreck: food, tools, and arms. Then he commenced building a boat so he could sail to Virginia and claim his dominion. Most of the settlers decided they did not want to go. They would rather stay in abundant Bermuda, where they might establish a new colony on their own terms. They dragged their feet to work, like the tortoise. Gates called them idlers. He organized them into work gangs, and at first tried cajoling them but then assigned to each gang an overseer from the ranks of his guardsmen. The sound of a bell mustered the settlers in the morning, and in the evening Gates counted them the way a warden counts prisoners. Discontent began with the sailors and quickly spread to the "major part of the common sort . . . of land men." Their complaints come down to us through Strachey, who, as Gates's secretary, called their arguments "churlish." Why continue working for the Company, the settlers wondered? In Virginia, "nothing but wretchednesse and labour must be expected." They would suffer "with many wants . . . there being neither that Fish, Flesh, nor Fowle" in Jamestown that was found easily in Bermuda. Especially since we know what they did not—that Jamestown was then suffering its notorious "starving time"—such arguments sound eminently reasonable, no matter how the narrative colored them. In Jamestown, the settlers reasoned, they would be virtual castaways anyway, lost to "friends and country." Why not stay in Bermuda then, where "pleasure might be inioyed"? Far "better were it for them, to repose and seate them [in Bermuda] where they should haue the least outward wants the while."[23]

The intellect behind this argument was a commoner named Stephen Hopkins. He explained to his fellow settlers that, while they each had signed a contract promising to obey the Company and to labor for some fixed time, so too had the Company promised to deliver them safely to Jamestown. The Company failed. The wreck of the *Sea Venture* invalidated the contract, as if immersion in the seawater dissolved it. Everyone was free to do what they wanted. They might follow Gates and his efforts to build a new boat and continue sailing to Virginia, or they might "decline from the obedience of the Gouernour, or refuse to goe any further, led by his authority (except it so pleased themselues)." Because they were castaways, even the "meanest" among them was only "bound each one to prouide for himselfe, and his owne family." On the shore of a Bermudan island, suspended between England and Virginia, cast into a wilderness, the survivors had been hurled into the state of nature. The young Thomas Hobbes was barely out of Oxford and just embarking on a grand tour, when Stephen Hopkins reasoned out the basis of modern political thought: outside of civil society, men were free to join any social contract they so desired.

William Strachey called Hopkins and his followers "outlawes." He was right—but in a sense he did not mean. Being castaway on a desert island removed them from the Company's authority. No law obtained in Bermuda, not even English law. In the wilderness, these fugitives were absolutely free until they bound themselves to some new rules of their own making. Each man would determine for himself and family whether or not to combine with others in a contract of mutual consent. Whatever government they formed would accord with their own wills. Hopkins and his fellows were living out the premise on which *Leviathan* and John Locke's *Second Treatise* would later erect their theories of government.

Shipwreck enabled this kind of thinking. Hopkins and his followers experienced the three-part psychological process identified by Steven Mentz: shock, immersion, and salvage. Figuratively speaking, the wreck of the *Sea Venture* washed away all previous political connections and obligations. The trauma of the storm, of the wreck, and of being castaway on a desert island emboldened the settlers. When their leaders enacted a train of abuses designed to reduce them under absolute despotism, they asserted their natural right to form new political associations according to their own wills.

Governor Gates had a different view. To think that way was insolence; to voice such an argument was conspiracy; to put it into action was mutiny. Over the ten months they were marooned on Bermuda, the castaways developed four conspiracies to escape from the Company's authority. One of these succeeded, because it was supported by Admiral Somers: the sailors decamped to another island beyond the scrutiny of Gates's guards. The three other plots involved most of the commoners and a few of the gentlemen. Had a vote been taken, they would have prevailed. But the corps du guard had the guns. Governor Gates foiled the first escape by marooning six ringleaders, without any supplies, on an inhospitable island. The most dramatic rebellion came just before the new ships were finished building. Gates executed a hotheaded discontent, a gentleman named Henry Paine, which triggered the spontaneous flight of several—perhaps dozens—of settlers. They fled to an uninhabited, remote spot in the islands, carrying with them all the means they needed to carve their own community out of the wilds: "Adises, Axes, Hatchets, Sawes, Augers, Planes, Mallets, &c." A neutral Admiral Somers brokered concessions from Gates, essentially renegotiating the contract between the governor and the settlers, which brought most of the fugitives back into camp. Three holdouts refused the new deal and continued hiding in the woods. Hopkins's own attempt to lead setters into the wilderness ended with his capture, trial, and a sentence of death. A broken man, he begged for clemency, which Governor Gates, facing an increasingly hostile workforce, found it expedient to grant. When Gates finally launched his homemade ships and headed for Jamestown, Hopkins, like most of the castaways, left Bermuda under threat of arms.[24]

What they found in Jamestown was even worse. The ill-governed colony was starving. Some settlers resorted to eating the dead. The Bermudan refugees, the survivors of shipwreck, became the saviors of Jamestown. Destitute as they were themselves, the Bermudans ended the "starving time" at Jamestown. Nevertheless, over the next couple of years, the Virginia Company imposed a slave labor camp even harsher than Gates's Bermuda. Again and again, settlers attempted to escape, not to start new colonies in the wilderness but to meld into the middle ground of the Algonquian towns on the Chesapeake. Many succeeded. But the Company captured some of the escapees, and to terrorize the remaining settlers it executed them in tortuous ways every bit as horrible as Spain's treatment of re-captured maroons.

The first several years of England's settlement in Jamestown produced maroons in both senses of the word. Some were victims of shipwreck, cast away, literally marooned. Others felt they were lost. Between the infrequent visits of resupply ships, they were effectively marooned in a strange wilderness, incompetently governed, and forced by the extremity of their circumstances into otherwise inconceivable choices. Most of those who stayed within the citadel of the English palisade died. Those who lived adapted to the frontier, even if that meant turning "savage." Just as Stephen Hopkins and the Bermudan castaways did, these settlers went through the psychological experience of shock, immersion, and salvage. Unlike the Pilgrims who would come to Massachusetts ten years later, they were transformed utterly by their encounter.[25]

Many of the settlers were also maroons in the original sense of that term. It might seem presumptuous to claim, as I am doing here, that many of Jamestown's white settlers were essentially the same as bound Africans who escaped Spanish slavery. The very notion of "white maroons," if engaged without qualifications, too easily can usurp a particularly ennobling and distinctly black aspect of American history. Those qualifications must always be acknowledged. The English bound for Jamestown consented to embark the ships. The maroons living in self-fashioned communities in the mountains of Panama and Jamaica, in the hinterland of Suriname, and the inaccessible recesses of Brazil did not; nor did the later maroons living among the Seminoles and in the Great Dismal Swamp. The degree to which the English settlers were duped by the Virginia Company—which history has not yet settled—does not erase this important distinction between them and people kidnapped from Africa or born into slavery. And, while the English settlers' chance of survival under Company rule in Virginia might have been similar to the Africans' chance of living out their natural lives in Spanish slavery, *if* the English survived they were confident that their freedom would be restored. They were bound not for life but for a term of years. Nevertheless, the points of similarity are important enough to claim that the original recorded instance of American democracy derived from *marronage*. The Bermudan castaways wanted to slip their binds and escape into the wilderness, where they would exercise freedom identical to that of black maroons. And their experience produced the first instance of social contract theory in the English tradition—long before that theory was explored by political philosophers.

We would do well to put this neglected patrimony into the anthologies of American literature, precisely because it anchors the past actually used by our culture—maroonage—to the values of *marronage*. A writer whose sense of maroonage was rooted in castaways of Bermuda could never pen *Tarzan*. And while we're at it, histories of the settlement of the east coast of the United States might begin not with Jamestown nor even Spanish Florida, but with two earlier episodes of true *marronage*: the maroons who escaped to the Carolina or Georgia coast in 1526, and the hundreds of black maroons near

Roanoke in 1585. Those who plunged into the wilderness, those transformed by contact with America, those who dared to claim authority over their own lives—escaped slaves, discontents, mutineers, outlaws—they are the stuff on which our dreams are made.

Notes

1. See Robert S. Tilton, *Pocahontas: The Evolution of an American Narrative* (New York: Cambridge, 1994).

2. *The Letters of Henry Adams*, J. C. Levenson, et al., eds., 2 vols. (Cambridge, MA: Harvard University Press, 1982): 287.

3. James W. Baker's *Thanksgiving: Biography of an American Holiday* (Hanover: University Press of New England, 2009) provides an authoritative and readable history of the holiday. For an example of early resistance to using the Pilgrims as a national myth of origin, see William Macon Coleman, *The History of the Primitive Yankees; or, The Pilgrim Fathers in England and Holland* (Washington, DC: Columbia, 1881).

4. Early America had "indeed been a Garden of the Gods," Becker suggested, and while he did quote John Winthrop's colonial propaganda over any of a dozen others he might have chosen, he gave Puritans little credit in the formation of American democracy. Becker, 143, 146.

5. Joseph Csicsila, *Canons by Consensus: Critical Trends and American Literature Anthologies* (Tuscaloosa: University of Alabama Press, 2004), 3. Though several critics have tackled the issue of canonicity in American literature, and many of these have studied the history of the college anthology, surprisingly few discuss the all-important issue of origins. Csicsila, for instance, has no interest in when exactly the Puritans Bradford, Bradstreet, Mather, or Winthrop became the supposed origin of American literary culture. As far back as the 1870s, Mathew Arnold suggested that the national anthology does the same cultural work in the modern, post-Darwinian world that the Bible performed in the pre-Darwinian world (see his "The Study of Literature").

6. He asserted that "the American soul" must "be made prominent in our school curriculums, as a guard against the rising spirit of experimental lawlessness which has followed the great war, and as a guide to the generation now molding for the future." Fred Lewis Pattee, *Century Readings for a Course in American Literature* (New York: Century Co., 1919), v. For a thorough discussion of canon formation, see Wendell Harris, "Canonicity," *PMLA* 106, no. 1 (January 1991): 110–21.

7. Edwin Greenlaw, *The Great Tradition: A Book of Selections from English and American Prose and Poetry, Illustrating the National Ideals of Freedom, Faith, and Conduct* (New York: Scott, Foresman, 1919), 162–64.

8. Malcolm Cowley, "The Puritan Legacy," *New Republic*, August 26, 1936, accessed May 25, 2018, https://newrepublic.com/article/79404/the-puritan-legacy.

9. Tomkins, 189; Csicsila, 14. For Mencken and Williams, see Reisling, 39–40. Tomkins sees this revision somewhat differently than I do; she detects a shift from the liberalism of the 1930s to the conservatism of the '50s and '60s. I should point out that some commentators, such as Max Weber, considered Benjamin Franklin to be a representative of Puritan or Pietist thought. In fact, Franklin is Weber's exemplar of the Protestant work ethic, which he labels the "spirit" of bourgeois capitalism (*The Protestant Work Ethic and the Spirit of*

Capitalism: The Talcott Parsons Translation Interpretations [New York: W. W. Norton, 2009], 22–24). The American anthologists made no connection between Plymouth or Boston Puritans and Franklin's Enlightenment thought.

The triumph of the Puritans reflected a shift in attitudes about what constituted "good" literature itself, away from edifying texts and towards aesthetically satisfying texts; one might say a shift from a political towards a *belles-lettres* approach to literary history. Texts once selected for how well they illustrated the development of American democracy were overtaken by texts of proven aesthetic value. Of course, we know today what American critics generally did not know until the 1970s: aesthetic sensibilities depend on political unconscious. Aesthetics judgments mask ideology. See, for example, Jane Tompkins's highly influential book *Sensational Designs: The Cultural Work of American Fiction, 1790–1860*, which discusses the factors, including ideological, that led to the rise of New Englanders in the American canon. Her study of Nathaniel Hawthorne's literary reputation is especially instructive.

The change was gradual. One 1935 anthology, *Major American Writers*, credited New York and Philadelphia writers Benjamin Franklin, James Fenimore Cooper, and Washington Irving with originating the American genius. Needless to say, a literary tradition that begins with Franklin's flight from Boston defines itself *against* the Puritan legacy. Pattee's anthology persisted on college syllabi, enlarging itself in several new editions into the 1960s (Csicsila, p. 10).

Historians shifted in the same direction. James Truslow Adams, who won a Pulitzer Prize in the 1920s for his history of New England, named his hugely influential 1931 book about the United States, *The Epic of America*. This monumental history, which popularized the concept of the "American Dream," held that the Mayflower Compact originated American society. "The novel situation of being free from all laws whatever," Adams explained, "faced the Pilgrims even before they landed from the *Mayflower*.... Some government was needful.... They simply avoided the possible dangers of anarchy or an iron dictator by agreeing to abide by the expressed *common* will." Adams cited the Puritan image of a "city set upon a hill," helping to initiate in the American consciousness our role as a beacon of self-determination. James Truslow Adams, *The Epic of America* (Boston: Little, Brown, and Company, 1931), 29, 45. Adams attributes the image of a city on a hill to another source. The originating role of the Pilgrims landing at Plymouth, the Mayflower Compact, and Puritan New England is even more evident in the first volume (*The Rise of the Union*) of Adams's monumental, multi-volume *The History of the United States* (New York: Charles Scribner's Sons, 1965; original copyright 1932), 1–63. Demonstrating Adams's influence, the Library of Congress instructs teachers to use *The Epic of America* to define the American Dream ("The American Dream," Library of Congress, n.d., accessed December 27, 2014).

10. *Concise Heath Anthology of American Literature, Volume 1: Beginnings to 1865* (New York: Cengage Learning, 2013); *The Norton Anthology of American Literature Shorter Eighth Edition*, eds. Nina Baym, et al. (New York: W. W. Norton, 2012).

11. Giles Gunn, ed. *Early American Writing* (New York: Penguin Books, 1994), 120.

12. Lyrics by Lynn Ahrens; first aired on ABC on March 1, 1975 ("Schoolhouse Rock!" *Wikipedia*, accessed January 17, 2016).

13. Philbrick, *Mayflower*, xiii–xiv; Nathaniel Philbrick, *Bunker Hill: A City, a Siege, a Revolution* (New York: Viking, 2013). "The City on the Hill" is the title of the first chapter.

14. Henry Luce, "The American Century," *Life*, February 17, 1941. Readers of my own generation probably hear the echoing phrase, "Truth, Justice, and the American Way," coined for the *Superman* television series in 1951, when Americans fully identified themselves with the

role of international beacon (see Lauren N. Karp, *Truth, Justice, and the American Way: What Superman Teaches Us About the American Dream and Changing Values within the United States*, thesis, Oregon State University, June 4, 2009, 45.). Dwight Eisenhower, inaugural address, January 20, 1953, delivered at the Capitol. Eisenhower Presidential Library, Museum and Boyhood Home, n.d., accessed December 2014. For a helpful discussion of the Puritan basis of "America's Messianic Beginnings," see Edward R. Schaffer, "The Myth of American Exceptionalism and Global Peace," in *Mythology: From Ancient to Post-Modern*, eds. Jürgen Kleist and Bruce A. Butterfield (New York: Peter Lang, 1992), 87–94. According to Schaffer, "American society was originally founded on [the Puritan's] messianic myth" (87).

15. Ronald Reagan, "Remarks at a dinner marking the 10th anniversary of the Heritage Foundation," October 8, 1983, The American Presidency Project, University of California, Santa Barbara, accessed May 25, 2018, http://www.presidency.ucsb.edu/ws/index.php?pid=40580&st=city+on+a+hill&st1=; John F. Kennedy, "City Upon a Hill" speech, January 9, 1961, Miller Center University of Virginia, accessed February 27, 2017, http://millercenter.org/president/kennedy/speeches/speech-3364. For a fuller discussion of the image in political rhetoric, see Joseph M. McShane, S. J., "Winthrop's 'City Upon a Hill' in Recent Political Discourse," *America*, October 1, 1988: 194–98. See also Richard M. Gamble, *In Search of the City on a Hill: The Making and the Unmaking of an American Myth* (London and New York: Continuum, 2012); "Remarks of the President at Fourth of July Celebration," The White House, Office of the Press Secretary, July 4, 2013, accessed January 7, 2015; Bercovitch, "A Model of Cultural Transvaluation: Puritanism, Modernity, and New World Rhetoric," keynote address, March 7, 1997, CUNY Renaissance Studies Conference, "Early Modern Trans-Atlantic Encounters: England, Spain, and the Americas." Often cited, this unpublished speech seems now to be unavailable online (see, for instance, Bernd Herzogenrath's bibliography in *An American Body/Politic: A Deleuzian Approach* [Dartmouth: Dartmouth College Press, 2010]).

16. I am using the term here as defined in Richard White's book, *The Middle Ground: Indians, Empires, and Republics in the Great Lakes Region, 1650–1810* (Cambridge University Press, 1991).

17. Paul Innes, *Epic* (New York: Routledge, 2013), 3.

18. "HYDROGEN BOMB," *New York Times*, January 18, 1950.

19. "DISTURBOR OF COMPLACENCY," *New York Times*, May 6, 1956.

20. Tompkins, 198.

21. Frank Miller, "Plymouth Adventure," *TCM.com*, accessed September 9, 2014.

22. More specifically, my argument leans on the elaboration of Turner's thesis in the work of Stanley Elkins and Erik McKitrick. See "A Meaning for Turner's Frontier, Democracy in the Old Northwest," in *The Turner Thesis: Concerning the Role of the Frontier in American History*, ed. George Rogers Taylor, 144–60; and Joseph Kelly, *Marooned: Jamestown, Shipwreck, and a New History of America's Origin*, 317–22.

23. William Strachey, *A true repertory of the wracke, and redemption of Sir THOMAS GATES Knight; vpon, and from the Ilands of the Bermudas: his coming to Virginia, and the estate of that Colonie then, and after, vunder the gouernment of the Lord LA WARRE, Iuly 15. 1610*. In Samuel Purchas, *Hakluytus posthumus; or, Purchas his pilgrims*. London: William Stansby, 1625, vol. 4., 1734–58. Quotations, 1743.

24. Strachey, 1744–45.

25. I have written about these events at greater length in *Marooned: Jamestown, Shipwreck, and a New History of America's Origin* (New York: Bloomsbury, 2018).

Secondary Source Bibliography

Adams, James Truslow. *The Epic of America*. Boston: Little, Brown, and Company, 1931.
Adams, James Truslow. *The History of the United States*. New York: Charles Scribner's Sons, 1965; original copyright 1932.
Baker, James W. *Thanksgiving: Biography of an American Holiday*. Hanover: University Press of New England, 2009.
Becker, Carl. *Our Great Experiment in Democracy: A History of the United States*. New York: Harper & Brothers, 1920.
Brooks, Van Wyck. *America's Coming of Age*. New York: B. W. Huesch, 1915.
Coleman, William Macon. *The History of the Primitive Yankees; or, The Pilgrim Fathers in England and Holland*. Washington, DC: Columbia, 1881.
Concise Heath Anthology of American Literature, Volume 1: Beginnings to 1865 (*The Norton Anthology of American Literature Shorter Eighth Edition*). Edited by Nina Baym et al. New York: W. W. Norton, 2012.
Cowley, Malcolm. "The Puritan Legacy." *New Republic*, August 26, 1936. Accessed May 25, 2018. https://newrepublic.com/article/79404/the-puritan-legacy.
Csicsila, Joseph. *Canons by Consensus: Critical Trends and American Literature Anthologies*. Tuscaloosa: University of Alabama Press, 2004.
Gamble, Richard M. *In Search of the City on a Hill: The Making and the Unmaking of an American Myth*. New York: Continuum, 2012.
Greenlaw, Edwin. *The Great Tradition: A Book of Selections from English and American Prose and Poetry, Illustrating the National Ideals of Freedom, Faith, and Conduct*. New York: Scott, Foresman, 1919.
Gunn, Giles, ed. *Early American Writing*. New York: Penguin Books, 1994.
Harris, Wendell. "Canonicity." *Publications of the Modern Language Association* 106, no. 1 (January 1991): 110–21.
Herzogenrath, Bernd. *An American Body/Politic: A Deleuzian Approach*. Dartmouth: Dartmouth College Press, 2010.
Innes, Paul. *Epic*. New York: Routledge, 2013.
Karp, Lauren N. *Truth, Justice, and the American Way: What Superman Teaches Us About the American Dream and Changing Values within the United States*. Thesis, Oregon State University, June 4, 2009.
Kelly, Joseph. *Marooned: Jamestown, Shipwreck, and a New History of America's Origin*. New York: Bloomsbury, 2018.
Levenson, J. C., et al., eds. *The Letters of Henry Adams*. Cambridge, MA: Harvard University Press, 1982.
Luce, Henry. "The American Century." *Life*, February 17, 1941.
McShane, Joseph M., S.J. "Winthrop's 'City Upon a Hill' in Recent Political Discourse." *America*, October 1, 1988, 194–98.
"A Meaning for Turner's Frontier, Democracy in the Old Northwest." In *The Turner Thesis: Concerning the Role of the Frontier in American History*. Edited by George Rogers Taylor, 144–60. New York: D. C. Heath and Company, 1972.
Miller, Frank. "Plymouth Adventure." *TCM.com*. n.d. Accessed September 9, 2014.
Pattee, Fred Lewis. *Century Readings for a Course in American Literature*. New York: Century Co., 1919.
Philbrick, Nathaniel. *Bunker Hill: A City, a Siege, a Revolution*. New York: Viking, 2013.

Philbrick, Nathaniel. *Mayflower: A Story of Courage, Community, and War*. New York: Viking, 2006.
Schaffer, Edward R. "The Myth of American Exceptionalism and Global Peace." In *Mythology: From Ancient to Post-Modern*. Edited by Jürgen Kleist and Bruce A. Butterfield, 87–94. New York: Peter Lang, 1992.
Tilton, Robert S. *Pocahontas: The Evolution of an American Narrative*. New York: Cambridge, 1994.
Tompkins, Jane. *Sensational Designs: The Cultural Work of American Fiction, 1790–1860*. Oxford, UK: Oxford University Press, 1986.
Weber, Max. *The Protestant Work Ethic and the Spirit of Capitalism: The Talcott Parsons Translation Interpretations*. New York: W. W. Norton, 2009.
White, Richard. *The Middle Ground: Indians, Empires, and Republics in the Great Lakes Region, 1650–1810*. Cambridge University Press, 1991.

Contributors

Richard Bodek is a professor of history at the College of Charleston and director of the European Studies program. He is especially interested in the twentieth century with a focus on popular culture, crime, and radical politics. His other works include studies of communist theater, a translation of a German novel banned by the Nazis, and articles about pulp literature and opera.

Claire P. Curtis is a professor of political science at the College of Charleston. She is the author of *Postapocalyptic Fiction and the Social Contract: "We'll Not Go Home Again"* (Lexington, 2010) and the co-editor of the special issue of *Utopian Studies* dedicated to Octavia Butler. She has published articles on Ursula Le Guin, Octavia Butler, and contemporary YA post-apocalyptic fiction. Most recently, she published "Standards of Justice for Human Being and Doing in Kim Stanley Robinson's *2312* and C. S. Friedman's *This Alien Shore*" in *Open Library of Humanities* and "The Politics of Living Together: Butler's Short Stories and Teaching Political Philosophy" in *Approaches to Teaching the Works of Octavia E. Butler*, edited by Tarshia Stanley. Currently she is writing a book on Martha Nussbaum's capabilities approach and contemporary post-apocalyptic fiction. As a political philosopher, she uses fiction as the experimental space of living together to analyze theories of justice. She teaches courses in the history of political thought, utopia/dystopia and the contemporary intersections of gender, theory, and law. She lives in Charleston, South Carolina.

Joseph Kelly is a professor of English at the College of Charleston and the director of the Irish and Irish American Studies program. He has published a wide range of social and cultural history, from the *Ulysses* obscenity trial to the evolution of slave ideology in the American South. His latest book is *Marooned: Jamestown, Shipwreck, and a New History of America's Origin*.

Simon Lewis has been teaching African literature at the College of Charleston since 1996. He edits the literary journal *Illuminations: An International Magazine of Contemporary Writing*, and directs the African Studies program and the *Carolina Lowcountry and Atlantic World* (CLAW) program. He is the author of *White Women Writers and Their African Invention* (University Press of Florida, 2003) and *British and African Literature in Transnational Context* (University Press of Florida, 2011), and has published numerous articles on authors such as Olive Schreiner, Nadine Gordimer, Dennis Brutus, Abdulrazak Gurnah, and Jhumpa Lahiri.

Steve Mentz is professor of English at St. John's University in New York City. His most recent book is *Shipwreck Modernity: Ecologies of Globalization, 1550–1719* (2015). He is the author of two earlier monographs, *At the Bottom of Shakespeare's Ocean* (2009) and *Romance for Sale in Early Modern England* (2006), and also editor or co-editor of four collections: *The Sea in Nineteenth-Century Anglophone Literary Culture* (2017), *Oceanic New York* (2015), *The Age of Thomas Nashe* (2013), and *Rogues and Early Modern English Culture* (2004). He has written numerous articles on ecocriticism, Shakespeare, and maritime literature and curated an exhibition at the Folger Shakespeare Library, "Lost at Sea: The Ocean in the English Imagination, 1550–1750" (2010). He blogs at The Bookfish, www.stevementz.com.

J. Brent Morris is associate professor of history, Humanities Department Chair, and Director of the University of South Carolina Beaufort Institute for the Study of the Reconstruction Era. Widely published in the fields of Southern, African American, and nineteenth-century American history, he is the author of a forthcoming monograph on the maroons of the Great Dismal Swamp.

Peter Sands is associate professor of English and Director of the Honors College at the University of Wisconsin-Milwaukee. He is president of the Society for Utopian Studies, and teaches and writes about science fiction and utopias, law and literature, cannibalism in literature, and emerging technologies.

Edward Shore is a historian and postdoctoral fellow at the Bernard and Audre Rapoport Center for Human Rights and Justice at the University of

Texas School of Law. His research explores the long-standing struggles of the black peasantry over land, natural resources, and autonomy in Brazil's Ribeira Valley. Since 2015, he has coordinated a project with the Advisory and Articulation Team to Rural Black Communities of the Ribeira Valley (EAACONE) and the Instituto Socioambiental to create a post-custodial digital repository of historical documentation concerning quilombos, working with their members to curate their own community-based archives and strengthen their legal claims to land and resources in the Atlantic Forest.

James O'Neil Spady is an associate professor of American History at Soka University of America. His first book is forthcoming from Routledge Press. He is at work on a second book that presents a fresh interpretation of the Denmark Vesey events of 1822.

Index

Aeneas, 82, 91
Aeneid, The, 91, 167
Africa, 30, 37, 39, 40, 44, 47, 48, 56, 84, 85, 86, 87, 119, 120, 121, 122, 123, 183
African Americans, xiv, 20, 41, 53n16, 163
Africans, xi, xxi, 6, 7, 17, 41, 47, 83, 93, 94, 119, 121, 126, 136, 183
Agamben, Giorgio, 33, 46
Amazon, 58, 59, 74n3
ambergris, 88, 89, 90, 91, 92, 93
American Revolution, 7, 49, 119, 172
Angola, 39, 89, 93
animals, 65, 103, 104, 105, 108, 109, 110, 111, 112, 114, 115, 147; alligators, xv, 5; bears, 5, 20, 146; bloodhounds, 8, 20; cattle, xi, 6, 55, 66, 72, 110, 113; hogs, 6, 85, 88, 90; snakes, xv, 6, 13, 20; sperm whales, 90; wildlife, 5, 109
apocalypse, 97, 138, 139, 179
Aptheker, Herbert, xii, 31
Arbella, 168, 173, 174
Argosy, 155
Article 68 of the Brazilian Constitution, 55, 56, 57, 58, 69, 70, 72, 73, 74, 75, 76
Atwood, Margaret, xix, 134–41, 143, 146, 147, 148, 149; *MaddAddam*, xix, 134, 135, 137, 138, 140, 141, 142; *Oryx and Crake*, 138, 145; *The Year of the Flood*, 138
Auster, Paul, 109

Baram, Uzi, xiii
Baxa, Paul, 150
Becker, Carl, 168
Bellamy, Edward, 134
Bercovitch, Sacvan, 173, 174
Berkhofer, Robert F., Jr., 104
Bermuda, xi, xviii, xx, 82, 83, 84, 85, 86, 87, 88, 89, 90, 91, 92, 93, 94, 95, 97, 99, 180, 181, 182, 183
Bernhard, Virginia, 88
Bikini Atoll, 178
Bilby, Kenneth, xiii
Blackwell, Jeannine, 99, 115
Bois-Caiman, 49
Bonaparte, Napoleon, 121, 122
Boston, Massachussetts, xiv, 133, 171
Botha, P. W., 130
Bradford, Dorothy, 174, 177
Bradford, William, xx, 167, 168, 169, 170, 171, 173, 174
Bradstreet, Anne, 170
Brazil, xv, xvi, 4, 55, 56, 57, 58, 59, 60, 61, 62, 64, 65, 67, 68, 69, 70, 71, 72, 73, 74, 118, 120, 183
Bridges, Lloyd, 177
Brooks, Van Wyck, 169, 170, 175
Burnham, Michelle, 99, 107
Burroughs, Edgar Rice, 179
Butler, Octavia, xx, 149, 150, 159, 160, 161, 162, 163; *Kindred*, xx, 150, 151, 160, 162

Index

Butler, Olivia, 21, 76, 83, 150, 151, 159, 160, 161, 162, 163, 164
Byrd, William II, 5, 6, 7

Camelot, xix, 154
Cameron, James, xvi
Canada, 10
Cananéia, 59
Canary Islands, 83, 88
Cape Verde Islands, 83
Caribbean, xi, xix, 4, 5, 85, 86, 87, 88, 119, 120, 121, 124, 167
Carolina Lowcountry, The, xii, 5, 18, 39
Carvalho, Matías José de, 61, 124
castaways, xi, xii, xv, xvi, xvii, xviii, xix, xx, xxi, 85, 88, 89, 90, 92, 93, 95, 97, 118, 119, 120, 124, 130, 131, 132, 145, 151, 152, 161, 164, 167, 179, 180, 181, 182, 183
Caviola, Hugo, 108, 113
Charleston, South Carolina, xiv, xvi, 7, 30, 31, 32, 33, 37, 38, 39, 40, 42, 43, 44, 47, 48, 49
Chesapeake, 5, 17, 171, 182
Christianity, xviii, 40, 48, 99, 100, 102, 107, 115, 157; church, 47, 48, 68, 152, 153
Christiansë, Yvette, xix, 118, 119, 120, 121, 122, 123, 124, 125, 126, 127, 128, 129, 130, 131, 132, 133, 135, 137; *Castaway*, 120, 121, 122, 123, 124, 125, 131; *Imprendehora*, 118, 120, 123, 124, 125, 127; *Unconfessed*, 119, 120, 128, 131
cimmarón, xi
Civil War, 8, 19, 49, 168
Clavin, Matthew, xiii
Clifford, Mary Louise, 119
Colombia, 57, 76n29
Columbus, Christopher, 83, 104, 126, 152, 167, 170
Confederate States of America, xiv, 8, 19, 151
coral, 82, 88, 93, 95
Courtship of Miles Standish, The, 168
Cowan, William Tynes, xvii
Cowley, Malcolm, 170
crops, 6, 13, 61, 65, 68, 90; beans, 13, 64, 65; cassava, 64, 65; rice, 55, 61, 62, 63, 64, 65, 66; tobacco, 7, 86, 88, 89, 91, 92, 93, 94
Crosby, Alfred, 84
Cuba, 86
Curitiba, 58, 71, 72

Da Gama, Vasco, 83, 120
da Silva, Daniel Domingues, 63, 119
Dampier, William, xii
Darwin, Charles, 176
Davies, John, xii
de Camp, L. Sprague, xx, 150, 154, 155, 156, 157, 158, 159, 160, 163, 164, 165, 167, 169; *An Elephant for Aristotle*, 159; *Lest Darkness Fall*, 8, 21, 150, 151, 153, 154, 155, 156, 157, 158, 159, 160; *The Arrows of Hercules*, 155; *The Bronze God of Rhodes*, 155
Defoe, Daniel, xi, xviii, 95, 97, 100, 104, 107, 125
Delany, Martin, xiv
Deliverance, 90
Dias, Bartholomew, 120
Die Wand (The Wall), xviii, 97, 98, 107, 108, 109, 110, 111, 112, 113, 114, 115
Diouf, Sylviane, xii, xiii, xiv, xvi, 5, 31
Don Quixote, 87
Donne, John, 86
Dos Santos Barboza, Guilherme, 56, 60, 61, 73
Douglass, Frederick, 9, 39, 44
Drake, Sir Francis, xi, xii, 86, 94
Drayton, Charles, 34, 46
Dunmore, Lord (John Murray), 7
dystopia, 98, 108, 109, 110, 111, 112, 113, 115, 135, 138; critical dystopia, 98, 108, 109, 110

Egerton, Douglas, 30, 32
Eisenhower, Dwight D., 173, 179
England, xii, xxi, 84, 85, 89, 90, 91, 99, 103, 107, 150, 167, 172, 181
Eniwetok Island, 176
Enlightenment, xix, 135, 147, 169
Eurocentrism, xviii, 83, 91
Europe, 19, 82, 84, 85, 86, 101, 107, 155, 156, 157, 160
Europeans, xii, xvi, xviii, 4, 82, 83, 84, 85, 86, 99, 100, 103, 104, 105, 109, 115, 178
exiles, xvi, 7, 131
Exodus, Book of, 171, 172, 174, 179, 180

Female American, The, xx, 97, 98, 99, 101, 107, 109, 114
Ferdinandez d'Oviedo y Valdez, Gonzalo, 85
Fisher, Carl, 108

Flávio dos Santos Gomes, 56, 57, 61, 71
Florida, xiii, 4, 183
Forbidden Planet, 178
Ford, John, 179
Foucault, Michel, xiv
Franklin, Benjamin, 169
Franklin, John Hope, xiii, 5
freedom, xv, xvii, xix, 3, 6, 10, 17, 18, 20, 30, 32, 40, 44, 48, 57, 60, 63, 69, 73, 83, 84, 91, 101, 119, 123, 124, 126, 127, 128, 129, 130, 131, 132, 136, 140, 153, 173, 183
Freitas, James, 56, 99, 107
French and Indian War, 168
French Guiana, 57
French Revolution, 49
Freud, Sigmund, 176, 178
Friday, 110, 113, 179
Fyfe, Christopher, 119

Garner, Margaret, 128
Gates, Sir Thomas, xx, 90, 166, 167, 180, 181, 182
Gell, Monday, 34, 40, 45, 46, 48
Genn, Leo, 177
Genovese, Eugene, xiii, 4, 31
Georgia, 38, 183
Gerrity, Sean, xvii
Gilman, Charlotte Perkins, 134
Gilroy, Paul, 121
Goering, Hermann, 158
Graves, Robert, 154, 158
Great Dismal Swamp, xiii, xiv, 4, 5, 6, 7, 8, 9, 10, 11, 12, 13, 14, 15, 16, 17, 18, 19, 20
Greenlaw, Edwin, 169
guerillas, 8, 11, 19
Gulf Stream, 84, 88, 93, 94
Gullah, xiv, 31, 33, 36, 37, 38, 39, 40, 42, 44, 45, 47, 48, 49, 56, 58
Gullah Jack, xiv, xvi, 30, 31, 32, 35, 36, 37, 38, 39, 40, 41, 42, 45, 46, 47, 49
gynotopia, 113, 114

Hahn, Steven, xiii, xiv
Haiti, xiv, 30, 48, 49
Haitian Revolution, 49
Harris, David, 119
Haushofer, Marlen, xviii, 97, 98, 103, 107, 108, 109, 110, 111, 112, 113, 114, 115

Heath Anthology of American Literature, 170, 171
Higgenson, Thomas Wentworth, xiv
Hispaniola, xi, 86
Hopkins, Stephen, 181, 182, 183
Howard, Rosalyn, xiii
hurricane, xi, 85, 87, 93, 94, 95, 167

Indigenes, 6, 15, 100, 119, 152, 174
Innes, Paul, 175
Ivaporunduva, 60, 61, 62, 63, 64, 65, 66, 67, 70, 71, 72, 73, 74

Jackson, Edmund, 3, 23n33
Jamaica, xiii, 4, 7, 57, 152, 167, 183
James, C. L. R., 121
Jameson, Frederic, 135, 136, 149
Jamestown, xviii, xx, 85, 87, 88, 90, 102, 121, 166, 167, 168, 170, 171, 180, 181, 182, 183
Jansen, Hendrina, 128
jeremiad, 174, 175
Johnson, Michael, 32, 35, 58
Jones, Christopher, 177
Jourdain, Sylvester, 89

Kai, Nubia, xvii
Kathrada, Ahmed, 130
Kazanjian, David, xvii
Kecht, Maria-Regina, 108
Kennedy, John F., 173
Kennedy, Lionel, 31, 35, 36
King, Martin Luther, Jr., xv
Krio, 119, 124

Leaming, Hugo Prosper, xiii
Lest Darkness Fall, xx, 150, 152–55
Levitas, Ruth, 113, 117, 135
Liberia, 40, 48, 53
Liberty Bell, The, 3
liminality, 119
Lincoln, Abraham, 160, 168
Lincoln, Steffens, 154
Linebaugh, Peter, 13
Locke, John, 181
Lockley, Timothy, xiii, 23
Loewen, James, 174
Longfellow, Henry Wadsworth, xiv, 168

Index

Lopez, Fernão, 120, 125, 131
Luce, Henry, 173, 179

MacNeil, Denise Mary, 107
Mandela, Nelson, 130–31
Maria, Joanna, 60–62, 70, 73
Maris-Wolf, Ted, xiii
maroons, xi–xxi, 3–20, 31–32, 41, 56–57, 61, 65, 69–70, 72, 84, 93, 103, 124, 139, 151, 180, 183; interior maroons, 13, 15
marronage, xii–xxi, 4–5, 8–9, 11, 31, 40–41, 43–44, 46–49, 58, 83, 99, 105, 118–19, 124, 128, 132, 148, 151, 161, 179, 183
Martyr, Peter, 86
Marvell, Andrew, 92
Massachusetts, 93, 166–71, 173–74, 183
Mather, Cotton, 169–70
Mayflower, xx, 166, 171–72, 177
Mayflower Compact, 172
McCarthy, Cormac, 109
McDowell, Tremaine, 98–99, 107
McMichael Anthology of American Literature, 170
Mencken, H. L., 169
Mentz, Steven, xvi–xix, 85–87, 178, 181
Mexico, xii, 87
Middle Atlantic, xiv
Midwest, xiv
Moore, Richard, 90–91
More, Thomas, 87, 113, 133
Morgan, Hank, xix, 149, 151–53, 155
Morgan, Philip D., 5
Morrison, Toni, 116, 128
Mouse on the Mayflower, 172
Mullin, Gerald, 31
Mullin, Michael, 4
Mussolini, Benito, 150, 158

New England, 16, 21, 170, 171, 172, 178, 180, 187
New York City, New York, xiv, xx, 168, 170–71, 174–75
Nielson, Leslie, 178
Norfolk, Virginia, 6, 19
North Atlantic Gyre, 85, 87
North Carolina, 5, 8, 18–19, 169

Norton Anthology of American Literature, 171
Norwood, Richard, 92

Obama, Barack, 173
Odysseus, xi
Of Plymouth Plantation, 167–68, 171–72
Oroonoko, 36–37
Ortner, Sherry B., 112

Paine, Henry, 182
Panama, xi–xii, 183
Panza, Sancho, 87
Paquette, Robert, 30, 32
Paraná, 55, 58
Patience, 89–90
Pattee, Fred Lewis, 169
Pearson, Andrew, 119
Pedro Cubas, 63–74
Penguin Anthology of American Literature, 171
Philbrick, Nathaniel, 171–72
Philip, Marie Nourbese, 131
Pilgrims, xx, 168–77
pirates, 82, 84, 108
plantation, xi, 5–6, 17–19, 31, 38–39, 41–42, 47–48, 55–57, 61–62, 65, 67, 103, 160–62
Plough, 90–91
Plymouth, 87
Plymouth Adventure, 176–78
Plymouth Plantation, 167, 170
Plymouth Plantation, Of. See *Of Plymouth Plantation*
Plymouth Rock, 171
Pocahontas, xviii, 99, 167
Pölsler, Julian, 108
posthuman, 82–84, 92–94
Price, Richard, ix, xv–xvi, 31, 57–58, 71
Price, Sally, xvi
Prospero, xvi, 178
Puritans, xx, 167–71, 174–76

Rath, Carlos, 59–60, 62
Reagan, Ronald, 136, 173–74
Rediker, Marcus, xiii
revolution, 16, 30, 33, 47–49, 126, 145
Rich, Richard, 90
Roanoke, xxi, 184

Robben Island, 119–20, 128, 130–31
Roberts, Neil, xv, xix, 119, 124, 126, 128, 132
Robinson, Kim Stanley, xix, 135–36, 138, 141–42, 144, 146–48
Robinson Crusoe, xvi, xviii, 97, 99; character, xi, xvi, 112–13, 125, 138, 179
robinsonade, xi, xviii, 97–99, 108, 112–13, 115
Rolfe, John, xviii, 88, 91–92, 168
Rome, 7, 82, 150–51, 154, 158

Saint Domingue, 42, 49
São Paulo, 55, 58–59, 62–63, 65–69, 72–74
São Pedro, 58, 68, 73, 75, 76, 77, 81, 85, 88
Saunders, Christopher, 119, 136
Sayers, Daniel O., xiii, 16
Schoolhouse Rock, 172
Schoolman, Martha, xvii
Sea Venture, xi, 166–67, 180–81
Seminoles, 4, 183; Black Seminoles, xvi
Shakespeare, William, xvi, xviii, 89, 178; *The Tempest*, xviii, 89, 178
shipwreck, xvi–xviii, xx, 63, 82–83, 85, 88, 90, 95, 134, 152, 167, 177–78, 181–82
Sierra Leone, 40–41, 48, 119, 124–25
slaves, xi, xii–xvi, xvii, xix, xxi, 5, 7, 10, 12, 17–19, 30–49, 55–73, 93–94, 101, 103, 118–21, 124–127, 128, 131, 151–53, 160–62, 163, 183, 184; as fugitives, xii–xiv, xvi, xx–xxi, 3–7, 9, 11, 18–20, 55–61, 63–65, 67, 70–72, 181–82; as recaptives, 124, 126; slavocracy, xiv
Smith, Adam, 154
Smith, D. K., 92
Smith, John, xviii, 99, 168, 170–71; *General History of Virginia*, 168
Somers, George, 89, 91–92, 167, 182
Sousa, Martim Afonso de, 59
South Carolina, xiii–xiv, 7, 38, 40, 42, 52
St. Helena Island, xix, 118–20, 127, 129
Stoler, Ann Laura, 33
Stowe, Harriet Beecher, xiv
Strachey, William, xxi, 90, 167, 178, 180–81; *A True Reportory of the Wracke and Redemption of Sir Thomas Gates Knight, upon and from the Ilands of Bermudas*, xx, 167, 178

Strother, David Hunter, 3
Suffolk, Virginia, 5, 11
Suriname, 57, 71, 183
Sweninger, Loren, xiii

Tarzan of the Apes, 179, 183
Thanksgiving, 168, 171–72, 174, 176–77
This Is America, Charlie Brown, 172
Thompson, Alvin O., 5
Thornton, John K., 39
Tidewater, 6–7
Tierney, Gene, 177
Tillich, Paul, xv
Titanic, xvi
Tomkins, Jane, 170, 176
Tracey, Spencer, 177
Turner, Frederick Jackson, 179
Turner, Nat, 7, 9
Tuscarora War, 7
Twain, Mark, xix, 151–56, 164; *A Connecticut Yankee in King Arthur's Court*, xix, 150–54

Underground Railroad, xiii, 10
United States, The, xiii–xiv, 4, 8, 151, 164, 167–69, 173, 175–77, 183
utopia, xiv, xviii–xix, 87, 97–100, 101, 104–5, 107, 110–14, 134–36, 138–42, 144, 146, 148
Utopia, 87, 93, 113, 134

van de Kaap, Sila, 120, 128
Vesey, Denmark, xiv, 32, 35–36, 40, 44–45, 48–49
Vesey Rebellion, xiv, 7, 30–32, 47–49
Virgil, 82, 91, 93, 167
Virginia, xiii, xx, 5–7, 11, 17–18, 20, 88–93, 98–100, 103, 168–71, 180–81, 183
Virginia Company, 83, 87, 89–91, 94, 166, 182–83; Second Charter of, 166

Walcott, Derek, 121
Walking Dead, The, 179
Waller, Edmund, 92
Washington, George, 16, 169
Washington Ditch, 17
weapons, 30, 45–46, 112, 155, 176, 178; arrows and arrowheads, 11, 15, 109; firearms,

11, 30; gunflints, 13–14; guns, 13, 48, 182; knives, 11, 15; pistols, 13; rifles, 13; swords, 11, 46
Weik, Terrence, xiii
Wells, H. G., 152
Williams, William Carlos, 170
Wingfield, Edward Maria, 102
Winkfield, Eliza Unca, 97–102, 110, 114–15
Winthrop, John, 168, 170–75
Wood, Marcus, 126
Worden, Nigel, 119
World War I, 168–69
World War II, xx, 158, 174–75, 177

zombie, xi, xix, 135, 179
Zuck, Rochelle Raineri, 99, 107
Zumbi, 56

www.ingramcontent.com/pod-product-compliance
Lightning Source LLC
Chambersburg PA
CBHW030622230426
43661CB00053B/2106